Exploring the Southwest States through Literature

Exploring the United States through Literature Series

Kathy Howard Latrobe, Series Editor

Exploring the Northeast States through Literature
Edited by P. Diane Frey

Exploring the Southeast States through Literature
Edited by Linda Veltze

Exploring the Great Lakes States through Literature
Edited by Kathy Howard Latrobe

Exploring the Plains States through Literature
Edited by Carolyn S. Brodie

Exploring the Southwest States through Literature
Edited by Pat Tipton Sharp

Exploring the Mountain States through Literature
Edited by Sharyl Smith

Exploring the Pacific States through Literature
Edited by Carol A. Doll

Exploring the Southwest States through Literature

Edited by Pat Tipton Sharp

State Editors
Cathy C. Bonnell, Arizona
Carol A. Sarath, New Mexico
Terri Parker Street, Oklahoma
Anita S. Baker, Texas

Exploring the United States through Literature Series
Kathy Howard Latrobe, Series Editor

Oryx Press
1994

The rare Arabian Oryx is believed to have inspired the myth of the unicorn. This desert antelope became virtually extinct in the early 1960s. At that time several groups of international conservationists arranged to have 9 animals sent to the Phoenix Zoo to be the nucleus of a captive breeding herd. Today the Oryx population is over 800 and nearly 400 have been returned to reserves in the Middle East.

Copyright © 1994 by The Oryx Press
4041 North Central at Indian School Road
Phoenix, Arizona 85012-3397

Published simultaneously in Canada

All rights reserved
No part of this publication may be reproduced or transmitted in any form or by any means, electronic or mechanical, including photocopying, recording, or by any information storage and retrieval system, without permission in writing from The Oryx Press.

Printed and Bound in the United States of America

(∞) The paper used in this publication meets the minimum requirements of American National Standard for Information Science—Permanence of Paper for Printed Library Materials, ANSI Z39.48, 1984.

Library of Congress Cataloging-in-Publication Data

Exploring the Southwest states through literature / edited by Pat
  Tipton Sharp.
    p. cm. — (Exploring the United States through literature series)
  Includes bibliographical references and indexes.
  ISBN 0-89774-765-8
  1. Southwestern States—Juvenile literature—Bibliography.
I. Sharp, Patricia Tipton. II. Series.
Z1251.S8E97   1994
[F787]
016.976—dc20   93-40814
                                                          CIP
                                                          AC

Contents

Series Statement   vii

Preface   ix

Contributors   xi

Arizona   1
    by Cathy C. Bonnell

New Mexico   21
    by Carol A. Sarath

Oklahoma   40
    by Terri Parker Street

Texas   61
    by Anita S. Baker

Directory of Publishers and Vendors   87

Author Index   95

Title Index   98

Subject Index   103

Series Statement

The *Exploring the United States through Literature Series* comprises seven annotated regional resource guides to selected print and nonprint materials for grades K-8. Each regional resource is divided into state sections identifying materials that relate to the history, culture, geography, resources, industries, literature and lore, and famous figures of the states in the region. The seven volumes cover the following regions and states:

- *Exploring the Northeast States through Literature:* Connecticut, Delaware, District of Columbia, Maine, Maryland, Massachusetts, New Hampshire, New Jersey, New York, Pennsylvania, Rhode Island, Vermont
- *Exploring the Southeast States through Literature:* Alabama, Arkansas, Florida, Georgia, Kentucky, Louisiana, Mississippi, North Carolina, South Carolina, Tennessee, Virginia, West Virginia
- *Exploring the Great Lakes States through Literature:* Illinois, Indiana, Michigan, Minnesota, Ohio, Wisconsin
- *Exploring the Plains States through Literature:* Iowa, Kansas, Missouri, Nebraska, North Dakota, South Dakota
- *Exploring the Southwest States through Literature:* Arizona, New Mexico, Oklahoma, Texas
- *Exploring the Mountain States through Literature:* Colorado, Idaho, Montana, Nevada, Utah, Wyoming
- *Exploring the Pacific States through Literature:* Alaska, California, Hawaii, Oregon, Washington

The materials included in these resource guides were selected because they can be used by teachers and librarians to enrich young people's understanding of the histories and contemporary cultures of the 50 states, and because they are suitable for use with young people from any of the regional or ethnic groups of the contemporary United States. Each annotation includes a brief description of the particular work, a comment on its usefulness or appropriateness, and at least one learning activity compatible with the identified interest level of the resource.

Purpose

The *Exploring the United States through Literature Series* offers teachers, school library media specialists, and public librarians valuable assistance in resource selection and user guidance. The suggested activities demonstrate each title's potential for involving young people in creative thinking and problem-solving and for inspiring teachers and librarians to invent other imaginative uses for the title. The series can also be used effectively by school library media specialists and teachers as they work together to develop curricular units and plan learning experiences about the geographic regions of the United States or about specific states. Reading, language arts, and social studies teachers will find the series particularly useful.

The series addresses needs created by the following recent and important educational trends:

1. The whole language approach to learning, especially the integration of literature, the arts, and social studies curricula
2. Rapidly changing social environments that demand flexible curricula and multiple learning resources
3. Multicultural education with an emphasis on multicultural diversity and a recognition of the importance of encouraging young people to accept and appreciate diversity

4. The position of the Curriculum Task Force of the National Commission on Social Studies (NCSS) that the social studies curriculum should include both breadth and depth

The NCSS emphasizes the discovery approach to learning and maintains that young people should develop an overview as well as immerse themselves in the details of history and social studies.

Scope

Each regional editor coordinated the contributions of state editors who brought to the series a familiarity with and understanding of the notable and special features of their states and regions. The state editors used their own judgment in selecting materials that could most effectively assist young people in learning and understanding the many dimensions of each state. The editors' goal was not to include a predetermined number of entries, but rather to select pertinent items of merit. Because there are similarities across the regions, a few titles appear in more than one state bibliography. These duplicate entries serve to reinforce students' experiences with the region or to take the title in a new direction with a different activity. Also, some books listed under only one state may be appropriate for other states as well.

Each state editor valued diversity—in subject matter, in time period, and in media. The editors sought to capture the past and present of each state by including not only books, but also such items as periodicals, computer programs, sound recordings, and videocassettes. A major goal of the series is to bring alive to young people each state's sights, sounds, tastes, music, stories and legends, natural environment, and people.

Activities

The state editors, who are professionally involved either directly or indirectly with the education of young people, have devised learning activities that can appropriately extend the work being described. Denoted by a diamond (♦) in each entry, the activities are designed to enhance young people's understanding of each state and to encourage further exploration of the topic at hand. The activities relate the work to young people themselves, to specific geographic areas, to associated disciplines and subjects, or to broader concepts within social studies.

Sources of Materials

Because of the diversity and regional or state focus of materials, no single jobber can deliver all the included items upon request. Therefore, a "Directory of Publishers and Vendors," including specialized sources for state and regional materials, has been included in each volume. The agencies and departments of state and local governments, state and local historical societies, and other state and local organizations are also excellent sources of informational materials.

Organization

Each volume is organized first by the states within the region (arranged alphabetically). Each state section is then subdivided into Nonfiction (by Dewey Classification), Biography (collective biography, then individual biography, alphabetically by subject), Periodicals, and Professional Materials (by Dewey Classification). Reference works listed in the Nonfiction section are identified immediately following the Dewey number.

In general, each bibliographic entry identifies Dewey Classification number, author, title, publisher or producer, ISBN or ISSN, date of publication or release, number of pages, black-and-white or color illustrations, cost of nonprint materials, any special purchasing information, and running time and format specifications for nonprint items. Each entry also includes an interest level designation and relevant subject headings, which have been based on the *Sears List of Subject Headings*.

Three indexes provide access by author, title, and subject. The state-by-state division allows teachers and librarians to access materials by state, and the Subject Index provides access to materials appropriate to more than one state and to topics with regional significance.

The Dewey Decimal Classification numbers, while appropriate for each volume's organization, are not offered as recommendations for cataloging/classification purposes. Many items are open to classification in more than one area.

—Kathy Howard Latrobe
Series Editor

Preface

Exploring the Southwest States through Literature is one of seven regional annotated bibliographies of print and nonprint materials for young people in grades K-8. The materials included in this bibliography will offer young people a deeper understanding of the histories and contemporary cultures of Arizona, New Mexico, Oklahoma, and Texas. Functioning as a selection tool or as a resource for reader guidance, this volume identifies about 460 items that are set in or focus on at least one of the four states often identified as the southwestern United States.

In addition to bibliographic data and subject headings, each entry includes a brief annotation (75-100 words). Each annotation describes the work, evaluates its merit, and suggests a follow-up activity [marked by a diamond (◆)] to encourage young people to extend the ideas or information in the work.

Materials in all media formats are considered, and the bibliographies may include significant professional materials. State contributors have selected only those items that they, from firsthand examination, can recommend for purchase or use. Most materials included are currently in print, but some are available only through small presses. Items that are out of print, but that are important resources and may still be available in libraries, are marked as out of print. Publisher addresses are included in the Directory of Publishers and Vendors.

Arizona

Arizona's rich tradition of Native American stories is evident in the available books and nonprint materials relating to the state. Many legends and myths are included in this guide, and the beauty of the text and the illustrations in them is remarkable. Also included are numerous books about specific tribes. Many of the books about Native Americans are now being written by Native Americans.

Desert life and desert creatures are popular topics for books about Arizona. Fiction and information books about the desert and its plant and animal inhabitants make up a large portion of the Arizona section.

Materials on Arizona history do not make up a major portion of the bibliography, and the same is unfortunately true for materials on current business and industry in Arizona. There is certainly a need for additional publications in these areas.

New Mexico

New Mexico, like Arizona, has many publications that relate to Native American contributions and to stories collected from Native Americans. New Mexico materials on Native Americans are both historical and contemporary in their treatment, and the quality of the publications is quite high.

The colorful history of New Mexico is a major focus of the New Mexico materials, including biographical materials. The Navajo Code Talkers from World War II, the Manhattan Project's Robert Oppenheimer, and numerous artists are a part of the New Mexico heritage represented in this section.

The difficulty in compiling the New Mexico bibliography was that the books and nonprint materials available are high caliber, but the choice of materials is limited. For this reason, the New Mexico bibliography has fewer titles than some of the other state sections.

Oklahoma

Three major concepts predominate in the Oklahoma publications: the Native American influence in the state, the economic impacts of the "dust bowl" and oil, and the southwestern culture of cowboys and homesteading.

The Oklahoma books and materials on Native Americans reflect a variety of perspectives. The rich cultural heritage is evident in the oral quality of the stories and the handsome illustrations that draw on Native American designs. Legal conflicts involving Native Americans and the reservations appear in several items.

Economic issues, as seen in information books and in fictional stories, are an important part of the Oklahoma materials. The Great Depression and the drought that caused the "dust bowl" are featured in numerous books and videos. These issues make for interesting reading, though some of the stories are gritty in their discussions of the extreme poverty and deprivation of the time. This poverty is contrasted in other materials with the wealth that the discovery of oil brought the state and its people. Economic development of Oklahoma is evident in many of the materials.

Will Rogers, cowboy culture, and homesteading are all part of another theme in the Oklahoma publications. The Land Rush and the settling of the West join stories of the western outlaw. From Edna Ferber, Wilson Rawls, Harold Keith, and S. E. Hinton come fictional stories set in Oklahoma that are loved far beyond Oklahoma's boundaries.

Texas

There is an expansiveness about the publications relating to Texas that matches the size of the state. Many outstanding materials are available, so many that the difficulty with this section was in trimming it to the best of the available materials. It is in the Texas resources that the cultural diversity of the southwestern portion of the United States is shown with most clarity. In both historical and contemporary Texas, the influence of the minority groups who settled in the Lone Star State has been highly significant, and this is evident in the quantities of books and other materials on minority groups. Fiction and nonfiction treatment of the history and current situation of minorities in the state proliferate.

From biographies about Texas rangers to stories about Susanna Dickinson, the woman Santa Anna allowed to leave the Alamo, the personalities in the stories are memorable, and it is here that the Texas list is most noteworthy. People like the legendary Pecos Bill or the nearly legendary Sam Houston provide excitement and interest to this list.

Texas independence is a major topic for the state, and the Alamo is remembered in many of these books. Fiction and nonfiction materials provide many opportunities for learning about the state's exciting history, and several books feature women who have contributed significantly to Texas and its development.

We welcome comments or suggestions of materials for future editions of this book, which can be sent in care of

Editorial Department
The Oryx Press
4041 N. Central Avenue, Suite 700
Phoenix, AZ 85012

Contributors

Regional Editor

Pat Tipton Sharp is chair of the Department of Curriculum and Instruction, School of Education, Baylor University, Waco, Texas. A professor in the School of Education, Dr. Sharp teaches children's literature and directs the Learning Resource Center. She has published articles and reviews in *School Library Journal, American Reference Books Annual,* and *Top of the News,* and has written chapters that appear in *Multicultural Aspects of Library Media Programs* and in *Public Relations for School Library Media Centers.*

State Editors

Anita S. Baker is associate professor of Curriculum and Instruction, School of Education, Baylor University, Waco, Texas. She is coordinator of the Teacher Recruitment Corps, a minority recruitment effort of Baylor University's School of Education, and a presenter at conferences at the local, state, and national levels. Several student organizations at Baylor have honored her as the outstanding female faculty member at the university.

Cathy C. Bonnell is library media specialist at Ironwood Elementary School in the Washington Elementary School District, Phoenix, Arizona. She is active in the Arizona State Library Association, serving as 1991-92 president of the School Library Media Division and the founding chairperson of the Children's Services Roundtable. She was named the Arizona Library Media Specialist of the Year in 1991 by the Arizona Educational Media Association.

Carol A. Sarath is library media specialist for the Gallup-McKinley County School District in Gallup, New Mexico. She is a member of the Advisory Council for Libraries for the State of New Mexico.

Terri Parker Street is an elementary school library media specialist in Norman, Oklahoma. A certified presenter in adult education, she has conducted numerous workshops on literature and literary activities, and teaches children's literature at the University of Oklahoma. She is also the co-author of *Literature-Based Art and Music* (Oryx, 1992) and of the forthcoming *Developing Learning Skills through Children's Literature: An Idea Book for K-5 Classrooms and Libraries, Volume 2* (Oryx, May 1994).

Arizona

by Cathy C. Bonnell

Nonfiction

291.212
Baylor, Byrd. *The Way to Start a Day.* Illus. by Peter Parnall. Scribner (0-684-15651-2), 1978. Unpaginated. Color illus. (Interest level: K-3).

Text and illustrations of this Caldecott Honor book describe people all over the world and throughout history celebrating the sunrise, beginning with Native Americans on the desert mesa. The author's very personal style and use of questions make the prose sound lyrical when read aloud.
♦ Readers who have experienced a sunrise may write or dictate their impressions, observations, and feelings. Others may be convinced to get up in time for a sunrise and record similar responses to the experience.
1. Sun worship.

291.212
The Way to Start a Day. (Videocassette). Best Film and Video, 1988. (Stories of American Indian Culture). 1/2" VHS, (12 min.). (Interest level: K-5).

Host Will Rogers, Jr., narrates this animated film version of the book by Byrd Baylor (*see* preceding entry). The film's illustrations are true to Peter Parnall's renderings of customs people around the world use to greet the day. Through imagination and Parnall's exquisite and colorful drawings, the enjoyable, positive story takes many different beliefs about dawn and extracts the beauty and wonder of a sunrise seen by all.

♦ After locating the four countries mentioned in the story, students may make a group mural to show how the four cultures greet the day.
1. Sun worship.

398.2
And It Is Still That Way: Legends Told by Arizona Indian Children; with Notes by Byrd Baylor. Charles Scribner's Sons (0-684-14676-2), 1976. 85p. (Interest level: K-4).

Forty-one short, traditional legends, each told by an Arizona Native American child and credited with the child's name, tribe, and school, were collected by Byrd Baylor as memories of stories from many tribes. When Native American legends are told today, they end with a statement such as "And it is still that way," or "It can happen like that now," so that listeners never feel that the legends are something from the past and finished. Using contemporary language, these tales recall the past and connect it with the present.
♦ Students may interview their ancestors to learn stories told in their families over the years and perhaps make a class compilation to be put into their school library.
1. Indians of North America—Legends.

398.2
Arrow to the Sun. (Videocassette). Films Incorporated, 1983. 1/2" VHS, (12 min.). $79.00. (Interest level: 2+).

This animated tale of the Acoma Pueblo Indians recounts the story of a boy's search for his father. The boy voyages on an arrow to the sun, undergoes trials in the sky village until he is recognized by his father, and then returns to Earth to spread the sun's warm delights. Used in conjunction with the book by Gerald McDermott (*see* p. 4), this color video provides an excellent example of Native American symbols integrated into story illustration.
♦ Students can experiment with animation using a video camera or by drawing on old, no longer needed 16mm film soaked in a solution of bleach diluted 50-50 with water. *Media Cookbook for Kids* by Mary Ellen Cravota (Libraries Unlimited, 1989) has instructions for bleaching film.
1. Acoma Indians—Legends.

398.2
Begay, Shonto. *Ma'ii and Cousin Horned Toad*. Illus. by author. Scholastic (0-590-45391-2), 1992. (Interest level: K-4).

Native American Shonto Begay weaves his own favorite childhood story of lazy, conniving Coyote, who takes advantage of his cousin Horned Toad until Horned Toad teaches him a lesson. This playful retelling, with Begay's richly imaginative paintings, captures the spirit and mystery of the Navajo world. The glossary of Navajo words and an afterword about Coyote and Horned Toad's place in the stories are particularly useful.
♦ Research about the coyote and the horned toad may lead students to write other adventure stories about these two desert dwellers.
1. Navajo Indians—Legends 2. Coyotes (Legendary character) 3. Horned toads—Folklore 4. Indians of North America—Legends.

398.2
Browne, Vee, reteller. *Monster Slayer: A Navajo Folktale*. Illus. by Baje Whitethorne. Northland Publishing (0-87358-525-9), 1991. 32p. Color illus. (Interest level: 1-4).

Twin brothers go in search of a terrible monster that is plaguing the Anasazi villages of the Southwest's canyon country, making villagers afraid to plant their crops. Retold and illustrated by Navajos Browne and Whitethorne, the story is magically alive with its strikingly bold and colorful pictures.
♦ Students may write or dictate and illustrate their own adventure about trying to rid the villages of a monster. A library or classroom display of the illustrations, along with the book, might encourage other students to do the same.
1. Navajo Indians—Legends 2. Indians of North America—Legends.

398.2
Carey, Valerie Scho, adapter. *Quail Song: A Pueblo Indian Tale*. Illus. by Ivan Barnett. Putnam (0-399-21936-6), 1990. (Interest level: K-4).

In this retelling of a Pueblo Indian trickster tale, Quail outwits the persistent Coyote. Colors and images reflect the Southwest setting. Children will quickly join in on the repetitive sounds the characters make and delight in the humor of this enjoyable tale told in the true storyteller tradition.
♦ The geometric shapes of the illustrations may inspire children to use cut-and-paste illustrations for a southwestern story of their own. Children may enjoy finding a special rock and painting it to look like the quail in the story.
1. Pueblo Indians—Legends 2. Indians of North America—Southwest.

398.2
Cohen, Caron Lee. *Mud Pony: A Traditional Skidi Pawnee Tale*. Illus. by Shonto Begay. Scholastic, Inc. (0-590-41525-5), 1988. (Reading Rainbow). 32p. Color illus. (Interest level: K-5).

This Reading Rainbow book is a traditional Skidi Pawnee hero tale of a boy who longs for a pony of his own. He shapes a pony out of mud, and Mother Earth turns the mud pony into a real one. As the boy becomes a powerful leader, the reader learns the rigors of village life and buffalo hunts. When the pony turns back to mud, the boy must find his own strength. The dreamlike illustrations of Shonto Begay, son of a Navajo medicine man, depict the world of ancient gods and animal beings that are still alive today in the myths of the Native American people.
♦ Students may shape their own ponies from clay and write a story about the adventures they would have if the pony came to life.
1. Indians of North America—Legends 2. Ponies—Folklore.

398.2
Cohlene, Terri. *Turquoise Boy: A Navajo Legend*. Illus. by Charles Reasoner. Rourke (0-86593-003-1), 1990. 47p. Color illus. (Interest level: K-4).

Turquoise Boy searches for something to make the Navajo people's lives easier in this retelling of a Navajo legend. Bold, colorful illustrations are accompanied with original photographs of Navajo people and their homes. A time line and glossary are included.
♦ Readers may make a dry sand painting as depicted in the book, or construct a model hogan using one of the three methods described in the history section.

1. Navajo Indians—Legends 2. Indians of North America—Legends 3. Indians of North America—Social life and customs.

398.2
Courlander, Harold. *People of the Short Blue Corn: Tales and Legends of the Hopi Indians.* Illus. by Enrico Arno. Harcourt Brace Jovanovich (0-15-260525-8), 1970. 189p. (Interest level: 4-8).

Folktales in this collection tell of the creation of the world, of deeds of courage and folly, and of magic and sorcery. Notes on Hopi oral literature at the end of the stories, a pronunciation guide, and a glossary make this book valuable for studying the Hopi culture.
♦ Students may choose any story in the collection and rewrite it, making their own version of a legend. Some students may wish to share their creations orally or in writing with other students.

1. Hopi Indians—Folklore 2. Indians of North America—Folklore.

398.2
Highwater, Jamake. *Anpao: An American Indian Odyssey.* Pictures by Fritz Scholder. Lippincott (0-397-31750-6), 1977. 256p. (Interest level: 6+).

Traditional tales from Great Plains and Southwest Native American peoples are woven into a single story that relates the adventures of a boy as he grows to manhood. This Newbery Honor book conveys the rich heritage of Native Americans by weaving old and new in the classic tradition of the Native American storyteller.
♦ Older students may learn one of the "lessons" or stories from the book well enough to tell it to younger students during a story session.

1. Indians of North America—Legends.

398.2
Hoyt-Goldsmith, Diane. *Pueblo Storyteller.* Photos by Lawrence Migdale. Holiday (0-8234-0864-7), 1991. 32p. Color photos. (Interest level: 3-5).

Crisp, full-color photos and first-person text relate the everyday life of 10-year-old April and her grandparents, as well as tell the Pueblo legend "How the People Came to Earth." The photographic essay portrays the ancient customs of pottery making, bread baking, and drum making. An index is included.
♦ Making fry bread in the classroom is exciting, especially since students can eat the end product.

1. Indians of North America—Social life and customs 2. Pueblo Indians—Legends.

398.2
Lacapa, Michael, reteller. *Antelope Woman: An Apache Folktale.* Illus. by author. Northland Publishing (0-87358-543-7), 1992. 41p. Color illus. (Interest level: 2-6).

"Respect all things great and small" is the theme of this Apache story, which features a beautiful young maiden and a stranger. The maiden follows the stranger through four magical hoops, and they both turn into antelopes. The story is told by a father to his son, giving the reader a sense of the warmth in the storytelling tradition. The book's boldly colored, geometrical illustrations enhance the tale, whose message is one of love and the need to honor family and all life.
♦ Students may paint their own renditions of the magical hoops, using the book for inspiration. The class can plan a schoolwide display to share their work with others.

1. Indians of North America—Folklore 2. Apache Indians—Folklore.

398.2
Lacapa, Michael. *The Flute Player: An Apache Folktale.* Illus. by author. Northland Publishing (0-87358-500-3), 1990. 32p. Color illus. (Interest level: K-4).

Of Apache/Hopi descent, Michael Lacapa tells the tale of a young Apache flute player whose music echoes from the walls of a southwestern canyon and captures the heart of a beautiful girl who dies of grief when the flute player goes on his first hunt. Bright colors and bold graphics accompany this story, which has been told by tribal elders for centuries.
♦ Students may enjoy experimenting with sounds on inexpensive wood flutes or recorders.

1. Apache Indians—Legends.

398.2
McDermott, Gerald. *Arrow to the Sun.* Illus. by author. Viking Press (0-670-13369-8), 1974. Unpaginated. Color illus. (Interest level: 2-4).

This Caldecott-winning adaptation of the Pueblo myth explains how the spirit of the Lord of the Sun was brought to the world of man. The stunningly bold and colorful illustrations by McDermott could tell the story alone, but the easy text makes enjoyable reading for all.
♦ Students may paint or color a version of their star shooting to the sun. Be sure to display the results for all to see.
1. Mythology, Pueblo Indians 2. Indians of North America—Religion.

398.2
Oughton, Jerrie. *How the Stars Fell into the Sky: A Navajo Legend.* Illus. by Lisa Desimini. Houghton Mifflin (0-395-58798-0), 1992. Unpaginated. (Interest level: 1-4).

Author Oughton and illustrator Desimini team to retell a powerful Navajo legend that provides a fanciful answer to the question children have asked for centuries about the origin of star patterns in the sky. Poetic language, combined with intense and dramatic paintings, beautifully invokes the desert settings and the grandeur of the night sky.
♦ Have students punch holes in a plastic coffee-can lid with a pen or pencil in the pattern of a constellation, and then have them color the lid with a permanent black marker. Place a piece of black paper around the can lid, and using a flashlight or an overhead projector, project the constellation through the lid onto a wall to accompany a student's discussion of the constellation shown.
1. Navajo Indians—Legends 2. Indians of North America—Southwest—Legends.

398.2
Rodanas, Kristina. *Dragonfly's Tale.* Illus. by author. Clarion Books (0-395-57003-4), 1992. 22p. Color illus. (Interest level: K-5).

Similar to Tony Hillerman's retelling of the same Zuni legend in *The Boy Who Made Dragonfly: A Zuni Myth* (*see* p. 23), and enhanced by strong visual images, this story reflects the Zuni people's concern with kindness to others and their respect for the gifts of nature. Colorful, vivid full-page illustrations by the author depict the vast panoramas of the Southwest.
♦ Students may wish to draw dragonflies or make pop-up insect books after seeing illustrations in informational books on insects.
1. Zuni Indians—Legends 2. Indians of North America.

398.2
Rucki, Ani. *Turkey's Gift to the People.* Illus. by author. Northland Publishing (0-87358-541-0), 1992. 32p. Color illus. (Interest level: K-4).

The animal people are threatened by flood and gather together to save themselves. Mr. and Mrs. Turkey are missing, but they become heroes after the others discover that the turkeys alone have remembered to save seeds crucial for replanting after the flood. The brilliant colors and sharply outlined characters in the illustrations add to the enjoyment of this traditional Navajo folktale.
♦ Students may plant seeds of various types in the classroom or on the school grounds and make turkeys using pine cones and feathers to watch over the growth.
1. Navajo Indians—Folklore 2. Indians of North America—Folklore 3. Animals—Folklore.

398.8
Griego, Margot. *Tortillitas Para Mama: And Other Nursery Rhymes/Spanish and English.* Illus. by Barbara Cooney. Henry Holt & Company (0-8050-0285-5), 1981. Unpaginated. Color illus. (Interest level: Preschool-2).

These rhymes and fingerplays in English and Spanish have been passed on in the oral tradition by generations of Spanish-speaking families. These familiar rhymes, accompanied with beautiful, rich, earth-tone illustrations that capture the authenticity of the Hispanic subjects, kindle feelings of warmth, security, and love.
♦ Older readers may teach the rhymes to or perform the rhymes for younger children, and then have the younger readers chant the rhymes together. Teachers may want to teach children the Spanish versions of nursery rhymes that students know in English and then compare the rhythm of the words in each language.
1. Nursery rhymes, Spanish 2. Nursery rhymes, English.

551.4
Mike, Jan M. *Desert Seasons.* Illus. by Samuel A. Mike. Treasure Chest Publications (0-

918080-49-5 pbk), 1991. Unpaginated. Color illus. (Interest level: K-4).

This Tucson, Arizona, author/illustrator team re-creates the four desert seasons, as a young narrator relates his favorite events for each one. The full-page airbrush illustrations create soft impressionistic scenes of desert animals, plants, weather, insects, customs, and sweeping vistas.
♦ Working in cooperative groups, students may duplicate in watercolor the seasonal changes on the desert as they construct a mural for the school or library.

1. Deserts 2. Seasons.

574.5
Baylor, Byrd. *The Desert Is Theirs.* Illus. by Peter Parnall. Scribner (0-684-14266-X), 1975. Unpaginated. Color illus. (Interest level: Preschool-3).

This Caldecott Honor Book examines the closeness of the Papago Indians to the harsh land that they share with all other living things. The simple lyrical text and dramatic illustrations give insight into an ecological philosophy of living in harmony with nature.
♦ Students may write reports to share with others concerning habitats and food chains of desert animals and cultural attributes of the Papago Indians related to living in harmony with nature.

1. Deserts 2. Ecology 3. Papago Indians—Social life and customs.

574.5
Guiberson, Brenda Z. *Cactus Hotel.* Illus. by Megan Lloyd. Holt (0-8050-1333-4), 1991. Unpaginated. Color illus. (Interest level: Preschool-3).

In describing the life cycle of the giant saguaro cactus of the Sonoran Desert, *Cactus Hotel* emphasizes the plant's role as a home for desert dwellers, and provides the young reader a visual delight. A fact page at the end of the text gives additional information about the life cycle of the saguaro and the people and animals it impacts.
♦ Students may wish to read *Desert Giant: The World of the Saguaro Cactus* by Barbara Bash (*see* p. 6) along with this book.

1. Cactus 2. Desert plants 3. Desert animals 4. Sonoran Desert.

574.5
Spencer, Guy J. *A Living Desert.* Photos by Tim Fuller. Troll Associates (0-8167-1169-0), 1988. (Let's Take a Trip). 32p. (Interest level: 2-6).

The description of plants and animals of the Arizona Sonoran Desert is accompanied with exquisite photographs introducing young readers to the many wonders of a green, living desert. The high-quality photography and easy-to-read but fact-filled text make this title an excellent resource for desert studies.
♦ Students who live near a desert may take a short walking tour and keep a log of and photograph plants and animals seen. Other students may make language webs that describe the desert plants and animals about which they have read.

1. Deserts—Southwest 2. Desert animals 3. Desert plants 4. Sonoran Desert.

574.5
Wiewandt, Thomas. *The Hidden Life of the Desert.* Photos by author. Crown (0-517-57355-5), 1990. 40p. Color photos. (Interest level: 1-4).

Through brief text and color photographs, taken in actual desert settings, the author shows Sonoran Desert events not often witnessed by humans: a desert tortoise eating prickly pear fruit, a long-nosed bat dining on century plant nectar, a female scorpion carrying her brood on her back, a desert iguana eating creosote bush flowers, and much more. The excellent quality of the photography and the chatty style of the text make this title very popular with students and teachers.
♦ Students may enjoy taking photographs of unusual animals, plants, or weather conditions to enter in an all-school photo contest.

1. Deserts—Southwest 2. Desert animals 3. Desert plants.

582.13
Magley, Beverly. *Arizona Wildflowers: A Children's Field Guide to the State's Most Common Flowers.* Illus. by D. D. Dowden. Falcon Press Publishing (1-56044-096-1), 1991. (Interpreting the Great Outdoors). 32p. Color illus. (Interest level: 4-6).

This field guide to 50 of Arizona's most common flowers is handsome and useful. Each flowering plant is beautifully illustrated by D. D. Dowden and described with its various common names and its botanical name. Cautionary notes are given for poisonous plants, as well as a glossary and a list of the best places to see wildflowers in Arizona.

♦ Take students on a search for wildflowers in your area, using this or another field guide appropriate to your area. Encourage students to draw or photograph the flowers, not pick them.
1. Wildflowers.

583
Bash, Barbara. *Desert Giant: The World of the Saguaro Cactus.* Illus. by author. Little, Brown & Co. (0-316-08301-1), 1989. Unpaginated. Color illus. (Interest level: 1-5).

A picture-book format helps readers gain a better understanding of the life cycle and ecosystem of the giant saguaro cactus, depicted in its habitat in the Sonoran Desert. The animals who live and feed off the saguaro are shown, as is the harvest ritual of the Tohono O'odham Indians, who for centuries have gathered the sweet fruit. The simple, easy-to-read text and appealing drawings by the author will help readers develop a better understanding of and a lasting respect for this giant of the desert. A related book on the same topic for the same general age group is *Cactus Hotel* by Brenda Guiberson (*see* p. 5).

♦ Students may draw a desert scene for a library or school display depicting how an animal uses the saguaro cactus. Also, using a simple sugar cookie recipe, students can make and roll out cookie dough, cut out cookies in the shape of a saguaro cactus, and bake them for a special treat.
1. Cactus 2. Desert plants 3. Ecology.

583
Busch, Phyllis S. *Cactus in the Desert.* Illus. by Harriett Barton. Crowell (0-690-01336-1), 1979. 34p. (Interest level: Preschool-3).

This simple, clear explanation of the adaptation of cacti to desert environments is illustrated with drawings depicting cross sections of several kinds of cacti. Much information is presented in an interesting manner for the youngest reader.

♦ Students may soak rigatoni noodles, standing up, in a baking pan of water that reaches half way up the noodles. The rigatoni noodles will swell in water as the cactus does when it absorbs and stores water for the plant's use during long dry periods. After 3-4 hours, students may record or dictate their observations and discuss differences in these noodles and dry noodles.
1. Cactus 2. Desert plants—Southwest.

583
Holmes, Anita. *The 100-Year-Old Cactus.* Illus. by Carol Lerner. Four Winds Press (0-590-07634-5), 1983. Unpaginated. Color illus. (Interest level: K-3).

This story offers one possible set of events for the first 100 years of the life of a saguaro cactus, as it grows from seed to adult plant in the Arizona desert. This informational book reads like a storybook; the events described show how the saguaro cactus provides food and shelter for desert animals and birds. Bold, lifelike illustrations enhance the text.

♦ Planting cactus seeds in pots or on the school grounds for an ongoing, all-school activity may keep students coming back to school to check the progress for years to come. Students may also make drawings, models, and/or dioramas of the saguaro at different stages of growth.
1. Cactus 2. Ecology—Arizona 3. Desert ecology.

591
Animal Trackers. (Computer software for Apple II). WINGS (No ISBN), 1989. Teacher's guide $139.95. (Interest level: 3-8).

In *Animal Trackers*, students try to identify an animal in a woodland, grassland, or desert biome using clues such as tracks, dens, broken brush, or scraps of food. Program users may choose from among three levels of difficulty. Students employ higher-level thinking skills to interpret clues they record on an online notepad and search for data about the characteristics of the animals in an online field guide. The interesting and enjoyable program gives students practice using many problem-solving skills such as examining assumptions, making organized lists, successive scanning, and information gathering.

♦ Students working in teams in the computer lab may share hypotheses and strategies to reach their goal of identifying the animal and discuss similarities and differences of animals that were identified. Students may enjoy playing a game of "20 Questions" using only questions that can be answered with "yes" or "no" to identify an animal they have studied. If possible, the class may take a field trip to a desert biome to look for animal signs, and then record their findings by drawing sketches or making plaster casts of deep prints.
1. Animal tracks.

591
Clark, Ann Nolan. *Along Sandy Trails.* Viking (0-670-11485-5), 1969 (out of print). 31p. Color photos. (Interest level: Preschool-3).

A young Native American girl and her grandmother walk along the sandy trails of their desert home and marvel at the beauty of the plants and animals they see. The intergenerational relationship is depicted in sensitive text and exquisite color photographs, which show the findings of the two walkers. Several customs of Native American life are described.
♦ Students may take a nature walk together to observe types of plants and animals, and then record their impressions and findings. They may also examine the area for signs of pollution, or organize a cleanup campaign for a playground or other area. Students may want to write letters to the local newspaper or to their elected officials concerning the need to protect the environment.
1. Indians of North America 2. Desert plants—Southwest 3. Desert animals—Southwest.

591.5
Coyote. (Videocassette). Encyclopaedia Britannica Educational Corporation, 1988. (Video Ways to Reading). 1/2" VHS, (12 min.). $99.00. (Interest level: Preschool-2).

Characteristic activities of coyotes in their natural habitat are presented in this video, which highlights both dramatic situations and everyday occurrences. The color video is repeated in three identical parts with key words appearing on the screen for use in reading instruction as the viewer watches a typical day in the coyote den.
♦ Students may discuss what they found out about the coyote and its habitat, and then collaborate on a class story about coyotes, which the teacher writes on a chart. Each student may illustrate the class story.
1. Desert animals 2. Coyotes.

591.5
George, Jean Craighead. *One Day in the Desert.* Illus. by Fred Brenner. Thomas Y. Crowell (0-690-04340-6), 1983. 48p. B/W illus. (Interest level: 3-6).

In this sensitive book, Jean Craighead George explains how the animal and human inhabitants of the Sonoran Desert of Arizona, including a mountain lion, a roadrunner, a coyote, a tortoise, and members of the Papago Indian tribe, adapt to and survive the desert's intense heat on a July day. Attractive drawings by Fred Brenner add to this beautiful description of the desert's fascination.
♦ Have students write a chronicle of a day in their community, perhaps focusing on extremes in their climate and the accommodation necessary.
1. Desert ecology 2. Sonoran Desert 3. Heat, Physiological effect 4. Papago Indians 5. Indians of North America—Arizona.

591.9
Kirk, Ruth. *Desert Life.* Photos by Ruth Kirk and Louis Kirk. Natural History Press for The American Museum of Natural History (0-385-02446-0), 1970. Unpaginated. Color illus. (Interest level: Preschool-4).

Full-color photographs and sparse, easy-to-read text depict the land, weather, plants, and animals of the unnamed American desert. This introduction to life in the desert will give readers a sense of the desert's beauty.
♦ Students may choose one of the animals introduced, do further research, then share their information with others in the class or school.
1. Deserts 2. Desert animals 3. Desert plants.

595.4
Mell, Jan. *The Scorpion.* Crestwood House (0-89686-520-7), 1990. (Wildlife, Habits and Habitat). 47p. Color photos. (Interest level: 2-6).

Photographs and text examine the physical characteristics, behavior, and natural environment of the scorpion, a desert creature sure to fascinate students. Stunning color photographs, an index, and a glossary make this a valuable tool for studying the scorpion.
♦ If possible, a trip to the insect section of the zoo will give students a firsthand view of the many types of scorpions. Students' enlarged drawings of the various types of scorpions could adorn a school gallery.
1. Scorpions.

598.2
Amon, Aline. *Roadrunners and Other Cuckoos.* Atheneum (0-689-30646-6), 1978. 87p. B/W illus. (Interest level: 4-8).

The desert roadrunner and other members of the cuckoo family are discussed, with emphasis on physical characteristics and behaviors. Only one chapter is devoted to the roadrunner, but readers will find the description of the bird's attack on a rattlesnake very exciting. Detailed black line drawings illustrate

the book, which also contains an index and extensive bibliography.
♦ Students may write a comic-book sequence about a day in the life of a desert roadrunner, then illustrate it in comic-book style, with frames for each part of the day.
1. Roadrunners 2. Cuckoos 3. Desert animals.

599.0979
Skramstad, Jill. *Wildlife Southwest.* Chronicle Books (0-8118-0216-8), 1992. 55p. Color photos. (Chronicle Junior Nature Series). (Interest level: 3-8).

Twenty-five animals often seen in the southwestern United States are profiled with details of each animal's habits as well as enemies and endangered status. Unusual creatures such as the ringtail, horned lizard, and desert tortoise along with the more familiar ones such as the coyote and mule deer are shown in excellent close-up, captioned photographs. The brief, informative text will help the reader develop a lasting appreciation and respect for creatures in our fragile environment.
♦ After a study of desert animals, students may form cooperative groups to poll students in the school about their favorite desert animal and then graph the voting results. Perhaps then the class could raise money to participate in the "adopt-a-pet" program of a local zoo by adopting the winning animal. Students may also plan a field trip to listen and look for wildlife in their area, sketching tracks and signs.
1. Desert animals—Southwest.

811
Baylor, Byrd. *The Other Way to Listen.* Illus. by Peter Parnall. Charles Scribner's Sons (0-684-16017-X), 1978 (out of print). (Interest level: Preschool-4).

A young boy and an old man explore the desert, listening to sounds around them and observing the beauty of nature. After hoping and trying, the narrator of the story is finally able to hear the hills singing, because he has learned wisdom and patience from his elder in this tender and lyrical story of an intergenerational relationship.
♦ A class may visit a local retirement or rest home, and after getting to know the residents, students may take a nature walk with a new friend listening for especially interesting sounds. Students may share and compare their experiences after returning to the classroom or media center.
1. Nature poetry 2. Deserts—Poetry.

811
Geis, Jacqueline. *Where the Buffalo Roam.* Ideals Children's Books (0-8249-5870-2 lib bind), 1992. Unpaginated. Color illus. (Interest level: Preschool-4).

This adaptation of the favorite song "Home on the Range" showcases the animals, plants, and geographical features of the American Southwest, highlighting endangered species. The familiar text adds additional interpretive verses. Flowing watercolors are framed in a unique design using tinted reproductions of prehistoric Native American drawings. A glossary is included.
♦ Students may prepare a class book of their own in which they adapt a favorite song.
1. Desert animals—Poetry 2. Southwestern States 3. Folk songs—United States.

811
Jernigan, Gisela. *One Green Mesquite Tree.* Illus. by E. Wesley Jernigan. Harbinger House (0-943173-35-3), 1989. Unpaginated. Color illus. (Interest level: Preschool-4).

One Green Mesquite Tree radiates the magic of the southwestern desert, a land humming with life in the smallest and most unexpected places. Large, colorful numbers, from one through 20, introduce young, native southwestern plants and animals through lively poetry and exquisite illustrations.
♦ Students can make their own counting books using action verbs to describe their favorite plants and animals; then the books can be added to the library media center collection for the whole school to use.
1. Deserts—Southwest 2. Counting.

811
Maher, Ramona. *Alice Yazzie's Year.* Illus. by Stephen Gammell. Coward, McCann & Geoghegan (0-698-20432-8), 1977 (out of print). (Interest level: 2-8).

Twelve free-verse poems chronicle the events and feelings of a Navajo girl's 11th year. Gammell's haunting illustrations join the insightful text to create a beautifully designed book.
♦ Students may write poetry or prose to record their own life experiences through the months of one year. Or students may construct time lines of events in their lives or in the lives of their families.
1. Navajo Indians—Poetry 2. Indians of North America—Poetry.

811
The Other Way to Listen. (Videocassette). Southwest Series, 1988. 1/2" VHS, (16 min.). $39.95. (Interest level: Preschool-4).

This live-action film, narrated by Will Rogers, Jr., gives the viewer a vicarious trip through the desert, as a young boy and an old man explore and listen to the world around them. The film is based on *The Other Way to Listen* by Byrd Baylor (*see* p. 8) and follows closely the text of that book. Through this video, we see cactus blooming and lizards sunning themselves, as well as enjoy a little magic and imagination.
♦ Students may sit quietly in the classroom, with the lights off, listening to all the sounds around them and writing down what they think they hear; then the class can compare the lists.

1. Nature poetry 2. Deserts—Poetry.

811.54
Jernigan, Gisela. *Agave Blooms Just Once.* Illus. by E. Wesley Jernigan. Harbinger House (0-943173-46-9; 0-943173-44-2 pbk), 1989. Unpaginated. Color illus. (Interest level: Preschool-3).

Illustrated verses from A to Z present 26 Sonoran Desert plants and animals, with a glossary for additional information. Stylized letter forms are based on Hohokam pottery designs, and geometric borders on each page set off the uncluttered and earth-colored illustrations.
♦ Students may write alphabet books (rhyming or not) about items that are important to them or found in their community. Then they can share the books with others in their school or library.

1. Nature poetry 2. Alphabet 3. Desert plants—Poetry 4. Desert animals—Poetry.

917.3
The Southwest. (Videocassette). National Geographic, 1983. (United States Geography Series). 1/2" VHS, (27 min.). $79.00. (Interest level: 4-8).

This National Geographic video focuses on the physical, cultural, and economic aspects of the geography of Arizona, Texas, New Mexico, and Oklahoma. Outstanding video photography is complemented by the narration in this outstanding documentary.
♦ After viewing this video, students may plan and produce a documentary film of their city or neighborhood. Arrange for the library media specialist to assist the students in taping the final product.

1. United States—Geography—Southwest 2. Oklahoma—Geography 3. Texas—Geography 4. New Mexico—Geography 5. Arizona—Geography.

917.91
Filbin, Dan. *Arizona.* Lerner (0-8225-2705-7 lib bind), 1990. (Hello U.S.A.). 72p. Color photos and illus. (Interest level: 3-8).

Color photos, maps, and illustrations combine with a brief, interesting text to introduce Arizona geography, history, industry, and people. A facts-at-a-glance section, a glossary, and an index make this a valuable research tool for intermediate-grade readers and for reluctant readers in junior high.
♦ Students may use this and other resources to write and illustrate a promotional brochure for Arizona, or they may write a letter to recommend the special features of Arizona to a friend who is planning a vacation.

1. Arizona—Description and travel 2. Arizona—History.

917.91
Heinrichs, Ann. *Arizona.* Childrens Press (0-516-00449-2), 1991. (America the Beautiful). 143p. Color photos. (Interest level: 4-8).

The reader is introduced to the geography, history, government, economy, industry, culture, historic sites, and famous people of Arizona. The full-color photographs, time line, various maps and map key (including the new county divisions), facts-at-a-glance section, and complete index make this volume very useful for doing research papers.
♦ Students may write a paper comparing a state they have lived in or visited and Arizona. Students may also want to outline a trip to Arizona, indicating all the sites they would like to visit and calculating the distances they will travel.

1. Arizona—Description and travel 2. Arizona—History.

970
Indian Boy of the Southwest. (Videocassette). Phoenix/BFA Films, 1983. 1/2" VHS, (19 min.). $260.00. (Interest level: 2-8).

Through scenes not often seen by persons outside the Native American culture, the viewer experiences Hopi family life, work, and the colorful seasonal rituals that enable the Hopi people to transmit the communal values

and survival skills that have kept their culture alive. The film helps students appreciate the cultural diversity of the many people of the Southwest by showing typical scenes of daily life and family relationships.
♦ Students may want to try making, painting, and firing clay pots, as shown in the film. The class may also grind corn into flour, make cornbread or corn tortillas, and listen to Native American tales while eating.
1. Indians of North America—Southwest.

970
Native Peoples of the Southwest. (Kit). The Heard Museum Shop and Bookstore, Heard Museum, 1987. 5 sets; each set includes slides, audiocassette, transparencies, teacher's resource binder, student booklets, and artifact. (Interest level: 2-8).

The Heard Museum, specializing in Native American art and artifacts, has produced five multimedia instructional packets that use specific Native American tribes to discuss these social studies topics: family life, community, archaeology and cultural history, the influences of environment, and cultural change. Each kit includes a teacher's resource binder, containing lesson plans, cassettes, slides, songs, and observations by tribal members, as well as overhead transparencies, 30 student booklets, and an authentic Native American artifact. The entire series, used together as a unit of study, will provide a wealth of information to integrate many content areas into the elementary curriculum, as well as provide hands-on artifacts for students to learn an appreciation of the diversity of these cultures.
♦ Students may plan a mini-festival for the school, complete with food and craft-making booths, highlighting the various topics and tribes they have studied.
1. Indians of North America—Southwest 2. Apache Indians 3. Hopi Indians 4. Anasazi Indians 5. Tohono O'Odham Indians 6. Navajo Indians.

970.004
Ancient Indian Cultures of Northern Arizona. (Videocassette). Finley-Holiday Film Corp. (National Parks and Monument Series). 1/2" VHS, (30 min.). $24.95. (Interest level: 3-8).

This video presents a history of the Anasazi and Sinagua civilizations and explores the ruins of five national monuments of Arizona: Montezuma's Castle, Wupatki, Tuzigoot, Walnut Canyon, and Sunset Crater. Color photography of the ruins and surrounding areas is accompanied with effective narration to help the viewer understand the impact of these ancient civilizations.
♦ After viewing the video, students may write a story about a child who might have lived in one of these locations many years ago.
1. Indians of North America—Southwest 2. Anasazi Indians 3. Sinagua Indians.

970.004
Keegan, Marcia. *Pueblo Boy: Growing Up in Two Worlds.* Photos by author. Cobblehill Books (0-525-65060-1), 1991. 48p. (Interest level: 2-6).

Schoolroom computers and Walkmans coexist with traditional Pueblo ceremonies and study in the life of Timmy Roybal, a 10-year-old Pueblo boy who is a member of the Corn Clan and lives in San Ildefonso Pueblo, New Mexico. Sharp, clear photographs and descriptive text depict the home, school, and cultural life of a young boy with whom readers can readily identify, and students will learn much about the Pueblo culture.
♦ Students may correspond as pen pals with students who live on reservations or in traditional Native American communities to compare and tell about each of their lifestyles. Pen pal names may be obtained by writing to Interior Department of the United States Government, Bureau of Indian Affairs.
1. Pueblo Indians—Biography 2. Pueblo Indians—Social life and customs.

970.004
Warren, Scott. *Cities in the Sand: The Ancient Civilizations of the Southwest.* Photos by author. Chronicle Books (0-8118-0012-1), 1991. 64p. Color photos. (Interest level: 4-7).

The well-researched text and full-color photographs work together to examine the world of three prehistoric peoples: the Anasazi, the Hohokam, and the Mogollon. Students will find the text interesting for informational reading and useful for research projects; teachers will rely on the authenticity of information to supplement textbooks.
♦ Collaborative groups of students may brainstorm about what might be left as remnants of our civilization after several hundred years if a catastrophe occurred. Students could then write individual stories about ar-

chaeologists coming upon the ruins and trying to learn about this society.
1. Anasazi Indians 2. Hohokam Indians 3. Mogollon Indians.

970.3
Corn Is Life. (Videocassette). Tellens, Inc., for the Museum of Northern Arizona. Museum of Northern Arizona, 1982. 1/2" VHS, (20 min.). $19.95. (Interest level: 2-8).

This video shows scenes of family life, work, and colorful seasonal rituals of a vital, 1,000-year-old Native American culture in northern Arizona and discusses the ways the Hopis pass on the communal values and survival skills that have kept their culture alive. Through scenes rarely seen by outsiders, the viewer will see the Hopi people living in ancient villages built on top of mesas rising from the floor of northern Arizona's desert land. The title of this video is given on the title screen as *Corn Is Life*; the label title is *The Hopi.*
♦ Students may try grinding various kinds of corn and making cornbread or corn tortillas.
1. Hopi Indians 2. Indians of North America—Southwest.

973.0497
Osinski, Alice. *The Navajo.* Childrens Press (0-516-01236-3 pbk), 1987. (A New True Book). 45p. B/W and Color photos. (Interest level: K-4).

This brief history of the Navajo of Arizona, Utah, and New Mexico includes customs, interactions with white settlers, and changes in traditional ways of life necessitated by modern civilization. Color and historic black-and-white photos, a glossary, and an index make this thin book rich in information and visual delights.
♦ Students may list 10 important facts they learned by reading this book, and then write a reaction to the adjustment the Navajos have made from traditional to modern culture.
1. Navajo Indians 2. Indians of North America.

973.04972
Sneve, Virginia Driving Hawk. *The Navajos: A First Americans Book.* Illus. by Ronald Himler. Holiday House (0-8234-1039-0), 1993. 32p. Color illus. (Interest level 3-8).

Navajo history, culture, and present life are described so that ceremonies, rituals, and beliefs may be understood. Ronald Himler's majestic illustrations capture the tribe's family life. The book begins with an excerpt from the Navajo creation story and continues through the historic change from a culturally and economically rich people to a people struggling to recapture their identity, all told in a gentle, nonjudgmental way.
♦ Students may choose an aspect described in the book such as the coming of the white men, family life, ceremony, or battle, and write a "What if . . . " story about a fictional character whose life is affected by this event or situation.
1. Navajo Indians 2. Indians of North America—Southwest.

979
Aylesworth, Thomas G. and Aylesworth, Virginia L. *The West: Arizona, Nevada, Utah.* Chelsea House Publishers (9-7910-1049-X), 1992. (State Reports). 64p. Color illus. (Interest level: 3-6).

Geographical, historical, and cultural aspects make this fact-filled book on three states interesting reading and provide excellent concise data for report writing. An index and bibliography add to the usefulness of the work, and extensive color photographs provide added information.
♦ Collaborative groups may take one topic from the book and research it further in the school media center to prepare an oral report to give for the class, perhaps accompanied with overhead transparencies prepared from selected photographs from the book.
1. Arizona.

979
Yue, Charlotte and Yue, David. *The Pueblo.* Houghton Mifflin (0-395-38350-1), 1986. 117p. B/W illus. (Interest level: 4+).

The world of the Pueblo is introduced through descriptions of how their elegant stone masonry cities were built high in the walls of sheer cliffs, and how the inhabitants mastered their environment and lived in harmony with it. Black-and-white line drawings, filled with absorbing detail, capture both the reality and the spirit of the Pueblo. A bibliography and an index are provided.
♦ Students may work in cooperative groups to build scale models of the Pueblo villages and display them in the library for all students to see.
1. Pueblo Indians 2. Indians of North America—Southwestern States.

979.01
Trimble, Stephen. *The Village of Blue Stone.* Illus. by Jennifer Owings Dewey and Deborah Reade. Macmillan (0-02-789501-7), 1990. 64p. (Interest level: 3-8).

Trimble chronicles the daily life of the Anasazi, who lived in elaborate pueblo villages in the Southwest before mysteriously fading from history around the beginning of the fourteenth century. Carefully researched vignettes of farming, hunting, pottery making, storytelling, and ceremonial life re-create the life of both the people and the now silent but still imposing ruins. An index, a glossary, an author's note, recommended additional resources, and a list of Anasazi ruins to visit are included.
♦ Students may build a scale model or diorama of an Anasazi village after further research.
1. Indians of North America—Southwest—Social life and customs 2. Pueblo Indians—Social life and customs 3. Cliff dwellers and cliff dwellings—Southwestern States.

979.1
Carpenter, Allan. *Arizona.* Childrens Press (0-516-04103-7), 1979. (The New Enchantment of America). 96p. Color photos. (Interest level: 4-8).

Focusing on the Grand Canyon State, Carpenter discusses its history, famous citizens, and places of interest in a readable text. Color photographs enhance the information, which is given in straightforward style with a handy reference section of "instant facts" and an index for easy research. Though the book is older, much of the information, especially the historical data, is still useful.
♦ Have students use other media center resources to update the "Handy Reference Section" with new information.
1. Arizona.

979.1
Cobb, Vicki. *This Place Is Dry.* Illus. by Barbara Lavallee. Walker (0-8027-6854-7), 1989. Unpaginated. Color illus. (Interest level: 2-5).

This overview of the life of plants, animals, and people of the Arizona Sonoran Desert includes a short history of the Hohokam and a description of the engineering accomplishment of Roosevelt Dam. Colorful drawings enhance this simple but thorough examination of desert life.
♦ Readers may write a story about what might happen and the various animals, plants, and people they might encounter on a camping trip to the desert. Students may do further research to find tips for safe camping in the desert.
1. Arizona—Description and travel 2. Deserts 3. Sonoran Desert.

979.1
Fradin, Dennis Brindell. *Arizona.* Childrens Press (0-516-03803-6), 1993. (From Sea to Shining Sea). 64p. B/W and Color illus. (Interest level: 4-6).

This interesting introduction provides data on the geography, history, industries, notable sights, and famous people of the Grand Canyon State. Attractive photographs and drawings, succinct information, a glossary, and an index enable students to learn much about the state.
♦ Have students research the Grand Canyon, the Saguaro National Monument, or one of the other highlights of Arizona and, if possible, plan a trip to visit it.
1. Arizona.

979.1
Heinrichs, Ann. *America the Beautiful: Arizona.* Childrens Press, 1991. (0-516-00449-2), 185p. B/W and Color illus. (Interest level: 4-8).

An overview of the state and its history is presented in simple text. Fascinating details and numerous black-and-white and color photographs make this book appealing to students, and an extensive "Facts at a Glance" section, which includes a capsule biographical section of famous Arizonans, makes this resource highly useful.
♦ Encourage each student to research an individual included in the "Important People" section of the book and write a week of diary entries this person might have written during a significant time in his or her life.
1. Arizona.

979.1
Love, Frank. *Arizona's Story: A Short History.* B/W illus. Pruett Publishing (0-87108-218-7), 1986, 1979. 185p. B/W illus. (Interest level: 6-8).

This second edition of a survey of Arizona history for middle school grades focuses on the many people who influenced the state's development. Black-and-white illustrations add to the information about the state, and an index provides a means for students to do research.
♦ Have student groups create an illustrated time line showing the special-interest stories

from the state that the author included at the end of each chapter in an "Additional Information" section.
1. Arizona—History.

979.1
Thompson, Kathleen. *Arizona.* Steck-Vaughn (0-8114-6769-4), 1991. (Portrait of America). Color and B/W illus. 49p. (Interest level: 3-6).

This attractive book discusses the history, economy, culture, and future of Arizona. Nearly half of each double-page spread in the book is made up of color photographs and illustrations of Arizona, its people, and its magnificent landscapes. Students will also find the state chronology, pertinent statistics, maps, and index in this slight volume useful.
♦ Students may do collaborative research on the annual Arizona events listed on page 48, writing for added information and planning an imaginary trip to various celebrations and fairs.
1. Arizona.

Biography

92 Nampeyo, Daisy Hooee
Fowler, Carol. *Daisy Hooee Nampeyo.* Dillon Press, 1977 (out of print). (The Story of an American Indian). 74p. B/W photos. (Interest level: 4-8).

This biography tells the fascinating story of noted potter Daisy Hooee Nampeyo, whose failing sight at age 11 took her from her Arizona home to California for surgery and school, then to France for art study before she returned to Arizona. Though this book is out of print, the quality black-and-white photographs provide an interesting introduction to the art and the life of an American artist.
♦ Locate a local potter who will demonstrate his or her art for the students, either in the classroom or on a field trip to the studio.
1. Nampeyo, Daisy Hooee, 1910-   2. Hopi Indians—Biography   3. Indians of North America—Biography   4. Artists.

92 O'Connor, Sandra Day
Bentley, Judith. *Justice Sandra Day O'Connor.* Julian Messner (0-671-45809-4), 1983. 125p. B/W photos. (Interest level: 4-8).

More detailed than the biographies by Beverly Gherman and Carol Greene (*see* preceding entries), Bentley's book delves deeper into the Arizona ranch life of O'Connor, her Stanford education, her Arizona political career, her family and community life, and the implications of being the first woman in U.S. history to be appointed to the Supreme Court. Actual family photographs of Justice O'Connor's life add reality to a useful biography.
♦ Students may write opinion papers expressing their views on a recent Supreme Court decision after researching the case.
1. O'Connor, Sandra Day, 1930-   2. United States. Supreme Court—Biography.

92 O'Connor, Sandra Day
Gherman, Beverly. *Sandra Day O'Connor: Justice for All.* Illus. by Robert Masheris. Viking (0-670-82756-8), 1991. 54p. B/W illus. (Interest level: 2-6).

This biography follows Sandra Day O'Connor from her childhood on an Arizona ranch, through her days as a young lawyer and an elected Arizona state senator, to her appointment as the first female to be named to the U.S. Supreme Court. Short chapters with interesting titles give this book the aura of a story told about a strong female fictional character; how nice to know it is a true story of a role model for all young people.
♦ Students may research careers using biographies or nonfiction books, and then write their thoughts about the potential advantages and disadvantages of a possible career choice.
1. O'Connor, Sandra Day, 1930-   2. United States. Supreme Court—Biography.

92 O'Connor, Sandra Day
Greene, Carol. *Sandra Day O'Connor: First Woman on the Supreme Court.* Childrens Press (0-516-06318-1), 1982. 32p. B/W illus. (Interest level: K-2).

This short biography chronicles the life of Sandra Day O'Connor, the first woman appointed to the U.S. Supreme Court, who grew up on a ranch on the border between Arizona and New Mexico and spent her adult life in Phoenix. The brief, simple text, accompanied with photos and sketches, gives the reader just enough details of Justice O'Connor's life and personality to make her a modern-day hero who achieved goals set in childhood.
♦ Students may write or dictate their career goals, then set a short-term goal for what they would like to learn this year in school.
1. O'Connor, Sandra Day, 1930-   2. United States. Supreme Court—Biography.

92 O'Connor, Sandra Day
Huber, Peter. *Sandra Day O'Connor*. Chelsea House (1-55546-672-9), 1990. 112p. B/W photos. (American Women of Achievement). (Interest level: 5-8).

A close examination of the life and career of the first woman appointed to the U.S. Supreme Court, Huber's biography explores the effect of the women's movement on Justice O'Connor's appointment as well as her judicial rulings and philosophies. Identifying with Justice O'Connor on a personal level, readers may be inspired to set similar high standards and goals for themselves, and they will enjoy reading this lively and interesting account of the unflappable rancher's daughter who had the vision to struggle against great obstacles to achieve her goals.

♦ Students may write a fictional essay or group of diary entries using Sandra Day O'Connor as the main character, but placing the events during another time period such as the Civil War or Ancient Egypt.

1. O'Connor, Sandra, 1930- 2. United States. Supreme Court—Biography.

92 Spielberg, Steven
Mabery, D. L. *Steven Spielberg*. Lerner Publications (0-8225-1612-8), 1986. 40p. B/W and Color photos. (Interest level: 3-6).

In this short biography, Mabery chronicles Steven Spielberg's early life and phenomenal success as a movie producer, director, and writer. Interesting photographs of Spielberg and his movies and an informal, accessible style make this portrayal fascinating reading; a list of Spielberg's movies through 1986 is included.

♦ Renting and watching one of Spielberg's movies, such as "An American Tail," will be sure to entice young readers to the creator's biography.

1. Spielberg, Steven 2. Motion picture producers and directors.

Fiction

Amigo. (Sound recording). Southwest Series, Inc., 1989. One sound cassette. $5.95. (Interest level: 2-5).

Byrd Baylor, reading her first published story, says, "The desert keeps its secrets hidden and only lets you in on a few of them—but I learn what I can and that is what I write about." As a child, Baylor's family lived near a prairie dog town, which fascinated her and was the inspiration for the book *Amigo* (see p. 15).

♦ Ask children to write about something in nature that they find fascinating.

1. Friendship—Fiction 2. Desert animals—Fiction.

Annie and the Old One. (Videocassette). American School Publishers/Random House, 1986. 1/2" VHS, Color, (14 min.). $71.00. (Interest level: K-5).

Based on the book *Annie and the Old One* by Miska Miles (see p. 18), this transferred video production of a filmstrip is narrated to the accompaniment of soft Native American-style background music. This color production effectively tells the subtle story of intergenerational love and impending death.

♦ Combine the study of this book/video with *The Goat in the Rug as Told to Charles L. Blood and Martin Link by Geraldine* by Charles Blood and Martin Link (see p. 16) to enable students to compare and contrast their common theme of weaving. Students may want to write about the death of an important person in their life.

1. Navajo Indians—Fiction 2. Indians of North America—Fiction 3. Weaving—Fiction 4. Grandparents—Fiction.

Annie and the Old One. (Videocassette). BFA Educational Media, 1976. 1/2" VHS, (15 min.). $205.00. (Interest level: K-5).

This live-action re-creation of the book *Annie and the Old One* by Miska Miles (see p. 18) follows the text exactly. The video, which tells the story of a Navajo girl who unravels a day's weaving on a rug whose completion she believes will mean the death of her grandmother, is very sensitively done.

♦ Have students compare and contrast their lives with Annie's in relation to family, housing, parents' work, school, leisure time, etc. Have students answer the question "Do you think you would have acted in the same way as Annie?" Introduce or follow the video with the book.

1. Navajo Indians—Fiction 2. Death—Fiction.

Armer, Laura Adams. *Waterless Mountain*. Illus. by Sidney Armer and Laura Adams Armer. David McKay Co. (0-679-20233-1), 1931. 212p. (Interest level: 5-8).

This 1931 Newbery Medal winner, set in northern Arizona, tells the story of a Navajo boy's quest to become a medicine man.

Through the eyes and mind of the hero, the reader experiences a vivid portrayal of the life of a tribe that has lived for centuries in northern Arizona, and becomes acquainted with the animals, trees, and prehistoric cliff dwellings of the West, as well as the mystical beauty of the legends and traditions of the Navajo.
♦ Students may write a diary entry for each adventure or chapter, putting themselves in the main character's place.
1. Navajo Indians—Fiction 2. Indians of North America—Fiction.

Baylor, Byrd. *Amigo.* Illus. by Garth Williams. Aladdin (0-689-71299-5), 1989, 1963. 48p. Color illus. (Interest level: 2-5).

Francisco, a young Mexican boy who wishes for a pet dog, finds a prairie dog town and patiently makes friends with one of the inhabitants, who also tames the boy for his own pet. This clever story, fresh with imagination, warmth, and humor, is told in rhythmic verse accompanied with dazzling, but subdued color illustrations depicting the desert.
♦ Students may write a further adventure of Francisco and his new pet using either the point of view of the boy or the prairie dog.
1. Friendship—Fiction 2. Desert animals—Fiction.

Baylor, Byrd. *Desert Voices.* Illus. by Peter Parnall. Charles Scribner's Sons (0-684-16712-3), 1981. Unpaginated. Color illus. (Interest level: Preschool-4).

Ten desert creatures speak for themselves, telling about their lives as a pack rat, jackrabbit, spadefoot toad, rattlesnake, cactus wren, desert tortoise, buzzard, lizard, coyote, and desert person, making it clear that the desert is their home. This author/illustrator team has an inimitable style that once again reflects a special philosophy about the lovely land portrayed.
♦ Students may choose a favorite desert animal to write about, perhaps using a first-person approach, and then draw the animal.
1. Deserts—Fiction 2. Desert animals—Fiction.

Baylor, Byrd. *Hawk, I'm Your Brother.* Illus. by Peter Parnall. Aladdin (0-689-71102-6), 1986. Unpaginated. (Interest level: Preschool-5).

Determined to learn to fly, young Rudy Soto adopts a hawk, hoping that their kinship will bring him closer to his goal. With Baylor's fluid prose style and Parnall's distinctive illustrations, the reader gets to know Rudy and the ways of the desert bird.
♦ Students may imagine what it might be like to fly like a hawk, and draw what they might see on their lofty trip. Students may view the video of the same title (*see* p. 17).
1. Hawks—Fiction 2. Flight—Fiction.

Baylor, Byrd. *I'm in Charge of Celebrations.* Illus. by Peter Parnall. Charles Scribner's Sons (0-684-18579-2), 1986. Unpaginated. Color illus. (Interest level: Preschool-4).

Byrd Baylor writes of her own experiences while living a rustic life in the desert: celebrating a triple rainbow, a chance encounter with a coyote, and other wonders of the wilderness. The personal memories and private celebrations, such as Rainbow Celebration Day and Dust Devil Day, give the reader a feel for the grand beauty in the simple things of life.
♦ Students may write of their own celebrations, recalling special memories of experiences they have had in nature. Students may view the video of the same title (*see* p. 17).
1. Deserts—Fiction.

Baylor, Byrd. *Moon Song.* Illus. by Ronald Himler. Scribner (0-684-17463-4), 1982. Unpaginated. B/W illus. (Interest level: 2-6).

After giving birth to Coyote Child and leaving him to fend for himself, Mother Moon listens for the moon song of all coyotes. Descriptive, lyrical language tells the reader about the environment and habitat of the coyote in legendlike prose with black-and-white drawings and bold geometric borders.
♦ Students may choose another desert animal and write a legend about an unusual characteristic of that animal.
1. Coyotes—Fiction 2. Moon—Fiction.

Bird, E. J. *The Rainmakers.* Carolrhoda (0-87614-748-1), 1993. 120p. B/W illus. (Interest level: 4-8).

Seen through the eyes of Cricket, a young Anasazi boy, this novel offers a glimpse into the everyday life of the ancient inhabitants of the American Southwest as Cricket; his best friend, Sheep; his grandfather; and a pet black bear travel from village to village bringing much-needed rain to their people. Exciting adventures along the way include tracking kidnappers and hunting bison. The imaginative and moving tale shows the reader what life may have been like for the Anasazi, who built elaborate homes in the cliffs and canyons of the southwestern United States before disappearing in approximately 1250 A.D.

♦ Students may research Native American dances and their significance, then write informative reports to share with their classmates. If possible, Native Americans could be invited to the school to demonstrate cultural dances, or students could travel to local events featuring Native American dancers.
1. Pueblo Indians—Fiction 2. Indians of North America—Southwest—Fiction 3. Bears—Fiction.

Blood, Charles L. and **Link, Martin A.** *The Goat in the Rug as Told to Charles L. Blood and Martin Link by Geraldine.* Illus. by Nancy Winslow Parker. Aladdin (0-689-71418-1 pbk), 1990, 1976. 40p. Color illus. (Interest level: Preschool-3).

Geraldine, a goat who lives in the Navajo Nation at Window Rock, Arizona, relates the process of making a Navajo rug—from the day the wool is clipped until the product is finished. The whimsical and amusing illustrations, with Geraldine's first-person narrative, make this title a treasure. The hardback edition by Parents Magazine Press is now out of print.

♦ Following the steps described in the book, students may try carding, spinning, dyeing and weaving yarn. For a simpler activity, students could weave a potholder or small rug from purchased materials, or a local weaver could demonstrate weaving on a loom.
1. Navajo Indians—Fiction 2. Rugs—Fiction 3. Weaving—Fiction.

Buchanan, Ken. *This House Is Made of Mud.* Illus. by Libba Tracy. Northland Publishing (0-87358-518-6), 1991. Unpaginated. Color illus. (Interest level: Preschool-2).

This gentle story captures the sun-washed beauty of life in the Sonoran Desert. Vibrant, but soft watercolors and simple, sensitive text describe how the lives of the members of a family are interwoven with the environment and the home they make from adobe.

♦ Readers may write or dictate descriptive paragraphs about what makes their house a home, or experiment in making an adobe hogan. A full unit of study about different types of homes or shelters could be introduced with this story.
1. Houses—Fiction 2. Deserts—Fiction 3. Southwestern States—Fiction.

Cole, Judith. *The Moon, the Sun, and the Coyote.* Illus. by Cecile Schoberle. Simon & Schuster (0-671-69628-9 pbk), 1991. Unpaginated. Color illus. (Interest level: 1-5).

Depicted in his natural desert habitat, Coyote, caught in a dispute between the Sun and the Moon, receives the gift of many improvements in his appearance, but must ultimately be satisfied with what he has. This original folktale is beautifully enhanced with Schoberle's rich watercolors, with the sun and moon fashioned after southwestern Native American kachinas.

♦ Students may construct models of Native American kachinas using empty toilet tissue rolls, feathers, and paint.
1. Coyotes—Fiction 2. Sun—Fiction 3. Moon—Fiction 4. Indians of North America—Folklore.

Desert Voices: A Reading by Byrd Baylor. (Videocassette). Arizona Game and Fish Department. 1/2" VHS, (13 min.). $15.00. (Preschool-4).

The author invites us to use our imagination for a trip to the desert. The video uses a combination of live footage and Baylor's illustrations of the animals from her book by the same title (*see* p. 15). One of the short chapters about buzzards has words that appear on the screen for the viewer to read along.

♦ Students may plan an imaginary trip to the desert, each suggesting some animal they would like to see.
1. Deserts—Fiction 2. Desert animals—Fiction.

Gila Monsters Meet You at the Airport. (Videocassette). Great Plains National Instructional Library, 1986. (Reading Rainbow). 1/2" VHS, (50 min.). $39.95. (Interest level: Preschool-5).

This Reading Rainbow episode #8 features the book *Gila Monsters Meet You at the Airport* by Marjorie Weinman Sharmat (*see* p. 19), read aloud in its entirety, followed by a visit to the desert with a biologist from the Arizona Game and Fish Department, who handles a live gila monster, compares heights of saguaro cacti on the Sonoran Desert, shows viewers the convergence of the Salt and Verde rivers, and points out various desert animals' tracks. The live footage of the desert and of some of its animal dwellers makes this video a very useful addition to a desert unit of study.

♦ Students may research animal tracks in the media center and search for and identify tracks on the playground or other location.
1. Deserts—Fiction 2. Gila monsters—Fiction.

Girl of the Navajos. (Videocassette; 16mm film). Coronet, 1977. 1/2" VHS; 16mm film, (15 min.). $250.00. (Interest level: 2-8).

In this film, Nannabah, a young Navajo girl, recalls her feelings of fear and loneliness the first time she herded her family's sheep into the canyon, but she remembers also the friendship formed with another young girl who had the same task. Typical Native American dress, life in a hogan, prayer customs, and the hard work of life on the desert are poignantly presented, with breathtaking views of the desert and its canyons. The video is based on *Nannabah's Friend* by Mary Perrine (*see* p. 19).
♦ Students may make clay dolls and a model hogan, as Nannabah did to pass the time of day while her sheep grazed.
1. Indians of North America 2. Navajo Indians.

Green, Timothy. *Mystery of Navajo Moon.* Illus. by author. Northland Publishing (0-87358-523-2), 1991. 48p. Color illus. (Interest level: K-4).

The author, who lives on the Navajo Indian Reservation in Arizona, has written and illustrated an original story, in a folklore style, about a young Navajo girl who goes on a magical ride through the night on a silvery horse. Bold, colorful borders accent the text, which depicts life in a hogan in the southwestern desert and dreamlike visions of the magical night ride.
♦ Students may want to draw or paint a night scene on black paper with fluorescent crayons or paints, perhaps adding their own touch of magic by including a favorite animal.
1. Horses—Fiction 2. Night—Fiction 3. Navajo Indians—Fiction 4. Indians of North America—Fiction.

Grossman, Virginia. *Ten Little Rabbits.* Illus. by Sylvia Long. Chronicle Books (0-87701-552-X), 1991. 32p. Color illus. (Interest level: Preschool-3).

A celebration of Native American traditions is blended into the rhymed text of a counting book, with a glossary and additional information about 10 tribes at the end of the story. Using rich colors, Sylvia Long, an Arizona illustrator, depicts rabbits in Native American costumes as the characters who dance, hunt, fish, and gather to tell stories.
♦ Working in cooperative groups, students may imitate the colorful, geometric designs accompanying the additional information at the end of the story, by designing and then coloring or painting a large rectangle to depict the rugs woven by Native Americans.

1. Indians of North America—Social life and customs 2. Counting.

Hawk, I'm Your Brother. (Videocassette). Southwest Series, Inc., 1988. 1/2" VHS, (24 min.). $39.95. (Interest level: Preschool-5).

This live-action video, narrated by Will Rogers, Jr., follows the Byrd Baylor book about young Rudy Soto's wish to learn to fly and the capture of a pet hawk (*see* p. 15). The breathtaking desert vistas and soaring hawk give viewers a firsthand look at the habitat and characteristics of this desert bird.
♦ Students may do research in the media center to learn what they would need to do to train an animal of their choice.
1. Hawks—Fiction 2. Flight—Fiction.

Henry, Marguerite. *Brighty of the Grand Canyon.* Illus. by Wesley Henry. Rand McNally (ISSN 0-02-743664-0), 1953. 222p. (Interest level: 4-8).

After an old prospector's mysterious death, his burro Brighty again roams the Grand Canyon. Brighty befriends Uncle Jimmy Owen, who helps solve the mystery of his friend's death. Brighty's experiences are described so effectively that the reader seems to be experiencing them along with the characters.
♦ Students may research the Grand Canyon in informational sources, and then compare the information on the Grand Canyon presented in nonfiction and in fiction.
1. Grand Canyon 2. Arizona—Fiction.

I'm in Charge of Celebrations. (Videocassette). Southwest Series, Inc., 1989. 1/2" VHS, (10 min.). $22.95. (Interest level: Preschool-4).

In this video Byrd Baylor reads her book *I'm in Charge of Celebrations* (*see* p. 15). The book describes Baylor's experiences living in the southwestern desert country that is her home, such as watching a triple rainbow with a jackrabbit alone on top of a hill, or seeing seven whirlwinds at once dancing in time to their own windy music. Viewers meet the author and hear her read aloud, motivating students to search for this and other books by Baylor.
♦ Students may write about a personal experience that has made them want to create a celebration.
1. Deserts—Fiction.

John, Naomi. *Roadrunner.* Illus. by Peter Parnall and Virginia Parnall. Dutton (0-525-38485-5), 1980. Unpaginated. Color illus. (Interest level: Preschool-2).

Rich in descriptive vocabulary, this story features a day in the life of a desert roadrunner as he observes other desert dwellers. This exciting adventure story has a simple text, coupled with excellent information about desert life.
♦ After researching the habitat, life, and enemies of the roadrunner, readers can construct a shoebox diorama depicting a roadrunner in a desert scene.

1. Roadrunners—Fiction 2. Desert animals—Fiction.

Johnson, Annabel. *I Am Leaper.* Illus. by Stella Ormai. Scholastic (0-590-43400-4), 1990. 105p. B/W illus. (Interest level: 2-5).

Leaper, a kangaroo rat who can communicate with humans, enlists the aid of a boy named Julian to help defeat a "monster" that has been terrorizing the desert where she lives. Readers will be on the edge of their seats reading this suspenseful book, and they will come away with new respect and concern for the gifts of nature.
♦ Readers may research ways their communities are working toward wildlife conservation.

1. Kangaroo rats—Fiction 2. Animal communication—Fiction 3. Wildlife conservation—Fiction.

Lowell, Susan. *The Three Little Javelinas.* Illus. by Jim Harris. Northland Publishing (0-87358-542-9), 1992. Unpaginated. Color illus. (Interest level: Preschool-8).

This southwestern adaptation of the familiar folktale "The Three Little Pigs" takes place on the Sonoran Desert, where Native American, Mexican, and Anglo cultures blend. A light touch of humor and a view of the plants and animals of the desert in early summer add to the enjoyment for readers of all ages.
♦ What a perfect lead-in to have student cooperative groups rewrite other well-known folk and fairy tales, adding a southwestern twist!

1. Pigs—Fiction 2. Coyotes—Fiction 3. Southwestern States—Fiction.

McLerran, Alice. *Roxaboxen.* Illus. by Barbara Cooney. Lothrop, Lee & Shepard (0-688-07592-4), 1991. Unpaginated. Color illus. (Interest level: K-4).

On a hill on the southeast corner of Second Avenue and Eighth Street, in Yuma, Arizona, there is a place once known as Roxaboxen, an imaginary town created by the author's mother and her childhood friends using rocks and wooden boxes. The author's very personal style of descriptive prose re-creates the magical world of childhood, and Barbara Cooney's inimitable style of illustration adds just the perfect touch of reality.
♦ After reading the book, readers may construct a model of Roxaboxen for display or real play. Also, as an entry in their journals, students could write about a dream play place. Older readers may be able to write about their favorite play activities as a younger child.

1. Play—Fiction 2. Imagination—Fiction.

Miles, Miska. *Annie and the Old One.* Illus. by Peter Parnall. Little, Brown and Company (0-316-57117-2), 1971. 44p. Color illus. (Interest level: K-5).

This is a Newbery Honor book about a Navajo girl who is taught by her grandmother that there is a time for all things to return to the earth. The story weaves the daily life and traditional customs of a Navajo extended family into the touching story of Annie, who is trying to postpone her grandmother's death.
♦ Combine the study of this book with *The Goat in the Rug as Told to Charles L. Blood and Martin Link by Geraldine* by Charles L. Blood and Martin A. Link (*see* p. 16), and have students compare and contrast the books' theme of weaving. Students may want to write about the death of an important person in their life.

1. Navajo Indians—Fiction 2. Indians of North America—Fiction 3. Weaving—Fiction 4. Grandparents—Fiction.

Miller, Edna. *Mousekin Takes a Trip.* Prentice Hall (0-13-604363-1 lib bind), 1976. Unpaginated. Color illus. (Interest level: Preschool-4).

Searching for food, a curious little white-footed woods mouse hops into a trailer and takes an unexpected trip to the southwestern desert, where he meets many unusual creatures and plants and endures some strange weather. End papers give the reader a map of the United States and labeled drawings of plants and animals that Mousekin encounters during his short visit to the desert.
♦ Using an atlas, students may plan a trip from their home to Arizona, calculating miles to drive each day and places to see along the way.

1. Mice—Fiction 2. Deserts—Fiction.

Nunes, Susan. *Coyote Dreams.* Illus. by Ronald Himler. Atheneum (0-689-31398-5), 1988. Unpaginated. Color illus. (Interest level: K-2).

At night coyotes come quietly into a suburban garden, bringing with them their special, magical southwestern world of sand, sagebrush, lizards, and rocks. Soft watercolors with illusionary overlays of coyotes create this world and evoke the magic of the ancient name "Coyotl."
♦ After researching or viewing resources about coyotes, students may draw a coyote in its desert habitat for a southwestern gallery in the classroom or library media center.
1. Coyotes—Fiction 2. Deserts—Fiction.

O'Dell, Scott. *Sing Down the Moon.* Houghton Mifflin (0-395-10919-1), 1970. 137p. (Interest level: 5-8).

The peaceful spring of 1864 in Canyon de Chelly in Arizona Territory is shattered by the arrival of Spanish slavers and of soldiers who burn crops, destroy fruit trees, and force the Navajos of the canyon to join their Native American brothers on the long march to Fort Sumner. In this exciting and suspenseful story, a young Navajo girl named Bright Morning escapes from her kidnappers but is finally forced to leave her ancestral home.
♦ Students may write a simulated diary that Bright Morning might have kept during her experiences.
1. Navajo Indians—Fiction 2. Indians of North America—Fiction.

Perrine, Mary. *Nannabah's Friend.* Houghton Mifflin (0-395-52020-7), 1989. 32p. Color illus. (Interest level: K-3).

On the first day Nannabah must herd the sheep to the canyon all by herself, she is lonely and afraid. This simply written story tells how Nannabah bridges the gap between the security of home and family and the world of responsibilities, and in the process she makes a friend.
♦ Using clay, students can make a model hogan and a friend to live in it. Use the book in conjunction with the video *Girl of the Navajos* (see p. 17).
1. Navajo Indians—Children—Fiction.

Sharmat, Marjorie Weinman. *Gila Monsters Meet You at the Airport.* Illus. by Byron Barton. Aladdin (0-689-71383-5 pbk; 0-02-782450-0), 1990. Unpaginated. (Interest level: Preschool-5).

A little boy, moving from New York to the Southwest, discovers that he had some misconceptions about his new home (including thinking that everyone rides horses and talks in a slow drawl, and that gila monsters meet you at the airport), as does a boy he meets in the airport, who sees New York as the habitat of gangsters, traffic, and alligators in the sewers. In four easy-to-read chapters, Sharmat's humorous look at misconceptions and exaggerations will help readers enjoy learning about life on either coast.
♦ Students may research the gila monster to learn more about the habitat and life of this desert reptile. Some students may want to research the alligator and decide if they think one could really live in the New York sewers.
1. Deserts 2. Southwestern States.

Skurzynski, Gloria. *Trapped in Slickrock Canyon.* Illus. by Daniel San Souci. Lothrop, Lee & Shepard (0-688-02688-5), 1984. 128p. (Interest level: 4-8).

A northern Arizona teenager overcomes his antagonism toward his preppy cousin as they struggle to survive a life-threatening adventure, in which they meet treacherous men and natural dangers in an Arizona canyon. While enjoying a suspenseful story, the reader learns about flash floods, broiling desert sun, cold desert nights, ancient rock paintings, and the rigors of rock climbing.
♦ Students may write about their own real experiences with nature, or imagine how they would react to the situation described in the book and write a diary account of their imagined adventure.
1. Wilderness survival—Fiction 2. Deserts—Fiction.

Periodicals

591.52

Arizona Wildlife Views. Arizona Game and Fish Department (ISSN 0882-5572). Monthly. (Interest level: 4-8).

Arizona's official wildlife magazine is a monthly publication of the Arizona Game and Fish Department, and is dedicated to conserving, enhancing, and restoring Arizona's diverse wildlife. Excellent photographs, illustrations, question-and-answer columns, and an event calendar make this a valuable, inexpensive resource for the classroom and media center.
♦ Students may begin their research on unusual and obscure animals with articles in this periodical, and then expand their study with other materials from the media center.
1. Desert animals.

917.91
Arizona Highways. Arizona Highways (ISSN 0004-1521). Monthly. (Interest level: All ages).

This monthly magazine of the Arizona Department of Transportation includes a wealth of information about attractions and outdoor activities in Arizona, as well as articles about historical sites, events, and people. Breathtaking photography of flora and fauna, interesting articles, and a policy of accepting no advertising make this an excellent periodical for the classroom and media center.
♦ Students may plan an imaginary road trip from their home to visit the sites and events in Arizona.
1. Arizona—Description and travel 2. Arizona—History.

Professional Materials

016.9791
Arizona Heritage: Bibliography of Materials and Directory of Authors, Illustrators and Storytellers for Teachers, Librarians and Parents. Arizona State Library Association/Children's Services Roundtable (No ISBN), 1992. 144p. (Interest level: Professional).

This excellent bibliography provides a listing of books and nonbook materials about Arizona for children in kindergarten through eighth grade. Materials are arranged alphabetically by author within categories set up by genre and by type of publication, and the work is indexed by author, title, and subject. Useful special features include a separate section on magazines; a list of area storytellers, authors, and illustrators who are available to talk about their work; and a list of publishers and vendors specializing in materials about the Southwest.
♦ Using the list of storytellers and authors, plan a program to introduce students to one of these Arizona artists.
1. Arizona—Bibliography.

New Mexico

by Carol A. Sarath

Nonfiction

305.8211
Navajo Moon. (Videocassette). Films for the Humanities, 1988. 1/2" VHS, (24 min.). $149.00. (Interest level: 3-7).
   Photographed in New Mexico and northern Arizona, this program gives the audience an inside look at the lives of three Navajo children. This sensitive and interesting "Young People's Special" includes information on history, arts, and current lifestyles of Navajo Indians living on the reservation.
♦ Have students write a letter to one of the three children in the program, contrasting one aspect of their lives with that of the child described in the video.
1. Navajo Indians—Children   2. Indians of North America—Children.

364.155
Green, Carl R. and **Sanford, William R**. *Billy the Kid.* Enslow Publishers, Inc. (0-89490-364-0), 1992. (Outlaws and Lawmen of the Wild West). 48p. B/W photos. (Interest level: 4-8).
   The brief and violent career of the outlaw is profiled in this portrayal of Billy the Kid, who gained notoriety through his actions in Lincoln County, New Mexico. This clearly written biography provides a realistic introduction to an outlaw who has inspired a cult of aficionados.
♦ Students can compare the myths and the realities of the life of Billy the Kid and other outlaws they research in the media center.
1. Billy the Kid   2. Outlaws—Southwestern States—Biography   3. Frontier and pioneer life—Southwestern States.

372.8
Nason, Thelma C. *No Golden Cities.* Crowell-Collier (ISBN not available), 1970 (out of print). 154p. B/W illus. (Interest level: 7+).
   More than 20 years before the Pilgrims landed at Plymouth Rock, Spain established a colony in what is now New Mexico. This very readable account of Don Juan de Onate's expedition into New Mexico in 1598 is full of drama and suspense, as the Spanish soldiers made long and difficult journeys in search of fabled wealth, but found no golden cities. The cruelty and disdain with which the New Mexico inhabitants were treated is remarkable.
♦ Have students rewrite the encounters between Spaniards and the Native Americans from the Native American point of view.
1. New Mexico—History—To 1848.

398.2
Arrow to the Sun. (Videocassette). Films Incorporated, 1983. 1/2" VHS, (12 min.). $79.00. (Interest level: 2+).
   This video of the Acoma Pueblo Indian tale animates Gerald McDermott's story of a boy's search for his father (*see* p. 23). An impressive visual story rich with Native American symbols, the video shows the boy traveling to the sun where he undergoes trials until he is able to return to Earth after his father recognizes him.
♦ Using "found objects" (buttons, dried corn and beans, etc.), students may create a mosaic featuring one or more symbols from the video/book.
1. Acoma Indians—Legends.

398.2
Baker, Betty. *Rat Is Dead and Ant Is Sad.* Illus. by Mamoru Funai. Harper & Row (0-06-020347-1 lib bind), 1981. 64p. Color illus. (Interest level: K-3).

This cumulative story, based on a Pueblo tale, involves Rat, who falls into a pot when he tries to see what is in it. As Ant, Jay, a tree, a sheep, a river, and others mourn because they believe Rat is dead, a horse finally puts an end to all the nonsense by going to look for himself. This folktale will delight early elementary-age children with its repetitious story line and its color illustrations by Mamoru Funai.
♦ Have students create an illustrated cumulative tale as a class activity; the teacher can start the story with two or three sentences to provide the setting, and then transcribe the dictation. The finished book may be catalogued and added to the school media center.

1. Pueblo Indians—Legends.

398.2
Browne, Vee, reteller. *Monster Slayer: A Navajo Folktale.* Illus. by Baje Whitethorn. Northland Publishing (0-87358-525-9), 1991. 32p. Color illus. (Interest level: K-9).

The Anasazi villages of northwestern New Mexico and eastern Arizona are under attack by monsters. The monsters are eating so many members of the tribe that the tribe is unable to plant corn, squash, beans, or peach trees, so the people are starving. Illustrated by Navajo artist, Baje Whitethorn, this stunningly beautiful retelling of a traditional Navajo myth recounts the naming of the hero Monster Slayer.
♦ Have students make up a "traditional" myth, complete with the naming of a hero. Encourage stories with an atypical hero, such as a child, a female, or a minority.

1. Navajo Indians—Legends.

398.2
Carey, Valerie Scho, adapter. *Quail Song: A Pueblo Indian Tale.* Illus. by Ivan Barnett. Putnam (0-399-21936-6), 1990. Unpaginated. Color illus. (Interest level: 1-4).

This book retells the traditional Pueblo Indian tale in which Coyote tries to take Quail's song to use as a lullaby for his own young. Quail, of course, manages to outwit Coyote in this strikingly illustrated story.
♦ Have students write "songs" for animals they are familiar with, using sounds such as the ki-ruu of the quail and the tsi-ka of the lizard.

1. Pueblo Indians—Legends   2. Indians of North America—Southwestern States—Legends.

398.2
Cohlene, Terri. *Turquoise Boy: A Navajo Legend.* Illus. by Charles Reasoner. Rourke Corp. (0-86593-003-1), 1990. 47p. Color illus. (Interest level: 4+).

In this retelling of a Navajo legend, Turquoise Boy searches for something that will make life easier for the Navajo and returns with the horse, which to this day is considered sacred. The illustrations are stunning, and the book contains an informative section on the history and culture of the Navajo.
♦ Have students investigate the history of the introduction of the horse to Native Americans and the impact of the horse on the cultures.

1. Navajo Indians—Legends   2. Navajo Indians—Social life and customs.

398.2
Hausman, Gerald. *Turtle Island Alphabet: A Lexicon of Native American Symbols and Culture.* Illus. by Barry Moser and Cara Moser. St. Martin's Press (0-312-07103-5), 1992. 204p. Sepia illus. (Interest level: 6+).

From arrow to zigzag, the symbol, its associated Native American legends, and its cultural significance are described for the reader. This volume represents the author's lifetime research and is the most comprehensive discussion available of Native American images and symbols.
♦ Have students choose a symbol and share the meaning, associated stories, and/or interpretations with others. Emphasis on ecological concerns may be encouraged.

1. Indians of North America—Dictionaries—Legends.

398.2
Hayes, Joe. *Coyote E. Native American Folk Tales.* 2nd ed. Illus. by Lucy Jelinek. Mariposa Publishing (0-933553-01-3), 1983. 80p. Color illus. (Interest level: 3-7).

Thirteen Native American folk tales, retold by New Mexico's premier storyteller, Joe Hayes, display Coyote's character as a combination of cleverness and foolishness. These coyote tales have wide appeal for children because they juxtapose humor and good sense.
♦ Have students write a coyote tale that illustrates coyote's cleverness and foolishness.

Suggest they add to the tale another animal not used in these 13 stories.
1. Indians of North America—Legends 2. Coyote (Legendary character).

398.2
Hayes, Joe, reteller. *The Day It Snowed Tortillas: Tales from Spanish New Mexico*. Mariposa Publishing (0-933553-00-5), 1985, 1982. 73p. Brown/White illus. (Interest level: 4-8).

This collection of folktales from Spanish New Mexico, collected and retold by noted storyteller Joe Hayes, includes the well-known story of "La Llorona" and eight other stories. These humorous tales are excellent for telling or for reading aloud.
♦ Young people may choose and then learn one of the stories to tell their classmates and tape record.
1. Folklore—New Mexico.

398.2
Hayes, Joe. *Heart Full of Turquoise*. Mariposa Press (0-933553-05-6), 1988. 75p. B/W and Color illus. (Interest level: 3-7).

Outstanding storyteller Joe Hayes presents eight northern New Mexico Pueblo folktales through print. This collection of traditional tales will please readers, and an audiocassette with the same title by Hayes is also available for listeners (*see* following entry).
♦ After students listen to stories, either on tape or as read by the teacher, have them discuss the book's oral quality, beginning with the question "What makes a story seem to be storytelling, not reading?"
1. Pueblo Indians—Folklore 2. Indians of North America—Legends.

398.2
Heart Full of Turquoise. (Sound recording). Trails West (0-939729-10-5), 1988. (70 min.). $9.95. (Interest level: 3-7).

Joe Hayes's tape of eight northern New Mexico Pueblo Indian folktales appeals to a wide range of students. Hayes's storytelling has a personal quality to it that reminds the listener of sitting around a campfire telling stories.
♦ As students listen to stories, either on tape or as read by the teacher (*see* preceding entry), have them prepare an illustration to match the action.
1. Pueblo Indians—Folklore 2. Indians of North America—Legends.

398.2
Hillerman, Tony, reteller. *The Boy Who Made Dragonfly: A Zuni Myth*. University of New Mexico Press (0-8263-0910-0 pbk), 1986, 1972. 81p. B/W illus. (Interest level: 3-9).

In this retelling of a Zuni Indian myth, a young Zuni Indian boy fashions a cornstalk dragonfly, which comes to life and helps the boy and his sister survive the winter. The children, who were abandoned by their parents, live to become leaders of the tribe. The story effectively portrays the values of thrift, humility, compassion, and sharing as a source of power, and as the basis for a loving and productive community.
♦ Using dried cornhusks, available in some grocery stores, in arts and crafts stores, or from a local farmer or gardener, students may fashion a cornhusk insect of their choosing and imagine a story involving the insect's coming to life.
1. Zuni Indians—Legends.

398.2
Lacapa, Michael. *The Flute Player: An Apache Folktale*. Illus. by author. Northland Publishing (0-87358-500-3), 1990. Unpaginated. Color illus. (Interest level: 3-6).

Based upon a traditional Apache folktale, this story is retold and richly illustrated by Apache Indian Michael Lacapa. The story of star-crossed lovers, one of whom plays a flute that "sounds like the wind blowing through the trees," is touchingly portrayed.
♦ The fate of the flute player is left open to imagination; students may write a paragraph describing what they think has happened.
1. Apache Indians—Legends.

398.2
McDermott, Gerald. *Arrow to the Sun*. Illus. by author. Viking Press (0-670-13369-8), 1974. Unpaginated. Color illus. (Interest level: 2-4).

This northern New Mexico Pueblo Indian legend, told with words and pictures, explains how the spirit of the sun was brought to the Pueblo world. The Caldecott Award winner uses traditional Native American images in a unique and most effective manner to illustrate the text with bold graphics and dramatic color.
♦ Using a construction-paper collage technique, students may choose and then re-create a Native American image or symbol from the story.
1. Pueblo Indians—Legends.

398.2
Martinez, Estefanita. *The Naughty Little Rabbit and Old Man Coyote: A Tewa Story from San Juan Pueblo.* (Combined entry). Childrens Press (0-516-05141-5), 1992. Book; audiocassette, (11 min.). (Interest level: K-6).

This traditional San Juan Pueblo tale relates the story of Rabbit, who outsmarts Coyote before he can eat Rabbit. The story is given first without words, through striking illustrations; the text of the story is printed on the last page. The cassette tape narration is by the author, a San Juan Pueblo Indian, who reads in a smooth easy voice.
♦ The book is designed to encourage students to learn to tell the tale of the Naughty Little Rabbit. Alternatively, students can write or narrate a story to go along with the illustrations.
1. Tewa Indians—Legends 2. Coyote (Legendary character).

398.2
Oughton, Jerrie. *How the Stars Fell into the Sky: A Navajo Legend.* Houghton Mifflin (0-395-58798-0), 1992. Unpaginated. Color illus. (Interest level: 2-6).

This retelling of the Navajo legend explains how Coyote, through his impatience, ruins the hard work of First Woman, who was carefully placing the stars into the sky. The author's poetic language, in combination with the distinctive color illustrations, creates a dramatic version of this Navajo story.
♦ Students may research Native American constellations and compare them to European constellations.
1. Navajo Indians—Legends.

398.2
Rodanas, Kristina. *Dragonfly's Tale.* Illus. by author. Clarion Books (0-395-57003-4), 1992. 22p. Color illus. (Interest level: K-5).

Two Zuni Indian children regain the Corn Maidens' blessings for their people with the aid of a cornstalk dragonfly. The richly colored and detailed illustrations by the author enhance the retelling of this traditional Zuni legend.
♦ As a class activity, have students re-create the village of Zuni as it appeared shortly after the arrival of the Spanish conquistadors.
1. Zuni Indians—Legends.

398.2
Stories at Sundown with Joe Hayes: An Evening of Storytelling in Santa Fe with Joe Hayes at the Wheelwright Museum. (Videocassette). Trails West Publishing, 1987. 1/2" VHS, (45 min.). (Interest level: 3+).

This evening of storytelling, videotaped at the Wheelwright Museum in Santa Fe, New Mexico, presents famed storyteller Joe Hayes telling typical New Mexico folktales. This presentation captures the essence of the oral tradition.
♦ Students may learn a folktale and tell their version to the class and/or tape it on video.
1. New Mexico—Folklore 2. Storytelling.

623.4
Szasz, Ferenc Morton. *The Day the Sun Rose Twice: The Story of the Trinity Site Nuclear Explosion, July 16, 1945.* University of New Mexico (0-8263-0767-1), 1984. 233p. B/W photos. (Interest level: 8+).

Early in the morning, just before dawn on July 16, 1945, the world's first atomic bomb was exploded at Trinity Site in the central New Mexican desert. This compelling story of the persons involved and the events leading up to the explosion discusses the extraordinary amount of cooperation and secrecy required for the bomb's development. An index and a bibliography are included.
♦ Have students choose three of the Los Alamos scientists and write a short biographical paragraph for each.
1. Atomic bomb—New Mexico 2. Los Alamos (N.M.)—Description.

709.01
Bahti, Tom. *Southwest Indian Arts & Crafts.* KC Publications (0-916122-92-1), 1983. 47p. B/W and Color photos. (Interest level: 6+).

Bahti features the artwork of major Native American tribes from New Mexico and Arizona: pottery, painting, silverwork, kachinas, weaving, and bead making. This introduction provides information about the history, symbolism, and processes involved in creating the distinctive Indian art of the Southwest. A bibliography is included.
♦ Have student collaborative groups focus on a New Mexico Indian tribe and an art form that is associated with that tribe for a class presentation on the artwork.
1. Indians of North America—Southwestern States—Art.

709.01
Indian Art of the Pueblos. (Videocassette). Encyclopaedia Britannica Educational Corp.,

1976. 1/2" VHS, (13 min.). $69.00. (Interest level: 4+).

Various Native American art forms appear in this video examination of the traditional materials, forms, and symbols that characterize the art created by the Pueblo Indians of New Mexico. This color video shows ceramics, basketry, weaving, and ritual dance as they are used by today's Pueblo Indians to interpret the history and religion of their ancestors.
♦ Students may work in collaborative groups, each researching one of the traditional art forms, then sharing information about the techniques along with photographic examples.
1. Indians of North America—Southwestern States—Art 2. Pueblo Indians—Art.

709.01
Indian Artists of the Southwest. (Videocassette). Encyclopaedia Britannica Educational Corp., 1972. 1/2" VHS, (15 min.). $79.00. (Interest level: 4+).

Native Americans of New Mexico demonstrate traditional arts and crafts, including Navajo silverwork and weaving, Zuni turquoise, Acoma pottery, and Hopi kachinas. Though somewhat outdated in narration, this production succeeds in presenting a basic overview of Native American artists' translation of history and tradition into beauty, and a teacher's guide is provided.
♦ Suggest that students research the origin of a particular Native American art form: Was it learned from the Spaniards, adopted from other Native Americans, or developed in response to a particular need?
1. Indians of North America—Southwestern States—Art.

738.2
Trimble, Stephen. *Talking with the Clay: The Art of Pueblo Pottery.* School of America Research Press (0-933452-15-2), 1987. 116p. Color photos. (Interest level: 7+).

Interviews with 60 artisans provide an eloquent discussion of traditional and contemporary pottery making. Words and pictures capture the feeling that Pueblo pottery embodies all the beliefs and values central to Pueblo culture.
♦ Have students build a clay pot from coils and finish the pot with Native American designs.
1. Pueblo Indians—Art 2. Pottery, Pueblo Indians.

745.592
Smith, MaryLou M. *Grandmother's Adobe Dollhouse.* New Mexico Magazine (0-937-206-03-2), 1984. 32p. Color illus. (Interest level: 3-9).

Through a description of his grandmother's adobe dollhouse, a young boy gives information about the architecture, art, food, and culture of New Mexico. The features of a traditional adobe house provide a starting point for a fascinating description of traditional Mexican-American and Native American social life and customs.
♦ Students can study traditional styles of architecture from other areas of the country or world and compare and contrast features.
1. New Mexico—Social life and customs 2. Dollhouses—New Mexico.

811
Clark, Ann Nolan. *In My Mother's House.* Viking (0-670-83917-5), 1991, 1941. 56p. Color illus. (Interest level: K-3).

A young boy uses simple, yet elegant language to describe his home and the people, land, plants, and animals that make up the Pueblo world. This Caldecott Honor book's original publication date was 1941, but the rhythm and dignity of this timeless book still give students a sense of knowing Native American children and sharing experiences with them.
♦ Have students write a simple poem describing a part of their day to mimic the way the author has provided description in a poetry format.
1. Tewa Indians—Poetry 2. Children's poetry, American 3. Indians of North America—Poetry.

811.5
Wood, Nancy. *Many Winters: Prose and Poetry of the Pueblos.* Doubleday (0-385-02226-3), 1974. 80p. B/W illus. (Interest level: 6+).

For the past 800 years, the Indians of Taos Pueblo have lived under Taos Mountain in the Rio Grande Valley of northern New Mexico, and this collection of prose and poetry reflects their connection to the land. The literature effectively portrays the timelessness of Native American philosophy through the prose and poetry of the Pueblo.
♦ Students may create a collage that represents the Native American philosophy of life discovered in these writings.
1. Taos Indians—Poetry.

912.78
Ferguson, T. J. and **Hart, E. Richard.** *A Zuni Atlas.* University of Oklahoma (0-8061-1945-4), 1985. (The Civilization of the American Indians Series). 154p. B/W photos and illus. (Interest level: 8+).

Using historical photographs and a variety of maps, the authors outline Zuni archaeology, ethnohistory, and history, as well as the current conditions of the Zuni tribe of northwestern New Mexico, in relation to the tribe's geographic environment. This comprehensive and well-researched volume provides an appreciation of the value of the Zuni traditions and of the relationship of the Zuni to their environment. A bibliography and index are provided.
♦ Have students choose a historical photo from the book and then research and report on the activity or location depicted.
1. Zuni Indians—Maps 2. Southwestern States—Maps 3. Zuni Indians—History—Maps.

912.789
Williams, Jerry L., ed. *New Mexico in Maps.* University of New Mexico (0-8263-0869-4), 1986. 469p. (Interest level: 7+).

This large compilation of maps of New Mexico includes a wide range of demographic data in map form. Maps describing economic conditions, historical geography, and social conditions are only a few of the many maps available in this useful collection.
♦ Have students choose a map, make an overhead transparency of it, and describe the conditions portrayed by the map to the class.
1. New Mexico—Maps.

917.89
Chilton, Lance. *New Mexico: A New Guide to the Colorful State.* University of New Mexico (0-8263-0732-9), 1984. 640p. B/W photos. (Interest level: 7-9).

This comprehensive overview of the state of New Mexico includes history, climate, geography, geology, politics, religion, arts, architecture, and literature. The book recommends 18 driving tours, which cover the length and breadth of the state.
♦ Students may use maps of New Mexico to trace one of the tours suggested. They may do math activities, such as timing how long the trip will take, or research activities, reporting on the places that would be visited on the tour.
1. New Mexico 2. New Mexico—Description and travel.

917.89
Varney, Philip. *New Mexico's Best Ghost Towns.* University of New Mexico (0-8263-1010-9), 1987. 204p. B/W photos. (Interest level: 7+).

This book describes ghost towns and suggests tours, complete with maps and directions, for every part of the state of New Mexico. Much fascinating history not usually available is included in this comprehensive guide to ghost towns.
♦ Use this book with *Untold Tales of New Mexico*, a video produced about New Mexico ghost town tales (*see* p. 32). Have students choose a ghost town and write a ghost story set in this location.
1. Ghost towns—New Mexico.

940.54
Kawano, Kenji. *Warriors: Navajo Code Talkers.* Northland Press (0-87358-513-5), 1990. 107p. B/W photos. (Interest level: 8+).

This is a photographic essay concerning the surviving Navajo Code Talkers, the Navajo Indians who devised the only secret code never broken by the Japanese during World War II. Japanese-born Kenji Kawano is the photographer of these sensitive and fascinating portraits, which will be of interest to students of World War II or to anyone interested in Native Americans.
♦ Interested students may research and write to each other in some of the codes used during World War II that were broken by the Japanese.
1. World War, 1939-1945 2. Navajo language 3. Navajo Indians—Portraits.

940.54
Navajo Code Talkers. (Videocassette). One West Media, 1986. 1/2" VHS, (27 min.). (Interest level: 8+).

Navajo Indians were recruited to develop a secret code based on the Navajo language, which was used during World War II and never broken by the Japanese. Interviews with the now elderly Navajo Code Talkers make up this informative oral history video, which documents the experiences of these individuals who participated in a little-known but crucial chapter of World War II history.

♦ Have student teams develop codes, and have other student teams attempt to decipher them.
1. World War, 1939-1945—Cryptography 2. United States—Armed forces—Indian troops—History.

970.004
Baylor, Byrd. *When Clay Sings.* Illus. by Tom Bahti. Charles Scribner's Sons (0-684-12807-1), 1972. Unpaginated. Color illus. (Interest level: 2-5).

On desert hillsides of New Mexico and Arizona, one can still find pieces of ancient Indian pottery buried in the sand. This poetic story creates a picture of the past by describing the Indian way of life as gleaned through the pieces of pottery left behind. The rich earth tones of the illustrations add to the beauty of the tribute.
♦ Have students design a clay plate and decorate it with an ancient Indian design.
1. Indians of North America—Southwestern States 2. Indians of North America—Art 3. Pottery.

970.004
My Country: A Navajo Boy's Story. (Videocassette). Barr Films, 1988. 1/2" VHS, (25 min.). $295.00. (Interest level: 4-9).

Seen through the eyes of a 12-year-old Navajo boy and his family, this video describes life on the Navajo reservation. The beauty of the changing seasons is shown, and some of the ancient beliefs and traditions of the Navajo are effectively introduced.
♦ Have students write a report on a specific Native American tribe in which they compare various aspects of life and culture in that tribe to those of the Navajo.
1. Navajo Indians.

970.004
Surviving Columbus. (Videocassette). PBS Video, 1992. 1/2" VHS, (120 min.). $89.95. (Interest level: 7+).

Surviving Columbus tells the story of the arrival in New Mexico of the Spanish explorers and their impact on the indigenous peoples. This intensely interesting color program, filmed, written, and narrated by members of New Mexico's pueblos, portrays the Spanish occupation as a period of hardships and oppression, and shows the Native American point of view on the Columbus quincentenary celebrations.

♦ Have students compare events in New Mexico history from a Native American, Hispanic, and Anglo point of view.
1. Pueblo Indians—History 2. New Mexico—History.

970.004
Taos Pueblo. (Videocassette). Bullfrog Films, 1987. 1/2" or 3/4" VHS, (9 min.). $165.00. (Interest level: 2-6).

The Taos Indian Pueblo in Taos, New Mexico, claims to be the oldest continuously occupied settlement in North America. This simple color video for elementary school students describes life in the pueblo, including bread baking, pottery making, and the making of adobe, which has kept the pueblo buildings in good repair for 1,000 years.
♦ Students may list and research the Native American tribes in their location. They may also identify traditions that are being passed on to the young people of the tribe.
1. Taos Indians—Social life and customs.

970.004
Wood, Leigh Hope. *The Navajo Indians.* Chelsea House Publishers (0-7910-1651-X), 1991. (The Junior Library of American Indians). 79p. B/W and Color photos. (Interest level: 5+).

This up-to-date history of the Navajo recounts their story from the migration from Alaska and Northwest Canada to today's reservation in New Mexico and Arizona, home to the largest tribe in the United States. This clearly written text provides highlights of 500 years of life in the American Southwest, and includes a brief description of the scandals rocking Navajo tribal government in the early 1990s. An index is included.
♦ Have students research the history of the development of the Navajo Tribal Council and its reorganization in 1990.
1. Navajo Indians.

970.1
Keegan, Marcia. *Pueblo Boy: Growing Up in Two Worlds.* Cobblehill Books (0-525-65060-1), 1991. Unpaginated. Color photos. (Interest level: 2-6).

Photographs and story describe the home, school, and cultural life of a young Native American boy growing up on the San Ildefonso Pueblo in New Mexico. This attractively photographed book follows Timmy Roybal as he

weaves back and forth between the modern world and the traditions of his tribe.
♦ Students may become pen pals with children in the San Ildefonso Pueblo Day School or other New Mexico pueblo schools by writing the All-Indian Pueblo Council, P.O. Box 3256, Albuquerque, New Mexico 87190.
1. Pueblo Indians—Biography 2. Pueblo Indians—Social life and customs 3. San Ildefonso (N.M.).

970.3
Clark, Ann Nolan. *Little Boy with Three Names: Stories of Taos Pueblo.* Illus. by Tonita Lujan. Ancient City Press (0-941270-59-9), 1990. 50p. B/W illus. (Interest level: 3+).

This fictional account describes the interactions of three cultures in the life of a Native American boy from Taos Pueblo, New Mexico. In describing a summer in Taos Pueblo, the story emphasizes the three cultures by giving the three names the boy has: his Indian name, his Hispanic church name, and his boarding school name. Clark presents a heartwarming account of Taos Pueblo life that realistically includes some of the conflicts involved in integrating three cultures.
♦ Have children describe themselves with three names. They can use names from home, school, relatives, church, sports, hobbies, etc. Have them write a paragraph for each name to explain why it fits them.
1. Taos Indians—Children 2. Indians of North America—Children.

970.3
Clark, Ann Nolan. *Little Herder in Autumn.* Illus. by Hoke Denetsosie. Ancient City Press (0-941270-47-5), 1988. 91p. B/W illus. (Interest level: 3-9).

Far more than a story of sheep herding, this English/Navajo narrative describes all facets of Navajo life dependent upon sheep raising, from food to rug weaving to selling lambs for cash. *Little Herder in Autumn* sensitively portrays traditional Navajo life through both the prose and the illustrations drawn by Navajo artist Hoke Denetsosie.
♦ The Navajo language is very difficult to read and speak, but students might enjoy copying a part of the Navajo translation and trying to learn how to pronounce some words, particularly if a special visitor who speaks the Navajo language could visit the classroom. Pages 85-91 contain a description of the alphabet, word and sentence structure, and a pronunciation guide.
1. Navajo Indians—Social life and customs.

970.3
Clark, Ann Nolan. *Sun Journey: Story of Zuni Pueblo.* Ancient City Press (0-941270-49-1), 1988. 85p. B/W illus. (Interest level: 4-9).

Clark describes a year in the life of a young Zuni boy who returns from boarding school to learn and relearn the ways of his people from his grandfather, the Sun Priest of Zuni. The authentic and fascinating description of rites, religions, and tradition covers events in Zuni life from planting to the capturing of baby eagles.
♦ Students may describe a day spent with a grandparent and a tradition passed on.
1. Zuni Indians—Social life and customs.

970.3
Wood, Nancy. *Hollering Sun.* Simon & Schuster (0-671-65192-7), 1972 (out of print). Unpaginated. B/W photos. (Interest level: 4-8).

Dramatic black-and-white photographs depict life in Taos Pueblo along with the philosophy and beliefs of the Taos Indians. This poetic book may help students understand both the depth and simplicity of life.
♦ Have students bring a photograph from home and write a poem or prose piece describing it, with emphasis on the emotional response the photo elicits.
1. Taos Indians.

973.04
Sneve, Virginia Driving Hawk. *The Navajos: A First Americans Book.* Holiday House (0-8234-1039-0), 1993. Color illus. 32p. (Interest level: 2-6).

In a mere 32 pages, the author is able to convey the complex history of the Navajo people from creation, through migration to North America, through the Spanish period, and from the Long Walk until modern times. Brightly illustrated and sensitively portrayed, the story of the Navajo is presented in this outstanding book on the subject.
♦ Have students investigate variations on the creation story, both those of the Navajo and other peoples.
1. Navajo Indians.

973.0497
Osinski, Alice. *The Navajo.* Childrens Press (0-516-01236-3 pbk), 1987. (A New True

Book). 45p. B/W and Color photos. (Interest level: K-4).

Part of the New True Book series, *The Navajo* offers an introduction to Navajo life, including historical aspects of the Long Walk to Fort Sumner, the introduction of sheep by the Spanish, modern Navajo arts and crafts, religion, and education. Simple text and numerous illustrations provide basic information readily accessible to young readers.
♦ Students may write letters to children living on the Navajo reservation, exchanging information about history, culture, and lifestyle. Secure addresses by writing to the Navajo Division of Education, P.O. Drawer N, Window Rock, Arizona 86515
1. Navajo Indians 2. Indians of North America.

973.04972
Doherty, Craig A. and **Doherty, Katherine M.** *The Apaches and Navajos.* Franklin Watts (0-531-10743-4), 1989. (A First Book). 64p. Color photos. (Interest level: 3-5).

Similarities and differences are evident in this book, which discusses the Apache and the Navajo Indians who currently reside in reservations in New Mexico and Arizona. This informative resource will help students gain knowledge of two fascinating Native American tribes, and the color photographs effectively supplement the text. An index and a bibliography are included.
♦ Have students choose a cultural attribute, such as agriculture, religion, or arts and crafts, and compare Navajo and Apache practices.
1. Apache Indians 2. Navajo Indians.

978.9
Anaya, Rudolfo A. *The Farolitos of Christmas: A New Mexico Christmas Story.* New Mexico Magazine (0-937-206-05-9 pbk), 1987. 32p. Color illus. (Interest level: 4-8).

Anaya relates the history of the northern New Mexico Christmas tradition of making farolitos, often called luminarias, by filling paper bags with sand and a candle. This charming book explains the tradition of lighting farolitos on Christmas Eve in the context of a touching fictional story of northern New Mexico life.
♦ Students may describe a family Christmas tradition, as well as make farolitos to light for an evening Christmas program.
1. New Mexico—Christmas.

978.9
Ashabranner, Brent. *Born to the Land: An American Portrait.* G. P. Putnam's Sons (0-399-21716-9), 1989. 134p. B/W photos. (Interest level: 5+).

In a southwestern New Mexico setting, this portrait of America deals with farming and ranching and the effort to maintain the tradition of the family farm. Telling a story of a community with deep roots, the author portrays the struggle of people determined that the way of life they know will not perish. A bibliography and an index are included.
♦ Have students describe the combination of influences impacting the survival of the family farm in New Mexico and in other states of the country.
1. Ranch life—New Mexico—Luna County
2. Agriculture—New Mexico—Luna County.

978.9
Carpenter, Allan. *New Mexico.* Childrens Press (0-516-04131-2), 1978. (New Enchantment of America). 96p. Color photos. (Interest level: 4-9).

Carpenter provides a concise, interesting, and easy-to-read overview of the history and culture of the people of the state of New Mexico. Due to the age of this book, the sections on education and mining are out of date, yet the basic historical and cultural information is accurate and interestingly presented. The book also includes 1980 census figures, a handy reference section, and a detailed index.
♦ Have students prepare a brief biography of a well-known individual associated with the state of New Mexico and indicate who, what, where, when, and why the individual contributed to New Mexico history.
1. New Mexico.

978.9
Erdoes, Richard. *Native Americans: The Pueblos.* Sterling Publishing Co. (0-8069-2745-3 lib bind), 1983. 96p. Color illus. (Interest level: 4+).

This book describes the history, the land, and the traditional and modern life of the Pueblo of New Mexico. Richly illustrated with historical and contemporary photographs, Erdoes' book provides images not readily found in other works, and the text is interesting. An index is provided.

♦ Have students locate and mark the pueblos described on an overhead transparency map of New Mexico.
1. Pueblo Indians—New Mexico.

978.9
Folsom, Franklin. *Red Power on the Rio Grande: The Native American Revolution of 1680.* Follett Publishing (0-695-80374-5 lib bind), 1973 (out of print). 144p. (Interest level: 6-9).

Told from the Native American viewpoint, this book chronicles the revolt of the Pueblo people of the Rio Grande Valley of New Mexico against the oppressive rule of the Spaniards in 1680. Well-written and compelling, the book gives the achievement of the Pueblo the recognition it deserves. A bibliography is included.
♦ Ask students to compare and contrast the history of the Pueblo Revolt from both the Spanish and Native American perspectives.
1. Pueblo Revolt, 1680 2. Pueblo Indians—History.

978.9
Fradin, Dennis. *New Mexico in Words and Pictures.* Childrens Press (0-516-03931-8), 1981. 45p. Color photos. (Interest level: 2-5).

Starting with the dinosaurs, this simply written history chronicles New Mexico's development through the present day. The book provides information on New Mexico cities, Native Americans, Spanish explorers, the Lincoln County War, geologic features, and the state legislature. The text is not divided into chapters, so the narration is uninterrupted through all the facets of the state, but a detailed index is provided.
♦ Have students search for the history of the nickname "Land of Enchantment." Ask students to create their own nickname for the state.
1. New Mexico.

978.9
Frazier, Kendrick. *People of Chaco: A Canyon and Its Culture.* W. W. Norton (0-393-30231-3), 1986. 224p. B/W photos. (Interest level: 9+).

Called the Ancient Ones or Anasazi by the present-day Navajo, the people of Chaco Canyon lived and flourished 900 years ago in this remote northwest New Mexico canyon. The fascinating story of these people includes architecture, technology, road building, astronomy, and trade with Indians as far away as Mexico. A bibliography and an index are included.
♦ Have students choose one aspect of the life and times of the people of Chaco Canyon and prepare an oral report.
1. Chaco Canyon (N.M.) 2. Archaeology—New Mexico—Chaco Canyon 3. New Mexico—Antiquities.

978.9
Hoyt-Goldsmith, Diane. *Pueblo Storyteller.* Holiday House (0-8234-0864-7), 1991. 26p. Color photos. (Interest level: 2-5).

A young Cochiti girl, living with her grandparents in the Cochiti Pueblo in northern New Mexico, describes her home and family and the day-to-day life and customs of her people. Through clear writing and photographs, Pueblo activities are described in the context of a grandparent-grandchild relationship.
♦ Have students locate Cochiti Pueblo on a map of New Mexico, and then compare and contrast the origin myths of several New Mexico Pueblos.
1. Cochiti Indians 2. Cochiti Pueblo (N.M.)—Social life and customs 3. Indians of North America—Southwestern States.

978.9
Jenkins, Myra Ellen and **Schroeder, Albert H.** *A Brief History of New Mexico.* University of New Mexico (0-8263-0370-6), 1974. 89p. B/W photos. (Interest level 7+).

This concise book highlights important periods of New Mexico's past and present. Descriptions of early people of prehistoric times, pueblo development, Spanish exploration, and ties to Mexico enhance understanding of the richness of New Mexico's multicultural heritage, and the index and bibliography assist in research use.
♦ Have students choose a period of New Mexico history and investigate it further. Have them compare and contrast it to the same period of time in another state.
1. New Mexico—History.

978.9
Kirgo, Julie. *New Mexico: Portrait of the Land and People.* American Geographic Publishing (0-938314-65-3), 1989. Color photos. 112p. (Interest level: 6+).

This love story about New Mexico is charmingly told by a clearly enthralled author. The handsomely photographed book praises the whole of the state including the landscape, the

people, specific geographic regions, the arts and crafts, the culture, and the food.
♦ This book may be used as a resource for students searching for photographs or information on various peoples and regions of the state.
1. New Mexico—Description and travel
2. New Mexico—History.

978.9
Magnificent New Mexico: Land of Enchantment. (Videocassette). State of New Mexico. Economic Development and Tourism Department, 1988. 1/2" VHS, (14 min.). (Interest level: 8+).

This presentation is an overview of the history of New Mexico and a guide to tourist activities across the state. Though the video was produced to lure tourists, it can be useful as a brief, interesting presentation to introduce students to the diversity of cultures and geography that are found in the state.
♦ After viewing, have students choose an area of New Mexico that they would like to visit, write the Economic Development and Tourism Department and local Chambers of Commerce for additional information, and prepare a complete itinerary. Students may also discuss the elements of propaganda present in the video and then script a video to promote their city or state. If possible, have students produce the video.
1. New Mexico—Description and travel.

978.9
Portrait of America: New Mexico. (Videocassette). Turner Publishers, 1989. (Portrait of America). 1/2" VHS, (46 min.). $99.00. (Interest level: 4-8).

The New Mexico video from the Portrait of America series contains descriptions of the major cities in the state, as well as such diverse areas as Lincoln County, Chaco Canyon, and Trinity Site in White Sands. This program contains an excellent overview of the state and highlights some of the features that combine to make New Mexico so diverse and interesting.
♦ Narrator Hal Holbrook discusses the evidence of human presence in New Mexico from earliest times; students may investigate these traces of human occupation.
1. New Mexico.

978.9
Reeve, Frank D. and **Cleaveland, Alice Ann.** *New Mexico: Land of Many Cultures.* Pruett Publishing (0-87108-265-9), 1986 (out of print). 262p. B/W photos. (Interest level: 6-8).

This third edition of a popular overview of New Mexico's history, from 20,000 years ago in the age of volcanoes to today, includes a discussion of the first Americans, Spanish settlement of New Mexico, the Santa Fe Trail, and modern history and government. A readable text and many black-and-white photographs provide interesting and useful information about the state and its inhabitants for student researchers.
♦ Students may prepare a time line, starting with important prehistoric events in New Mexico's history and ending with events of today.
1. New Mexico—History.

978.9
Roberts, Calvin A. and **Roberts, Susan A.** *New Mexico.* University of New Mexico (0-8263-1048-6), 1988. 215p. B/W photos. (Interest level: 8+).

Three cultures that have strongly influenced New Mexican history include the Spanish, the Indian, and the Anglo-American, and this book explores their contributions to New Mexico's cultural and social history. From Billy the Kid to Robert Oppenheimer, the state's famous and infamous personages are discussed in this readable and informative volume. A bibliography and an index are included.
♦ Have students describe the influence of the three cultures on current culture and traditions that are apparent in New Mexico today.
1. New Mexico—History.

978.9
Roberts, Susan A. and **Roberts, Calvin A.** *A History of New Mexico.* University of New Mexico Press (0-8263-1264-0), 1991, c1986. 365p. B/W and Color photos. (Interest level: 7-8).

By adding a sixth unit on New Mexico's role in the modern world to this revised edition of a 1986 textbook, the authors bring students of New Mexico's history to the end of the 1980s. Another interesting addition to this respected work is a section in the chapter review entitled "Things You Can Make and Do," which actively involves students in learning New Mexico history.
♦ Have students make a poster or drawing of one of New Mexico's symbols and describe how the symbol represents New Mexico.
1. New Mexico—History.

978.9
Simmons, Marc. *New Mexico!*. Peregrine Smith (0-87905-135-3), 1983. 328p. B/W photos. (Interest level: 4-8).

This textbook discusses New Mexico's history, government, economy, geography, and culture. This comprehensive account emphasizes Native American and Hispanic American contributions and discusses the problems of progress. An index, a teaching guide, and maps are provided.
♦ Have students choose one of New Mexico's counties and identify its location and the site of its county seat on a map of the state. They could then write a paragraph describing an interesting place or institution in the county.
1. New Mexico.

978.9
Stein, R. Conrad. *America the Beautiful: New Mexico*. Childrens Press (0-516-00477-8), 1988. 144p. Color photos. (Interest level: 4+).

This overview of the history and culture of New Mexico describes the uniqueness of the land and people, while emphasizing that New Mexico is definitely one of the United States. This is a comprehensive treatment, which covers all geographic areas of the state while expressing a respect and admiration for the magical qualities of the Land of Enchantment. The color photographs contribute significantly to the text.
♦ Have students research New Mexico's contribution to the atomic age.
1. New Mexico.

978.9
Untold Tales of New Mexico. (Videocassette). Centre Productions, 1987. 1/2" VHS, (27 min.). (Interest level: 8+).

As the New Mexicans telling the stories point out, some New Mexico ghost towns are home to a number of fascinating tales that are not found in any history books. From the stories, enhanced by the photography of the majestic New Mexico landscape, the viewers gain a sense of Old West history, tradition, and color.
♦ Have students write a ghost story based on a real New Mexico ghost town. Use *New Mexico's Best Ghost Towns* by Philip Varney (*see* p. 26) or *Haunted Highways* by Ralph Looney (University of New Mexico, 1968).
1. New Mexico—History 2. Ghost towns—New Mexico.

978.9004
Sun Dagger. (Videocassette). Bullfrog Films, 1982. 1/2" or 3/4" VHS, (28 min.). (Interest level: 7+).

The discovery in Chaco Canyon, New Mexico, of a celestial calendar that was constructed more than 1,000 years ago changed anthropologists' views of the Anasazi. This video, narrated by Robert Redford, describes the complex workings of the calendar and the prehistoric culture of the Indians who built it.
♦ Have students research other prehistoric calendar sites, including their locations, what is known about them, how they functioned, when they are believed to have been built, and their similarities to or differences from the Sun Dagger.
1. Chaco Canyon (N.M.)—Antiquities 2. Pueblo Indians—Astronomy 3. Indians of North America—Calendar.

978.92
Radlauer, Ruth Shaw. *Carlsbad Caverns National Park*. Childrens Press (0-516-07742-2), 1987. 48p. Color photos. (Interest level: 2-6).

This book describes the physical features and plant and animal life of this national park located in the southern New Mexico desert. This simply written account provides students with information concerning stalactites, stalagmites, resident bats, and plants and animals that live in the surrounding desert.
♦ Have students investigate the life cycle of the millions of bats who inhabit Carlsbad Caverns.
1. Carlsbad Caverns National Park (N.M.).

978.942
Sotnak, Lewann. *Carlsbad Caverns*. Crestwood House (0-89686-403-0), 1988. 47p. Color photos. (Interest level: 2-6).

Sotnak's book describes the plant and animal life of Carlsbad Caverns of southern New Mexico, as well as provides a history of the discovery of the caves and the development of the famed national park. Children will enjoy the natural history aspects of the caverns portrayed in this clearly written and photographed book.
♦ Have students do research to compare and contrast the habitats of other large caves with that of Carlsbad Caverns.
1. Natural history—New Mexico—Carlsbad Caverns National Park 2. Carlsbad Caverns National Park (N.M.).

979
Anderson, Joan. *Spanish Pioneers of the Southwest.* Dutton (0-525-67264-8), 1989. Unpaginated. B/W photos. (Interest level: 4-8).

More than 20 years before the Pilgrims arrived on the eastern coast, Don Juan de Onate led troops and settlers into the northern portion of New Spain, now northern New Mexico, in order to establish the first colony of Europeans in the New World. Photographed on location at El Rancho de Golondrinas, a living museum of early Spanish/New Mexican life, this excellent work re-creates a view of life in the mid-1700s.
♦ Students may trace the journey of Don Juan de Onate from Mexico to New Mexico.
1. Southwestern States—History—To 1848
2. Spaniards—Southwestern States—History
3. Frontier and pioneer life—Southwestern States.

979
Yue, Charlotte and **Yue, David.** *The Pueblo.* Houghton Mifflin (0-395-38350-1), 1986. 117p. B/W illus. (Interest level: 4+).

The pueblos of northern New Mexico are described in this book, which focuses on the structure of pueblo dwellings, pueblo life, kivas, gardens, and churches. The book provides a good overview of pueblo communities and the lives of pueblo residents. A bibliography and an index are provided.
♦ Have students research the common elements and distinctive traits of the 19 New Mexico pueblos or the 8 Hopi pueblos located in Arizona.
1. Pueblo Indians 2. Indians of North America—Southwestern States.

979.01
Petersen, David. *The Anasazi.* Childrens Press (0-516-01121-9), 1991. (A New True Book). 45p. Color photos. (Interest level: 2-4).

Petersen describes the homes, culture, and way of life of the Anasazi, who disappeared more than 700 years ago from northern New Mexico and the other Four Corners states. This account provides much information on the ancestors of the Pueblo Indians in an easy, yet accurate book. An index is included.
♦ Have students locate the major Anasazi sites on a map of the Four Corners area.
1. Pueblo Indians—Antiquities 2. Anasazi Indians—Social life and customs.

979.01
Trimble, Stephen. *The Village of Blue Stone.* Illus. by Jennifer Owings Dewey and Deborah Reade. Macmillan (0-02-789501-7), 1990. 64p. B/W illus. (Interest level: 6-9).

Text and illustrations re-create daily life throughout the year 1100 A.D. in a Chaco Canyon pueblo in northern New Mexico. This simply written book provides students with insight into daily life and customs of the Anasazi, ancestors of the Pueblo. A bibliography, a glossary, and an index are included.
♦ Have students choose an activity or custom (basketweaving, marriage, burial, etc.) and compare it with the same aspect in modern day Pueblo life.
1. Pueblo Indians—Social life and customs
2. Cliff dwellers and cliff dwellings—Southwestern States.

979.01
Warren, Scott. *Cities in the Sand: The Ancient Civilizations of the Southwest.* Chronicle Books (0-8118-0112-1), 1992. 55p. Color photos. (Interest level: 5-8).

This book discusses the discoveries of the major archaeological sites of three major groups of Native Americans that lived in New Mexico, Arizona, Utah, and Colorado: the Anasazi, Hohokam, and Mogollon. This beautifully photographed volume is an important addition to the collection of works for children on the prehistoric Native Americans who populated the Southwest.
♦ Have students prepare a chart that compares and contrasts the cultures of the three major groups of Indians discussed.
1. Southwestern States—Antiquities 2. Pueblo Indians—Antiquities.

Biography

92 Martinez, Maria
Nelson, Mary Carroll. *Maria Martinez.* Dillon Press (0-87518-038-8), 1972. (The Story of an American Indian). 77p. B/W photos. (Interest level: 3-6).

Maria Martinez, famed Pueblo potter, was born around 1885 in the small Indian village of San Ildefonso Pueblo, New Mexico. The story of her life and of the skill she achieved as a potter provides a realistic account of pueblo life in the 1900s.

♦ Using the coil method, students can build their own handmade pottery.
1. Martinez, Maria 2. New Mexico—Biography.

92 Naranjo, Michael
Nelson, Mary Carroll. *Michael Naranjo.* Dillon Press (0-87518-111-2), 1975 (out of print). (The Story of an American Indian). 66p. B/W photos. (Interest level: 4-8).

Michael Naranjo is a Pueblo Indian sculptor who grew up observing nature and exploring the countryside around Santa Clara Pueblo, New Mexico. This simply written biography describes Michael's discovery of his artistic abilities after a grenade explosion left him sightless after only two months in Vietnam.
♦ Have students research the art of sculpture, other famous sculptors, and specific artwork created by Michael Naranjo.
1. Naranjo, Michael 2. Pueblo Indians—Biography.

92 Oppenheimer, Robert J.
Rummel, Jack. *Robert Oppenheimer: Dark Prince.* Facts on File (0-8160-2598-3), 1992. (Makers of Modern Science). 140p. B/W photos. (Interest level: 7-9).

Robert Oppenheimer: Dark Prince chronicles the life, times, and work of the man who spearheaded the Manhattan Project that was so shrouded in secrecy atop a lonely mesa in Los Alamos, New Mexico. This comprehensive account includes a thorough discussion of the political environment that preceded and followed the development of the atomic bomb and the end of World War II.
♦ Have students debate the positive and/or negative effects of the Manhattan Project and the development of the atomic bomb on world history. This biography includes a bibliography and an index.
1. Oppenheimer, Robert J. 2. Atomic bomb—United States—History 3. Physicists—United States—Biography.

92 Velarde, Pablita
Nelson, Mary Carroll. *Pablita Velarde.* Dillon Press (0-87518-037-X), 1971 (out of print). (The Story of an American Indian). 58p. B/W photos. (Interest level: 4-8).

Pablita Velarde is a famous Tewa Indian artist who was born in Santa Clara Pueblo, New Mexico. This clearly written biography tells of the successes and hardships in Pablita's life as she struggles to revive and reinterpret traditional Pueblo Indian art forms in an effort to preserve them. The stresses involved in living in both the Pueblo and Anglo worlds are recounted.
♦ Students can further research the art of Pablita Velarde or the traditional and contemporary styles of other Indian artists.
1. Velarde, Pablita 2. Pueblo Indians—Biography.

92 Wauneka, Annie Dodge
Nelson, Mary Carroll. *Annie Wauneka.* Dillon Press (0-87518-053-1), 1972 (out of print). (The Story of an American Indian). 66p. B/W photos. (Interest level: 4-8).

This is the story of Annie Dodge Wauneka, the first woman ever elected to the Navajo Tribal Council and a Medal of Freedom winner. Clearly and simply written, this biography details Wauneka's many contributions, especially in health education and disease prevention.
♦ Have students research the TB epidemics that affected the Navajo and Wauneka's efforts to eliminate the disease among her people. Students may then research the current resurgence of the disease among the general population and hypothesize reasons for its reemergence as a health problem.
1. Wauneka, Annie Dodge 2. Navajo Indians—Biography.

Fiction

Annie and the Old One. (Videocassette). BFA Educational Media, 1976. 1/2" VHS, (15 min.). $205.00. (Interest level: K-5).

This video tells Miska Miles's story (*see* p. 37) about a Navajo girl's attempts to prevent her grandmother from dying. The beautiful, sensitive illustrations and the lyrical text of the book are re-created in a live-action video which is true to the spirit of the original work.
♦ Have students plan and draw the design for a rug after researching the wide variety of designs used in Native American weaving.
1. Navajo Indians—Fiction 2. Death—Fiction.

Armer, Laura Adams. *Waterless Mountain.* David McKay (0-679-20233-1), 1931. 212p. B/W illus. (Interest level: 5-8).

This story of Younger Brother, a Navajo boy, and his training in the Navajo Way is related with sensitivity and understanding. Winner of the 1931 Newbery Award, *Waterless Mountain* may be considered by some students

to be dated, but it is a classic that has historic value.
- ♦ Have students imagine and describe a safe place to store treasures (much like Younger Brother's cave) and the treasures they would keep there if they could.
1. Navajo Indians—Fiction.

Baylor, Byrd. *Before You Came This Way.* E. P. Dutton (ISBN not available), 1969 (out of print). 32p. Color illus. (Interest level: K-5).

Petroglyphs, drawings on the canyon walls of New Mexico, Arizona, and west Texas, prompt questions about the lives and purposes of their prehistoric creators. This poetic evocation of the past explores what life may have been like when the drawings were made and discusses the beginnings of art, found here in one of its simplest forms.
- ♦ Have students draw a replica of a petroglyph found in this book or another and describe what the symbol means to them.
1. Rock drawings, paintings, and engravings—Fiction 2. Anasazi Indians—Fiction.

Baylor, Byrd. *One Small Blue Bead.* Illus. by author. Charles Scribner's Sons (0-684-19334-5), 1992. Unpaginated. Color illus. (Interest level: 2-5).

A boy makes it possible for an old man in their Anasazi tribe to go in search of his dream—to prove the presence of other tribes in distant locations. This poetic account of the meeting of two prehistoric peoples is richly illustrated in Baylor's distinctive style.
- ♦ Provide students with an artifact—a bead, pottery shard, picture of a pictograph, or other available item—and have them put into poetry a description of the person or event that caused the item to be made, shared, lost, etc.
1. Man, Prehistoric—Fiction 2. Stories in rhyme.

Blood, Charles L. *The Goat in the Rug.* Four Winds Press (0-02-710920-8), 1984, 1976. Unpaginated. Color illus. (Interest level: 2-4).

On the Navajo reservation, Glenmae the weaver makes a rug from the wool provided by Geraldine the goat. Through this reprint of Geraldine's tale, the reader learns not only about the care and pride with which a Navajo rug is made, but also about cooperation between friends.
- ♦ Have students describe the steps involved in weaving a Navajo rug from start to finish. Students may then list and illustrate the procedures for doing some task in a book of their own.
1. Navajo Indians—Fiction 2. Rugs—Fiction 3. Goats—Fiction.

Blume, Judy. *Tiger Eyes.* Bradbury Press (0-02-711080-X), 1981. 206p. (Interest level: 8+).

Resettled in the city of Los Alamos, New Mexico, after the violent death of her father, Davey Wexler recovers from the loss. This sensitive young adult novel uses the New Mexico setting to explore grief and coming of age.
- ♦ Have students research the history of the city of Los Alamos and its role in the development of the atomic bombs dropped on Japan to end World War II.
1. Death—Fiction.

Burroughs, Jean M. *Children of Destiny: True Adventures of Three Cultures.* Sunstone Press, 1975 (out of print). (Living History). 92p. B/W illus. (Interest level: 7+).

Children of Destiny is a collection of 12 short historical fiction stories spanning the years from 1590 until 1920 and detailing the lives of New Mexico children from all areas of the state. Each intriguing story is prefaced by a short paragraph that provides historical background. A bibliography is included.
- ♦ Student collaborative groups may select one event in New Mexico history and prepare a report or write a fictional memoir to share with the class.
1. New Mexico—Children—Fiction.

Duncan, Lois. *Summer of Fear.* Little, Brown & Co. (0-316-19548-0), 1976. 217p. (Interest level: 6-9).

After moving to New Mexico after the death of her parents, Cousin Julia takes over Rachel's bedroom and almost usurps Rachel's place in the family. Rachel finally realizes that Cousin Julia is a witch. This thriller maintains the suspense until the very last minute.
- ♦ Have students research witchcraft and share some of the various superstitions involving witches, such as the belief that a witch cannot be photographed.
1. Witchcraft—Fiction 2. New Mexico—Fiction.

Girl of the Navajos. (Videocassette; 16mm film). Coronet, 1977. 1/2" VHS; 16mm film, (15 min.). $250.00. (Interest level: 1-5).

Filmed on the Navajo reservation, this video shows a young girl who expresses her fear and loneliness concerning her first experience at

herding the family's sheep into the canyon by herself. Based on the book, *Nannabah's Friend* by Mary Perrine (*see* p. 37), this video is a sensitive portrayal of a young Navajo girl's first day on her own.
♦ Ask students to describe a time when they felt lonely. Have them describe their feelings and what they did to feel better.
1. Navajo Indians—Fiction 2. Indians of North America—Fiction.

Green, Timothy. *Mystery of Navajo Moon.* Illus. by author. Northland Publishing (0-87358-523-2), 1991. 48p. Color illus. (Interest level: 2-4).

Wilma Charley, a Navajo girl who lives on the Navajo reservation, takes a wonderful ride on a beautiful pony under the spell of a Navajo Moon, or was it just a dream? This richly illustrated book captures some of the magic of a clear night in the land of the Navajo.
♦ Students can argue pro or con as to whether Wilma's experience was real or a dream, using facts from the story to prove their point, or students can write and illustrate a dream sequence of their own.
1. Navajo Indians—Fiction.

Hillerman, Tony. *Dance Hall of the Dead.* Harper & Row (0-06-011898-9), 1973. 166p. (Interest level: 7+).

Dance Hall of the Dead, the Zuni name for the place called Heaven, is a murder mystery set in the western New Mexico reservations of the Ramah Navajos and the Zuni Indians. Hillerman provides an exciting story while sharing with the readers authentic aspects of Zuni and Navajo culture and a glimpse at the animosity sometimes shared by the two tribes.
♦ Have students locate Zuni and Ramah on a map of New Mexico and then compare and contrast the history and culture of the two tribes.
1. New Mexico—Fiction 2. Indians of North America—Fiction 3. Mystery and detective stories—Fiction.

Hillerman, Tony. *Listening Woman.* Harper & Row (0-06-011901-2), 1978. 200p. (Interest level: 7+).

Navajo police officer Joe Leaphorn finds himself involved in murder and mystery that ranges from the Navajo reservation to Santa Fe, New Mexico. Seeking revenge for historical crimes, the Buffalo Society kidnaps a group of Boy Scouts and holds them for ransom in this page-turning thriller, which includes fascinating information on Navajo history, religion, and culture.
♦ Students may further investigate the history of the atrocities for which the fictional Buffalo Society was seeking revenge, including Wounded Knee, the Sand Creek massacre, and the Olds Prairie Murders.
1. Navajo Indians—Fiction.

Hillerman, Tony. *Thief of Time.* Harper & Row (0-06-015938-3), 1988. 209p. (Interest level: 7+).

The setting of Chaco Culture National Historical Park in northwest New Mexico provides the backdrop for this novel, which combines anthropology and Navajo culture in a thrilling mystery. The flawless interweaving of Navajo culture with the intrigue of murder and the black market trading of Anasazi pots provides a thoroughly enjoyable read.
♦ Students may investigate the national and tribal parks and monuments in the Four Corner area of the United States that interpret the culture and history of the Anasazi.
1. Navajo Indians—Fiction.

James, J. Alison. *Sing for a Gentle Rain.* Atheneum (0-689-31561-9), 1990. 211p. (Interest level: 8+).

Alternating between the present-day story of a young man and his grandfather and the story of a young Anasazi girl and her grandfather from 700 years ago, this intricate tale brings the two together through song and dreams. With historical accuracy, the life of the Anasazi Indians is portrayed in an understanding manner; an intimate scene between the two protagonists is recorded.
♦ Have students prepare a diorama of an Anasazi village and its daily life.
1. Pueblo Indians—Fiction.

Krumgold, Joseph. *... And Now Miguel.* Harper & Row (0-690-04696-0), 1953. 245p. (Interest level: 5-9).

Twelve-year-old Miguel Chavez, who lives in northern New Mexico, has one wish: to accompany the men of his family on the long sheep drive to the Sangre de Cristo mountains for the summer season. The warmth and dignity with which the Chavez family is portrayed add poignancy to the dilemma that faces Miguel after his wish is fulfilled.
♦ Students may select and research the various cultures that raise and herd sheep as a livelihood throughout North America and the world.
1. New Mexico—Fiction.

Mazzio, Joann. *The One Who Came Back.* Houghton Mifflin (0-395-59506-1), 1992. 178p. (Interest level: 7-8).

When Eddie Chavez disappears after cutting school to spend the day in the Sandia Mountains east of Albuquerque, Eddie's best friend Alex must convince the police and everyone else that he had nothing to do with Eddie's death. This engaging story follows Alex as he mourns his friend and tries to unravel the mystery.
♦ Students can write a description of how they would have reacted to Eddie's disappearance in terms of notifying the police and telling adults.
1. New Mexico—Fiction   2. Missing persons—Fiction   3. Mystery and detective stories—Fiction.

Miles, Miska. *Annie and the Old One.* Little, Brown & Co. (0-316-57117-2), 1971. 44p. Color illus. (Interest level: K-5).

In this story, a Navajo girl comes to an understanding that she can not hold back the hands of time when it comes to the approaching death of her grandmother. This sensitive portrayal cuts across cultures in its story about Navajo family life and the relationship between young and old.
♦ Introduce or follow the book with the video of the same title (*see* p. 34). For those teachers who have a need or desire to broach the subject of death with their students, this story can introduce the topic and lead into a discussion.
1. Navajo Indians—Fiction   2. Death—Fiction.

O'Dell, Scott. *Sing Down the Moon.* Houghton Mifflin (0-395-10919-1), 1970. 137p. (Interest level: 5-9).

This Newbery Honor book presents a moving story, through the eyes of a young Navajo girl, of the tragic Long Walk of the Navajo from their homeland to Fort Sumner, New Mexico. O'Dell tells this very personal story of the suffering and the courage of the Navajo in lyrical prose.
♦ Students can further research the event in history called the Long Walk of the Navajo Indians. They may then compare this event with similar instances in the history of other Native American tribes.
1. Navajo Indians—Fiction.

Paul, Paula G. *Dance with Me, Gods.* Dutton (0-525-66760-1), 1982. 138p. (Interest level: 7-8).

Thirteen-year-old Pakatu, a San Juan Pueblo Indian boy, is coming of age in the time of the Pueblo Revolt of 1680. His mixed emotions are sensitively and realistically portrayed as his usually peaceful people wage war against the Spanish who have banned the Pueblo religion.
♦ Students can compare activities taking place in other geographic locations in the United States and the world during the year 1680.
1. Pueblo Revolt, 1680—Fiction   2. Pueblo Indians—Fiction   3. Indians of North America—New Mexico—Fiction.

Perrine, Mary. *Nannabah's Friend.* Houghton Mifflin (0-395-52020-7), 1989. 32p. Color illus. (Interest level: K-3).

Nannabah is lonely and fearful on her first trip to herd the sheep into the canyon alone. Nanabah makes a friend and gains independence in this simple, but effective story of a young Navajo girl and her new responsibility.
♦ Have students brainstorm a list of new things they have been fearful of doing or encountering, the feelings they had beforehand, and the way they dealt with their feelings. Students will enjoy seeing the video or film entitled *Girl of the Navajos*, which is based on this book (*see* p. 35).
1. Navajo Indians—Children—Fiction.

Perrine, Mary. *Salt Boy.* Houghton Mifflin (ISBN not available), 1968. 31p. Color illus. (Interest level: K-3).

Salt Boy wanted only one thing from his father; however, after finding the courage to ask, he was told that the time was not right. This simply written tale is the story of Salt Boy's earnestness and bravery, which wins his father's respect. The moving story focuses on the deep, unspoken feelings between a Navajo boy and his father.
♦ Have students tell of something they wish for but have been told to wait until they are older. Discuss reasons for waiting and why it seems so hard to do.
1. Navajo Indians—Children—Fiction.

Professional Materials

372.8
Cleaveland, Alice Ann. *Geography Skills in a New Mexico Setting.* Pruett Publishing (0-

87108-263-2 student workbook; 0-87108-264-0 teacher's guide), 1985. 187p. (Interest level: Professional).

Using maps of New Mexico as the basis for learning about the geographical concepts of direction and scale, the student workbook has many activities to enhance students' understanding, and the teacher's manual provides answer keys and enrichment exercises. This unique workbook, suitable for grades 4-8, and the teacher's guide incorporate math, history, and language arts in a study of geography.
♦ Many activities are included in the workbook and teacher's guide for measuring distance, using scale, tracing historical routes, and using a compass.

1. New Mexico—Study and teaching 2. Geography—Study and teaching.

372.8
Otero, George. *Teaching about New Mexico History and Culture.* Center for Teaching International Relations, University of Denver (No ISBN), 1977 (out of print). 108p. (Interest level: Professional).

This collection of teacher-tested ideas for teaching about New Mexico and its people is geared to grades one through eight. This excellent resource is out of print, but the activities are varied, innovative, and highly useful.
♦ Some of the interesting ideas include telling New Mexico folktales, making time capsules, learning about the Albuquerque Balloon Fiesta, using postcards, and baking bread.

1. New Mexico—Study and teaching.

970.004
The Chaco Legacy. (Videocassette). PBS Video, 1980. 1/2" VHS, (58 min.). $59.95. (Interest level: 9+).

Nine hundred years ago, in northwestern New Mexico, the area of Chaco Canyon was a religious and technological hub of activity. This color video discusses the complex architecture and technology used by the Chacoans and the possible reasons for the abandonment of the community by its inhabitants.
♦ Have students build a diorama or scale model of a scene they imagine might have occurred during the period in which the Chaco civilization flourished. Use *Chaco Canyon: Archaeology and Archaeologists* by Lister and Lister (*see* entry on this page) and *People of Chaco: A Canyon and Its Culture* by Frazier (*see* p. 30) for reference.

1. Chaco Canyon (N.M.) 2. Archaeology—New Mexico—Chaco Canyon 3. New Mexico—Antiquities.

978.9
Chavez, Thomas E. *An Illustrated History of New Mexico.* University Press of Colorado (0-87081-265-3), 1992. B/W photos. 253p. (Interest level: Professional).

This professional resource compiles photographs, illustrations, and quotations on important events and people in New Mexico history. The stated purpose of this unique book is to stimulate the reader into realms of discovery about the state, and it effectively achieves its goal.
♦ As students study a particular time in history, they may locate quotations and information originating in that period.

1. New Mexico—History—Pictorial works.

978.9025
New Mexico Blue Book. New Mexico. Office of the Secretary of State. (No ISBN), 1993-94. 226p. B/W and Color illus. (Interest level: Professional).

This semiannual publication, available free from the Office of the Secretary of State of New Mexico, includes current directory information, historical information, state symbols, and a description of the executive, legislative, and judicial branches of the state. This timely sourcebook provides government officials' names, telephone numbers, and offices, tribal data, and travel sites; the maps and photographs are also useful. A special feature is the listing of artwork that was created as a part of the New Deal art projects of 1933-43 in New Mexico.
♦ Teachers and students may use this resource to request information from schools, legislators, or other entities in New Mexico as they study the state.

1. New Mexico—Directories.

978.982
Lister, Robert H. and **Lister, Florence C.** *Chaco Canyon: Archaeology and Archaeologists.* University of New Mexico (0-8263-0756-6), 284p. B/W photos. (Interest level: 9+).

The Listers describe the discovery of and subsequent archaeological studies done on this remote northwest New Mexico canyon, which contained a sizable and advanced civilization for several thousand years. Though somewhat technical for the eighth-grade student, this book provides important historical background on the culture considered to be the ancestor of modern-day Pueblo Indians.

♦ Interested students may prepare a time line of archaeological studies done in Chaco Canyon, including important discoveries made by each.

1. Chaco Canyon (N.M.) 2. Archaeology—New Mexico—Chaco Canyon 3. New Mexico—Antiquities.

Oklahoma

by Terri Parker Street

Nonfiction

299
Howard, James H. with **Lena, Willie**. *Oklahoma Seminoles: Medicines, Magic, and Religion.* University of Oklahoma (0-8061-2238-2), 1984. (Civilization of the American Indian Series). 279p. B/W illus. (Interest level: 8+).

The customs and practices of the Oklahoma Seminoles are examined with emphasis placed on those that are unique to the tribe. This volume is a comprehensive resource on a side of Seminole life that is fast disappearing as younger generations become more acculturated and adopt "pan-Indian," intertribal customs rather than the old tribal ways. A bibliography and an index are included.
♦ Erect a target on a tall pole and teach the class to play the single pole ball game Howard describes. Allow young people to use their hands rather than the ballsticks Seminole males traditionally use.

1. Seminole Indians—Religion and mythology 2. Seminole Indians—Medicine 3. Seminole Indians—Rites and ceremonies 4. Indians of North America—Oklahoma—Religion and mythology 5. Indians of North America—Oklahoma—Rites and ceremonies 6. Indians of North America—Oklahoma—Medicine.

305.4
Women in Oklahoma: A Century of Change. Oklahoma Historical Society (0-941498-28-X), 1983. 214p. B/W illus. (Interest level: 7+).

This collection of essays presents views of some contributions women have made to Oklahoma's history and culture. Each essay focuses on one distinct group or area of achievement, making it easy to examine specific interests. An index makes research even easier.
♦ Students can list individually the 10 women each considers to be major figures in today's Oklahoma, and justify their choices. The class can develop a time line showing women's contributions to Oklahoma society. Have the class select 10 women from the individual lists that they agree to be major figures in shaping or guiding modern Oklahoma and place them on the time line appropriately.

1. Oklahoma—History—Women 2. Women's history—Oklahoma.

324.2
Oklahoma Legislature—But What Do They Do in There?. (16mm film). Oklahoma State University, A.V. Center, 1976. (30 min.). $9.00 for 2-day rental. (Interest level: 7+).

This film traces the legislative process as a bill is considered for adoption. Through this film, students can visualize the actual steps in passage of a bill through the Oklahoma House and Senate.
♦ Have students participate in a mock legislative session. Students should be assigned to committees where "bills" will be proposed, examined, and either tabled or sent to the entire class legislature for action.

1. Oklahoma—Politics and government.

328.73
Albert, Carl and **Goble, Danny**. *Little Giant: The Life and Times of Speaker Carl Albert.* University of Oklahoma (0-8061-2250-1), 1990. 388p. B/W illus. (Interest level: 8+).

This is the autobiography of Carl Albert, Speaker of the House of Representatives, who

was short of stature but loomed large in conviction, determination, and influence. This volume is as valuable for its insight into congressional politics as for its depiction of Albert's life. An index is included.
♦ Visit the state capitol to observe the state legislature in session. Following the field trip, have students write a brief paper comparing and contrasting the observed operation of the legislature with Albert's memoirs of the workings of Congress.
1. Albert, Carl Bert, 1908- 2. Legislators—United States—Biography 3. United States. Congress. House—Biography 4. United States. Congress. House—Speaker—Biography.

332.1
Zweig, Phillip L. *Belly Up: The Collapse of the Penn Square Bank.* Crown (0-517-55708-8), 1985. 500p. B/W illus. (Interest level: 8+).

The rise and fall of the Penn Square Bank and the widespread effects of its collapse on American banking are examined in detail. Thorough documentation gives credence and authenticity to information and contentions about what many consider the most disastrous economic event since the Great Depression. An index is included.
♦ Invite a local banking leader to visit the class and discuss the effects of the Penn Square Bank failure. Students may prepare interview questions regarding specific effects on the local, state, and national economy.
1. Penn Square Bank 2. Bank failures—United States.

353.976 (Reference)
Directory of Oklahoma. 43rd ed. Oklahoma Department of Libraries (1-880438-00-3), 1991. 792p. B/W and Color illus. (Interest level: 2+).

This directory, an accepted authority on the state, gives a wide range of information about state government, education, history, and statistics. Charts and maps supplement the text. Biennial publication ensures that the data contained in the volume is current and makes it an invaluable resource for every school collection.
♦ Ask students to assume that massive budget shortfalls demand that 10 percent of state government be eliminated and another 40 percent receive budget cuts. Using the information in the directory, students can make recommendations about which agencies, departments, or other institutions could be abolished and which should continue without reductions, justifying each answer.
1. Oklahoma—Politics and government 2. Oklahoma—Statistics.

355.3
Franks, Kenny A. *Citizen Soldiers: Oklahoma's National Guard.* University of Oklahoma (0-8061-1862-8), 1984. 234p. B/W illus. (Interest level: 7+).

Thoroughly documented text and photographs chronicle the history of the Oklahoma National Guard from its inception as a territorial militia through World War II, Korea, and beyond. The oversize volume covers all aspects of the Oklahoma National Guard but focuses largely upon the meritorious service of the 45th Division Thunderbirds. A bibliography, index, and color maps add to the usefulness of the book.
♦ As an extension, arrange a field trip to the Forty-fifth Infantry Division Museum in Oklahoma City if possible. If a field trip is impractical, arrange for a former or current guardsman to visit the classroom and discuss the role the National Guard plays in peacetime.
1. Oklahoma. National Guard—History 2. Oklahoma. Air National Guard—History.

371.9
Stanley, Jerry. *Children of the Dust Bowl: The True Story of the School at Weedpatch Camp.* Crown (0-517-58752-3), 1992. 85p. B/W illus. (Interest level: 5+).

This photodocumentary follows the struggles and emigration of "Okies" and then focuses on the farm labor camp where a dedicated educator and 50 children built their own school. Fervent text and period photographs blend to form an inspiring portrait of displaced people determined to make a better future. An index and maps are included.
♦ This compelling story gains new relevance when one considers the plight of the homeless in modern America. After sharing the book, have children write a story from the viewpoint of a homeless child of today.
1. Weedpatch Camp (C.A.)—Schools 2. Depressions—1929—Weedpatch Camp.

372.6
Etter, Jim M. *Between Me and You and the Gatepost: Rural Expressions in Oklahoma.*

New Forums (0-913507-16-4), 1990. 55p. B/W illus. (Interest level: 3+).

Many of the colorful expressions used in rural Oklahoma speech are examined and explained in short text. Young readers and newcomers to the state will find the explanations of Oklahoma idioms and other figures of speech fascinating and informative.
♦ Students may each select an expression from the book, copy it and a short explanation on a sheet of art paper, and create an original humorous illustration showing the literal meaning.
1. Speech—Oklahoma.

394.26
Rosser, Linda Kennedy. *Christmas in Oklahoma: Past and Present.* Western Heritage (0-86546-041-8), 1982. 122p. (Interest level: 5+).

Oklahoma traditions, practices, and foods for a joyous holiday are presented. Anecdotes of Christmases past and festive recipes, many of them from Oklahoma's ethnic groups, are the highlights of this volume.
♦ Students can share excerpts from the book with other classes, perhaps over the school intercom, during the holiday season. Work with the home economics teacher to allow some students to prepare and share with the class selected recipes from the volume.
1. Christmas—Oklahoma 2. Christmas—Oklahoma—Cookery.

398
Wise, Lu Celia. *Mini Myths and Legends of Oklahoma Indians.* Oklahoma State Department of Education and Lu Celia Wise (No ISBN), 1978. 64p. Color illus. (Interest level: K+).

This is a collection of 16 folktales from Oklahoma Indian tribes, accompanied by full-color illustrations, many of them reproductions of paintings by well-known Native American artists. The author succinctly introduces young readers to the culture and folklore of Oklahoma Indians in the preface and in notes accompanying the illustrations, which will be appreciated by all those interested in Native American art. A bibliography and glossary are included.
♦ After sharing the stories and illustrations in the volume, have older students choose, read, and illustrate tales from one of the books in the bibliography. Label each piece with the name of the folktale and display on a bulletin board captioned "The Art of Indian Folklore."

1. Folklore—Oklahoma 2. Indians of North America—Folklore.

582
McCoy, Doyle. *Roadside Wild Fruits of Oklahoma.* University of Oklahoma (0-8061-1626-9), 1980. 96p. Color illus. (Interest level: 3+).

Color illustrations and succinct descriptions of wild fruits found throughout the state are included in this guide. This definitive volume bears witness to McCoy's undisputed authority on Oklahoma plants.
♦ Students may use the text as a field guide for identifying fruits found during nature walks or field trips by the class. Bring native fruits, jams, or preserves to class so students may sample the distinct flavors of wild fruits such as blackberries or sand plums.
1. Roadside flora—Oklahoma—Identification 2. Fruit—Oklahoma—Identification.

582.13
McCoy, Doyle. *Oklahoma Wildflowers.* Doyle McCoy (0-8061-1556-4), 1987. 206p. Color illus. (Interest level: 3+).

Over 280 wildflowers found in the state are identified through brief descriptions and color photographs. The arrangement of flowers by color groups and the concise text facilitate use as a field guide while the glossary and index make the volume a useful reference source.
♦ If the season is appropriate, students may select blooms and bring them to class to be pressed and preserved in a wildflower collection. As an alternative, students may help collect or purchase seed to sow a wildflower bed at the school or a nearby park or recreation area.
1. Wild flowers.

582.16
McCoy, Doyle. *Roadside Trees and Shrubs of Oklahoma.* University of Oklahoma (No ISBN), 1981. 116p. Color illus. (Interest level: 4+).

Close-up color photographs illustrate the leaves, often accompanied by seeds or blossoms, of over 150 common trees and shrubs. Illustrations of the entire plant form would make this book more useful as an identification tool, but it nonetheless remains a valid resource on Oklahoma flora. A bibliography, a glossary, and an index are included.
♦ Bring several leaves from common trees or shrubs to the classroom. Challenge the stu-

dents to use McCoy's book to identify the plants from which each leaf was taken.
1. Trees—Oklahoma.

598.1
Sievert, Gregory and **Sievert, Lynnette**. *A Field Guide to Reptiles of Oklahoma*. Oklahoma Department of Wildlife (No ISBN), n.d. 96p. Color photos. (Interest level: K+).

Over 100 species and subspecies of reptiles are briefly described. Color photographs of 80 of the most common Oklahoma reptiles and maps showing the usual habitat range of each greatly facilitate the use of this slim volume. A bibliography and glossary are included.

♦ Invite a herpetologist or naturalist to speak to the class, bringing live specimens for the students to observe. The students may wish to participate in creative writing from the viewpoint of a favorite reptile.
1. Reptiles.

598.2
Sutton, George Miksch. *Fifty Common Birds of Oklahoma and the Southern Great Plains*. University of Oklahoma (0-8061-1439-8), 1984, 1977. 114p. Color illus. (Interest level: 4+).

Sutton's guide helps students identify many birds found throughout Oklahoma. Outstanding illustrations are the forte of this book, which is sure to delight bird-watchers of all ages.

♦ Make bird feeders from empty 3-liter bottles and hang them outside the classroom windows. Students can use Sutton's book to identify birds that visit the feeder and record the species and number of sightings on a classroom graph.
1. Birds—Oklahoma 2. Birds—Great Plains 3. Birds—Pictorial works.

641.5
Pirtle, Caleb, III. *The Land Where We Belong*. Leisure Time (0-9626682-4-9), 1990. 217p. Color illus. (Interest level: 4+).

Recipes are accompanied by a historical travelogue of Oklahoma. Cookery featuring made-in-Oklahoma ingredients is only half the appeal of this volume, which also contains information on Oklahoma personalities and tourist attractions, many of which are largely unknown.

♦ Arrange a field trip to one or more of the sites mentioned in the narrative. Conclude the study by having a sampling party featuring foods from the cookbook.
1. Cookery, American—Southern style 2. Oklahoma—Description and travel.

780
Savage, William W., Jr. *Singing Cowboys and All That Jazz: A Short History of Popular Music in Oklahoma*. Illus. by Rebecca Bateman. University of Oklahoma (0-8061-1648-X), 1983. 185p. B/W illus. (Interest level: 7+).

The author expounds upon "the Oklahoma history nobody knows," the story of popular music and musicians with roots in the Sooner State. The author contends that "culture ignored is culture lost," and readers of this work will be pleasantly surprised at the volume and quality of music with Oklahoma links. A bibliography, discographical references, and an index are included.

♦ With the music teacher, plan and prepare a brief program featuring the music of Oklahoma and its musicians. Present the program for parents or another class.
1. Music, Popular (Songs, etc.)—Oklahoma—History and criticism.

799.8
Gridley, Marion E. *Maria Tallchief*. Dillon (0-87518-060-4), 1973. 74p. B/W illus. (Interest level: 4-7).

The life of Bette Marie Tall Chief, from birth through her career as prima ballerina Maria Tallchief, is presented. The initial chapter, focusing on the Osage Indians, Tallchief's tribe, lends the added dimension of cultural insight to this examination of the heart and soul of an artist.

♦ Invite a local ballet student or instructor to demonstrate essential ballet steps and movements for the class. If possible, arrange a field trip to see a performance of a classical ballet.
1. Tallchief, Maria, 1925- 2. Ballet.

808.092
At Home with an Oklahoma Author. (Videocassette). Oklahoma State Department of Education, Media Section, 1988. 9 videocassettes, 1/2" VHS, (9 to 15 min. per segment). Free to public schools in Oklahoma. (Interest level: 3+).

Each of the 9 segments features an interview with a different author from the Sooner State, including S. E. Hinton, Dian Curtis Regan, and Bill Wallace. Students will gain insight into the

role and responsibility of an author as the writers discuss their lives and work.
♦ After viewing the video, students may participate in a unit focusing on the writings of one or more Oklahoma authors, many of whom are willing to visit schools. Let the students make, balance, and hang mobiles featuring objects from that author's works.
1. Authors, American—Oklahoma.

813
Daly, Jay. *Presenting S. E. Hinton.* Twayne (0-8057-8203-6), 1987. 127p. B/W illus. (Interest level: 7+).

This book details the life of S. E. Hinton, the author of young adult books, and critically analyzes her works. The insightful and extremely thorough analyses of Hinton's books make this an excellent reference tool for teachers and students studying the Oklahoma author's work. A bibliography and an index supplement the text.
♦ Students may select a scene from one of Hinton's books and adapt it into a reader's theater script. Students can share a brief overview of Hinton's life with the class and culminate with the reader's theater presentation.
1. Hinton, S. E.—Criticism and interpretation
2. Young adult fiction, American—History and criticism.

911.76
Historic Oklahoma Map Series. (Maps). Oklahoma Heritage Association, 1990. B/W and Color maps. (Interest level: 4+).

Twelve maps, available folded or unfolded, pinpoint specific aspects of Oklahoma, including biographical data on noted citizens, entertainment sites, transportation, sports, geology, and other topics. This map collection is unsurpassed in its variety, containing information not found in any other collection or format.
♦ Develop students' map skills by having the young people plan an Oklahoma tour itinerary that would include one historic site, one entertainment center, a forgotten community, and the home of a noted Oklahoman. Plot the tour on a laminated road map, showing the complete route to be followed.
1. Oklahoma—Maps.

911.76
Morris, John W., Goins, Charles R., and McReynolds, Edwin C. *Historical Atlas of Oklahoma.* 3rd ed. University of Oklahoma (0-8061-1991-8), 1986, 1974. 167p. (Interest level: 4+).

This compilation of 83 maps, some of which are in color, marks geographical features and regions, historical sites, and political divisions. Clear explanations accompany each of the maps in this well-arranged collection, making this an indispensable reference tool for all Oklahoma libraries and valuable for other libraries. A bibliography and an index are included.
♦ Students may select two or more maps from the collection and reproduce them as a map with an overlay or series of overlays. Have students research to determine what, if any, correlation exists between the information shown on the two types of maps, i.e. between geographical features and political boundaries.
1. Oklahoma—Historical Geography—Maps
2. Oklahoma—History.

917.3
The Southwest. (Videocassette). National Geographic, 1983. (United States Geography Series). 1/2" VHS, (27 min.). $79.00. (Interest level: 4-8).

This National Geographic video focuses on the physical, cultural, and economic aspects of the geography of Oklahoma, Texas, New Mexico, and Arizona. Outstanding video photography is complemented by the narration in this outstanding documentary.
♦ Students may plan and produce a documentary film of their city or neighborhood. Arrange for the library media specialist to assist the students in taping the final product.
1. United States—Geography—Southwest
2. Oklahoma—Geography 3. Texas—Geography 4. New Mexico—Geography 5. Arizona—Geography.

917.6
Deering, Ferdie J., ed. *Look at Oklahoma.* Oklahoma Publishing Co. (No ISBN), 1975. 160p. B/W and Color illus. (Interest level: K+).

The majority of illustrations in this photoessay were first published in ORBIT, the magazine of the *Sunday Oklahoman* newspaper. The photographs in this collection are well captioned and present a panorama of scenes detailing the variety found in the Sooner State.
♦ Students may collect or take a series of photographs dealing with a subject of their

choice. Organize and caption each photograph to present a photoessay on the topic.
1. Oklahoma—Description and travel.

917.66
Argo, Burnis and **Ruth, Kent.** *Oklahoma Historic Tour Guide.* Illus. by Jim Argo. Crossroads Communications (0-916445-34-8), 1992. 355p. Color illus. (Interest level: 7+).

Fascinating characters from Oklahoma's past are revealed as readers travel the state through the pages of this volume. Over 100 maps and color photographs extend the text of this descriptive tour. An index is included.
♦ Students may select and research a character from the text and then dress in costume to present oral reports from the perspective of each character.
1. Historic sites—Oklahoma—Guidebooks 2. Oklahoma—Guidebooks 3. Oklahoma—Tours.

917.66
Atlas of Oklahoma. Oklahoma State University (No ISBN), 1991. 180p. (Interest level: 4+).

This collection of over 75 maps illustrates a wide range of properties of Oklahoma, including physical features, climate, resources, economics, industry, demographics, history, and politics. The Oklahoma State University Cartography Laboratory was responsible for the preparation of these computer graphics maps, which are very clear and reproduce well, making this a vital part of every library collection. Charts, a glossary, and a bibliography enhance the text.
♦ Reproduce the political map from this volume and have students use the map to chart the election results in various statewide races. Students should fill in the map to show which candidate or stand on an issue carried each area.
1. Population—Oklahoma—Statistics 2. Oklahoma—History 3. Oklahoma—Maps 4. Oklahoma—Atlases.

917.66
Burchardt, Bill. *Oklahoma.* Illus. by David Fitzgerald. Graphic Arts Center (0-912856-57-2), 1979. 128p. Color illus. (Interest level: K+).

The panorama of Oklahoma is displayed in full-color photographs with brief captions. Text takes a backseat to the breathtaking illustrations in this oversize volume, occupying only the final 10 pages.

♦ As a follow-up, students can create a filmstrip or video based on excerpts from the text. Students may select a favorite passage, write dialogue as needed, and illustrate the scenes on a blank filmstrip or videotape a live performance for later viewing.
1. Oklahoma—Description and travel.

917.66
Debo, Angie. *Oklahoma, Foot-loose and Fancy-free.* Greenwood (0-313-23085-4), 1981, 1949. 258p. B/W illus. (Interest level: 8+).

A pioneer historian who experienced Oklahoma's history firsthand vividly, Debo goes beyond mere portraiture to include a thoughtful analysis of the causal relationships behind prevailing conditions and attitudes. An index is included.
♦ Much has changed in Oklahoma since the initial publication of this book. Have students use an analytical approach to explain how recent historical developments have altered attitudes and perceptions of Oklahoma and Oklahomans.
1. Oklahoma—Description and travel 2. Oklahoma—History.

917.66
Wilson, Steve. *Oklahoma Treasures and Treasure Tales.* University of Oklahoma (No ISBN), 1976. 325p. B/W illus. (Interest level: 7+).

Folklore of lost gold mines and hidden caches is explored and the plausibility of the tales is examined in this oversize volume. Extensive historical research and documentation give credence to the collected stories of Oklahoma treasure troves. Maps and a bibliography are included.
♦ After reading the book, students may select and give the teacher a written description of a "treasure site" and then develop a map to lead others to that location. For a more challenging assignment, students may encode the map so "uninitiated" readers would have to decode the puzzle to find the site.
1. Treasure—Trove—Oklahoma 2. Legends—Oklahoma 3. Oklahoma—Gold discoveries.

917.664
Ellenbrook, Edward Charles. *Outdoor and Trail Guide to the Wichita Mountains of Southwest Oklahoma.* In-the-Valley-of-the-Wichitas

(0-941634-01-9), 1991, 1983. 130p. B/W illus. (Interest level: 7+).

Informed descriptions of sites and trails evoke images of the beautiful region. Hiking enthusiasts will find much useful information in this guide, including universal safety tips for hiking or camping. Charts and a bibliography are included.
- ♦ Students may wish to help in the preparation of a hiking trail on or near the school campus. Young people could act as guides, taking class groups through the trail and pointing out spots of interest.

1. Oklahoma—Description and travel 2. Hiking—Oklahoma.

970.004
The Coming of the Indians. (Videocassette). Sigma Educational Media, 1987. (The Story of Oklahoma Series). 1/2" VHS, (13 min.). $100.00. (Interest level: 7+).

This video briefly looks at Oklahoma's first inhabitants and the removal of the Five Civilized Tribes to Indian Territory. This production is noteworthy for its treatment of Sequoyah and his efforts to develop an alphabet for the Cherokee language.
- ♦ Students may assume the role of an Indian who has survived the Trail of Tears. Have students write letters to an imaginary relative or friend describing the hardships endured and the new life in Indian Territory.

1. Indians of North America—Oklahoma 2. Indians of North America—Oklahoma—Five Civilized Tribes.

970.1
Debo, Angie. *A History of the Indians of the United States.* University of Oklahoma (0-8061-1888-1), 1970. (The Civilization of the American Indian Series). 450p. B/W illus. (Interest level: 8+).

A comprehensive account of Native Americans is presented from pre-Columbian times through the mid-twentieth century. Debo challenged the "white man's" version of history and, in so doing, produced what remains as the definitive volume on Native American history. A bibliography and an index are included.
- ♦ Students may work with the art teacher to develop a time-line mural of Indian history in pictorial form. Stage an exhibit to display the completed artwork and allow students to explain the historical relevance of the visual images.

1. Indians of North America—History.

970.5
Debo, Angie. *And Still the Waters Run: The Betrayal of the Five Civilized Tribes.* University of Oklahoma (0-8061-1903-9), 1972, 1940. 417p. B/W illus. (Interest level: 8+).

This volume was among the first to challenge the accepted version of the history of United States government dealings with Native Americans, documenting the unscrupulous policies that victimized the inhabitants of Indian Territory. The author's thorough research is obvious throughout this compelling story of official exploitation and disenfranchisement of the Five Civilized Tribes. A bibliography and an index supplement the text.
- ♦ Students may compare and contrast Debo's version of white settlement in Oklahoma with the standard "white man's" history. Have the youth use those comparisons and individual research to determine what, if anything, could or should be done to redress the wrongs done to Native Americans in the nation's past.

1. Five Civilized Tribes—Government relations 2. Indians of North America—Government relations 3. Indians of North America—Indian Territory.

976
Aylesworth, Thomas G. and **Aylesworth, Virginia L.** *South Central: Arkansas, Kansas, Louisiana, Missouri, Oklahoma.* Chelsea House (1-55546-561-7), 1988. (Let's Discover the States Series). 64p. B/W and Color illus. (Interest level: 2-4).

With its concise format, this book addresses the regional similarities and individual distinctions in the states that make up the south central United States. Beautiful full-color photographs and simple maps enhance the information on geography, history, and people of each state. A bibliography and an index are included.
- ♦ Create an Oklahoma collage using photographs from newspapers or surplus back issues of Oklahoma-based periodicals. As an alternative, students can use photographs or original drawings to illustrate an original class book on Oklahoma people and places.

1. Southwestern States.

976.6
The Beginnings. (Videocassette). Sigma Educational Media, 1987. 1/2" VHS, (15 min.). $100.00. (Interest level: 7+).

The geography, climate, and early inhabitants of the land that is now Oklahoma are

featured in computer graphics, reproductions, and live film footage. This video is of special interest because it is one of the few materials to include the Spiro Mounds.
♦ Students may make models of the Spiro Mounds and write a brief paragraph analyzing their importance as an archaeological site. Arrange with the media specialist to display the models and writing in the media center along with Oklahoma artifacts, which students or teachers may contribute.
1. Oklahoma—Description and travel 2. Oklahoma—History 3. Oklahoma—Spiro Mounds.

976.6
Bicha, Karel D. *The Czechs in Oklahoma*. University of Oklahoma (0-8061-1618-8), 1980. (Newcomers to a New Land Series). 81p. B/W illus. (Interest level: 7+).

The contribution of Czechs to Oklahoma society is examined. The Czech influence in Oklahoma, while small, remains in isolated areas of the state, and this volume will be of interest to those who wish to go beyond the Czech or Kolache Festival. A bibliography is included.
♦ Students may write the Chamber of Commerce in Prague or Yukon, the largest centers of Czech population in Oklahoma, to request information on local events celebrating that ethnic heritage. Some students may wish to bring Czech food to share with the class, i.e. kolach or kielbasa sausage.
1. Oklahoma—History—Czechs.

976.6
Blackburn, Bob L. *Images of Oklahoma: A Pictorial History*. Oklahoma Historical Society (0-941498-36-0), 1984. 228p. Sepia illus. (Interest level: 3+).

Photographic reproductions, topically arranged, evidence the rich blend of cultures in Oklahoma's heritage. Each section of this oversize volume is prefaced by a one-page introduction to the topic, and all photographs are well captioned with succinct descriptions.
♦ Students may select a topic from the book to research in the school media center. Help the students prepare overhead transparencies of selected photographs from the book to display as each presents the selected topic in an oral report to the class.
1. Oklahoma—Photographic history 2. United States—History—West—Photographic history.

976.6
Carlile, Glenda. *Buckskin, Calico, and Lace*. Southern Hills (0-9628214-0-3), 1990. 116p. B/W illus. (Interest level: 5+).

Stories about 19 famous and infamous Oklahoma women are collected in this slim volume. For years Carlile performed characterizations of territorial women and, after much coaxing, collected the orations into this book, which offers a discerning look at the feminine contribution to the state. A bibliography is included.
♦ Students may wish to visit one of the sites mentioned in the text, such as the Overholser Mansion in Oklahoma City or the Ferguson home in Watonga, both of which are now state museums. Students also may create original illustrations for a story in the collection.
1. Women—Oklahoma 2. Oklahoma—Biography.

976.6
Carpenter, Allan. *Oklahoma*. Illus. by Phil Austin. Childrens Press (0-516-04136-3), 1979. (Enchantment of America Series). 96p. Color illus. (Interest level: 4-8).

In simple text and scenic photographs, this book takes a general look at the state and its history. Fascinating details and little-known facts enhance the standard information and increase the book's appeal to intermediate readers.
♦ Encourage students to locate and mark on a map the cities and towns most strongly associated with prominent Oklahomans, including the noteworthy citizens Carpenter introduced. Display the map and photographs of famous Oklahomans on a bulletin board labeled "Oklahoma Roots, Global Influence."
1. Oklahoma.

976.6
Collings, Ellsworth and **England, Alma M**. *The 101 Ranch*. University of Oklahoma (0-8061-1047-3), 1986. 256p. B/W illus. (Interest level: 7+).

The quintessential Oklahoma ranch comes to life in this definitive chronicle. This faithful account merges meticulous research and complete documentation with straightforward style. An index is included.
♦ After reading this book, students may wish to investigate the history of Wild West shows. The class can create original posters

advertising the various shows and their star attractions.
1. 101 Ranch, Oklahoma 2. Ranch life—Oklahoma 3. Oklahoma—History.

976.6
The Dust Bowl. (Videocassette). Bennett Media, 1988. (Oklahoma Heritage). 1/2" VHS, (25 min.). (Interest level: 5+).

This black-and-white program was originally produced in the early 1960s using newsreel footage and black-and-white film to detail how economic factors and the advent of modern farming equipment combined with severe drought and fierce winds to create the dust bowl of the mid-1930s. The quality of some film, especially the newsreel clips, is poor, but the production accurately explains the causes of the ecological disaster in a concise and clear manner.
♦ After viewing the film, young people may research techniques of modern farming designed to prevent a recurrence of the huge dust storms. Students may also imagine themselves living in dust bowl Oklahoma and write a letter to a relative or friend describing the situation and the struggle to survive on the land.
1. Oklahoma—History 2. Dust storms.

976.6
Erickson, John R. *Panhandle Cowboy.* Illus. by Bill Elizey. University of Nebraska (0-8032-1803-6), 1980. 213p. B/W illus. (Interest level: 7+).

The life of a modern working cowboy is depicted in a narrative that is both amusing and informative. The author's personal experience as a cowboy and ranch manager combine with a wry sense of humor to produce an account reminiscent of the humor of Will Rogers.
♦ As a follow-up, visit the media center to locate a copy of Russell Freedman's *Cowboys of the Wild West* (Clarion, 1985). Ask students to compare and contrast the life and role of the modern cowboy with those Freedman portrays.
1. Erickson, John R., 1943- 2. Crown Ranch, OK 3. Ranch life—Oklahoma—Beaver County 4. Beaver County, OK—Social life and customs 5. Cowboys—Oklahoma—Beaver County—Biography 6. Beaver County, OK—Biography.

976.6
Faulk, Odie B. *Oklahoma: Land of the Fair God.* Windsor (0-89781-173-9), 1986. 341p. B/W and Color illus. (Interest level: 5+).

The colorful history of Oklahoma from Coronado to the mid-1980s is detailed with an added chapter on companies that are leaders in Oklahoma business and industry. The Oklahoma Historical Society collected the extensive photographs, drawings, and maps which enrich the narrative in this oversize volume. A bibliography and index are provided.
♦ Have students choose a local business, research the company, and interview the owner or manager regarding the company's contributions to the local community. Share this information with the class in an oral or visual report.
1. Oklahoma—History 2. Oklahoma—Description and travel 3. Oklahoma—Industries.

976.6
Fradin, Dennis. *Oklahoma in Words and Pictures.* Childrens Press (0-516-03936-9), 1981. 47p. Color photos. (Interest level: 2-5).

This brief introduction to Oklahoma points out some of the unique aspects of the 46th state. Color photographs, a facts-in-brief section, and a concise chronology add appeal to this simple narrative and make it useful for beginning research efforts.
♦ After sharing the book, review the five themes of geography (location, place, human/environment interactions, movement, and regions) with the class. Let students prepare book reviews in which they analyze how the book addresses each of the five themes.
1. Oklahoma.

976.6
Franklin, Jimmie L. *Journey toward Hope.* University of Oklahoma (0-8061-1810-5), 1982. 256p. B/W illus. (Interest level: 7+).

Franklin examines the condition of Oklahoma African Americans before statehood days to contemporary times. The author goes beyond the issues of injustice and civil rights to examine elements of the African American community that lend it strength, vitality, and unity. An index is included.
♦ Young people may identify aspects of their community that promote positive ethnic attitudes and aspects of their community that further tension and misunderstanding among groups. Allow students to share their conclu-

sions in class and exchange ideas for promoting the positive while eliminating the negative ideas and practices.
1. African Americans—Oklahoma—History 2. Oklahoma—History 3. Oklahoma—Race relations.

976.6
Fugate, Francis L. and **Fugate, Roberta** B. *Roadside History of Oklahoma.* Mountain Press (0-87842-279-X), 1991. (Roadside History Series). 456p. B/W illus. (Interest level: 8+).

A tour of towns and sites in Oklahoma is presented in historic sections, accompanied by passages that highlight particular events or situations. The highly readable narrative is thorough and accurate, with a regional map preceding each section. A bibliography and index are included.
♦ Ask students to find at least one historic fact of interest about their hometown or other designated location in this large volume. Students may design a picture postcard for the selected site.
1. Oklahoma—History, Local 2. Automobile travel—Oklahoma—Guidebooks 3. Oklahoma—Description and travel—1991—Guidebooks 4. Historic sites—Oklahoma—Guidebooks.

976.6
Gilbert, Claudette Marie. *Oklahoma Prehistory.* University of Oklahoma Stovall Museum/Oklahoma Archeological Survey (No ISBN), 1980. 80p. B/W and Color illus. (Interest level: 4+).

This slim volume presents archaeological information on Oklahoma from 25,000 B.C. to 1700 A.D. Interested readers will find accurate data presented in a clear manner that requires no background in archaeology to comprehend. A bibliography is included.
♦ Students may wish to participate in a simulated archaeology dig. Students also may visit an actual dig site or a local museum displaying prehistoric artifacts.
1. Oklahoma—History 2. Archaeology 3. Oklahoma—Antiquities.

976.6
Gregory, Robert. *Oil in Oklahoma.* Leake Industries (No ISBN), 1976. 90p. B/W and Color illus. (Interest level: 4+).

Text and illustrations explore the lives of major oil people and the impact of the oil industry on the state. Of particular interest are the chapters on the Osage Indians, victims of a mass murder scheme, and Thomas Gilcrease, founder of the Gilcrease Museum in Tulsa.
♦ Students may research the art holdings and major artists represented in the Gilcrease Museum collection. Children may consult the art teacher or media specialist to obtain reproductions of works by those artists to display in the classroom as students share their research findings.
1. Oklahoma—History—Biography 2. Petroleum industry and trade—Oklahoma.

976.6
Hard Times in Oklahoma: The Depression Years. Oklahoma Historical Society (0-941498-32-8), 1983. (The Oklahoma Series). 207p. (Interest level: 7+).

This collection of essays deals with the effects of the Great Depression on Oklahoma citizens. The essays on children and farmers, and the photoessay by Kenneth Hendrickson, Jr., are likely to be of most interest to general readers. An index is provided.
♦ Students may imagine themselves to be a child during the depression and write a journal detailing daily activities and emotions. As an alternative, students could interview an older adult about his or her experiences during the Depression.
1. Oklahoma—History 2. Oklahoma—Political history 3. Oklahoma—Depressions—1929 4. Depressions—1929—Oklahoma.

976.6
Heinrichs, Ann. *Oklahoma.* Childrens Press (0-516-00482-4), 1988. (America the Beautiful Series). 144p. B/W and Color illus. (Interest level: 4-8).

Text and captioned illustrations present concise information about the state and its people, including biographical sketches of noted Oklahomans. A facts-in-brief section, chronology, index, and thorough maps make this volume a good reference source for intermediate readers.
♦ Students may create an "Oklahoma Trivia" game based on the reading. The game may be played periodically to reinforce basic information about the state.
1. Oklahoma.

976.6
Hoig, Stan. *The Oklahoma Land Rush of 1889.* Oklahoma Historical Society (0-941498-41-7), 1984. 288p. B/W illus. (Interest level: 8+).

This volume is a well-researched, documented account of events leading up to and including the run for the unassigned lands. Anecdotes enliven the account, lending humor and new interest to a familiar subject. A bibliography and an index are included.
♦ Students may develop a mock courtroom to reenact one or more of the cases discussed in the text. Arrange to present the mock trials for younger students as they observe Oklahoma '89er Day.

1. Oklahoma—History—Land Rush, 1889 2. Oklahoma—History 3. United States—History.

976.6
Indians, Outlaws and Angie Debo. (Videocassette). Institute for Research in History and WGBH Educational Foundation/PBS Video, 1988. (The American Experience). 1/2" VHS, (60 min.). $59.95. (Interest level: 8+).

The life of Angie Debo, the determined Oklahoma historian who challenged the traditional view of Native American history, is examined in this color video production. Debo's inspiring story is one of perseverance, courage, and intelligence, told through narration and by Debo herself.
♦ After viewing the program, students may examine the difficulties Debo encountered while trying to establish herself as a serious scholar. Instruct the young people to analyze those obstacles, determine whether they stemmed from sexual or professional prejudices, and justify their answers.

1. Debo, Angie, 1890-1988 2. Oklahoma—History.

976.6
Jackson, Robert B. *The Remarkable Ride of the Abernathy Boys.* Levite of Apache (0-918634-6-3), 1989, 1967. 70p. B/W illus. (Interest level: 3-6).

A simple narrative recounts the daring round-trip of Temple and Louis "Bud" Abernathy from Frederick, Oklahoma, to New York City to meet Theodore Roosevelt in 1910. The author details the colorful aspects of the journey and gives necessary explanations while glossing over the mundane to maintain a brisk pace sure to appeal to young readers.
♦ Have students use road atlases to plan a trip from their hometown to New York City. Urge groups to use math problem-solving skills to figure the total distance to be traveled (compare to the distance given on p. 63 for the boys' journey), number of days needed to complete the round-trip, and approximate total fuel cost given an average price per gallon.

1. Abernathy, Louis 2. Abernathy, Temple 3. United States—Description and travel.

976.6
Morgan, Anne Hodges and **Strickland, Rennard**, eds. *Oklahoma Memories.* Illus. by Dick Gilpin. University of Oklahoma, Norman (0-8061-1767-2), 1981. 308p. B/W illus. (Interest level: 7+).

This collection of largely firsthand accounts of Oklahoma life includes selections from pre-statehood through the late 1970s. Brief personal anecdotes make history come alive for readers.
♦ Young people may interview a grandparent or senior citizen regarding memories of earlier life in their state. Share the accounts with the class orally or in written form.

1. Oklahoma—Biography 2. Oklahoma—Social life and customs 3. Frontier and pioneer life—Oklahoma.

976.6
Morris, John W. *Ghost Towns of Oklahoma.* University of Oklahoma (0-8061-1420-7 pbk), 1978. 229p. B/W illus. (Interest level: 7+).

The rise and fall of over 100 Oklahoma ghost towns are explained by political and economic factors. Maps and specific instructions for finding these ghost towns encourage interested readers to seek out and explore many of the locales included. An index is provided.
♦ Students may write a paragraph in which they assume the role of the last inhabitant of a ghost town. Urge the young people to describe the emotions they feel as they watch their hometown die around them.

1. Cities and towns, ruined, extinct, etc.—Oklahoma 2. Oklahoma—History, Local.

976.6
Names We Never Knew. (16mm film). Oklahoma State University, A.V. Center, 1975. (27 min.). $11.00 for 2-day rental. (Interest level: 7+).

The artist Charles Banks Wilson narrates a history of the Oklahoma people. Although Wilson is noted for his paintings of famous citizens, such as Will Rogers and Sequoyah, he lucidly explains in this color production why he prefers to paint the common people.

♦ Arrange for the class to visit a local art museum or art gallery showing a display of Oklahoma art. Let students research noted Oklahoma artists (i.e., Wilson, Jerome Tiger, or Bert Seabourn) and share their findings with the class.
1. Oklahoma—History 2. Social life and customs—Oklahoma 3. Artists, American.

976.6
Oil. (Videocassette). Sigma Education Media, 1987. (The Story of Oklahoma). 1/2" VHS, (16 min.). $100.00. (Interest level: 5-9).

This video chronicle addresses the discovery of oil and the industry's development into a major factor in Oklahoma's economy. Reproductions of photographs and actual newsreel footage lend authenticity to the production.
♦ Ask students to list the first 10 things each would do if oil were discovered on their land and they became suddenly wealthy. Urge the children to discuss and justify their choices.
1. Petroleum 2. Oklahoma—Industries.

976.6
Oklahoma: New Views of the Forty-sixth State. University of Oklahoma (0-8061-1651-X), 1982. 308p. (Interest level: 8+).

Six essays offer new perspectives on Oklahoma's history, economics, farmers, politics, and literature and how they resembled and differed from those in other states. The noted scholars who contributed to this collection write with authority and accuracy, with Anne Morgan's essay on literature of the state being of special merit.
♦ As a follow-up to the reading, have students choose and read one of the books Morgan mentioned. Each student may prepare and present a book talk about the work.
1. Oklahoma—History—Addresses, essays, lectures.

976.6
Oklahoma Land Runs. 1889!. (Videocassette). Sigma Educational Media, 1987. 1/2" VHS, (12 min.). $100.00. (Interest level: 2-6).

Computer graphics, maps, and film footage detail the various land openings that allowed white settlement in Oklahoma. The video addresses the need for audiovisual materials about Oklahoma that present information on the elementary level.
♦ After viewing, allow students to participate in a re-creation of the Land Run of 1889. Students may stake homesteads on the playground or other designated area and determine what improvements each will make on the land.
1. Oklahoma—History 2. Oklahoma—History—Land Rush, 1889.

976.6
Oklahoma Our State. (Videocassette). Sigma Educational Media, 1987. 1/2" VHS, (11 min.). $100.00. (Interest level: 2-6).

This video introduction to the state focuses on Oklahoma's location, resources, cities, heritage, and symbols. Colorful computer graphics are combined with film footage and clear narration to give an overview for young learners.
♦ Have children research the Indian symbols in the Great Seal of the State of Oklahoma to determine what significance each holds and to which tribe it is related.
1. Oklahoma—History 2. Oklahoma—Description and travel.

976.6
Oklahoma Run. (Game). M.B.O.P., 1988. (Interest level: 2-7).

This board game, patterned after the classic Monopoly, features Oklahoma sites, characters, and events. Intermediate-age children can learn about the state as they acquire property, build, and drill for oil on the game board.
♦ Introduce the game to the class by having each student select one of the game cards and visit the media center to research the Oklahoma character, locale, or situation mentioned on the card. As students move around the board, have them share the information they found and locate and mark each site on a map of the state.
1. Oklahoma—History.

976.6
Outlaws and Lawmen. (Videocassette). Sigma Educational Media, 1987. (The Story of Oklahoma). 1/2" VHS, (22 min.). $100.00. (Interest level: 4-9).

This program explains how Indian Territory became a haven for white criminals because Native American courts had no jurisdiction over whites and describes the efforts of Judge Isaac Parker and his deputies to bring justice to the land. Color live-action re-creations and reproductions of old photographs help bring to life the wild side of territorial life, a subject sure to appeal to intermediate-age students.
♦ The outlaw life is often glamorized in movies and television. Ask students to compare and

contrast the reality of that life as depicted in this video with the fantasy portrayed in the media.
1. Outlaws—Oklahoma—History 2. Oklahoma—History.

976.6
The Plains Indians. (Videocassette). Sigma Educational Media, 1987. (The Story of Oklahoma). 1/2" VHS, (16 min.). $100.00. (Interest level: 4-8).

The conflict between the nomadic existence of the Plains Indians and the demands of white settlers is detailed in this video. Color footage and reproductions of paintings and vintage photographs, along with informative narration, demonstrate the hardships and dignity of the Plains Indians in Oklahoma's past.
♦ Visit the Museum of the Great Plains in Lawton or another museum that focuses on the Plains Indians. After the field trip, students may construct a model of a Plains Indian village complete with tepees and travois illustrating the mobility of the nomadic people.
1. Indians of North America—Oklahoma 2. Oklahoma—History.

976.6
Roots of Oklahoma. (Slides/audiotape). A. Y. Owen, 1979. (22 min.). $7.00 for two-day rental. (Interest level: 4+).

Color slides and narration present the Charles Banks Wilson murals *Roots of Oklahoma*. This pulse-synchronized program makes viewers aware that paintings are often more than art; they are also history.
♦ Students may discuss the research an artist must do before painting a historical work. Explain the term anachronism and allow students to create original illustrations of a historical scene, adding a minimum of three anachronisms to each scene.
1. Oklahoma—History 2. Art, American.

976.6 (Reference)
Shirk, George H. *Oklahoma Place Names.* University of Oklahoma (0-8061-2028-2 pbk), 1965, 2nd ed. 1974. 268p. (Interest level: 4+).

This directory includes entries noting the location, post office dates, and origins of over 3,500 geographical names. The second edition of this reference tool corrects errors found in the original volume and includes several new entries. Maps and a bibliography are included.

♦ Groups of children can use the alphabetical list of geographical locations in an atlas to select several Oklahoma locations with interesting names. Use Shirk's volume to discover the origin of each place name and share that information with the class.
1. Names, Geographical—Oklahoma.

976.6
Smith, Jack H. *Oklahoma—A Land and Its People: Early Views and History in Picture Postcards.* Vestal (0-911572-80-5), 1989. 122p. Color illus. (Interest level: 5+).

Picture postcards offer a glance at Oklahoma's history and the people who made it. These reproductions offer a panorama of the state as it once was.
♦ Students may find scenes depicted in these postcards that no longer exist. Have students choose one such scene and draw original postcards that show the scene as it now appears.
1. Postcards—Oklahoma 2. Oklahoma—Description and travel 3. Oklahoma—History, Local—Pictorial works.

976.6
Sooner Saga. (Videocassette). Oklahoma State University, A.V. Center, 1982. (Oklahoma Heritage Series). 1/2" VHS, (54 min.). $13.00 for two-day rental. (Interest level: 4+).

This black-and-white production follows Oklahoma history from before Oklahoma's admission to the Union to the Diamond Jubilee of 1982. Many original photographs are reproduced in this video, which focuses on the people and personalities that make up the Sooner State.
♦ After viewing, let students recall the major events and personalities that are associated with the state. Have students vote on the people and events that they consider most important in Oklahoma history, tabulate the votes, and create a class "Oklahoma Hall of Fame," admitting the top five as charter members.
1. Oklahoma—History.

976.6
Strickland, Rennard. *The Indians in Oklahoma.* University of Oklahoma (0-8061-1674-9), 1980. (Newcomers to a New Land Series). 171p. B/W illus. (Interest level: 8+).

This in-depth study of the contribution Native Americans have made to Oklahoma includes a sympathetic account of the tribes'

treatment by the U.S. government. Extensive research and documentation lend authenticity to this thorough examination of Oklahoma's Native American population.
♦ Students may contact tribal governments or research in the media center to discover how the tribes have progressed during the decade since the publication of this volume. Invite a Native American to visit the class and share information about tribal culture.
1. Indians of North America—Oklahoma 2. Oklahoma—History.

976.6
Thompson, Kathleen. *Oklahoma.* Raintree (0-86514-456-7), 1986. 48p. Color photos. (Interest level: 2-5).

Brief text gives an excellent overview of Oklahoma and its history. Large print and a simple, straightforward style make this information book easily readable for early or reluctant readers. Maps and an index are provided.
♦ Point out that the chronology at the back of the book contains an error in one of the dates (1907 is listed as the year the capital moved from Guthrie to Oklahoma City). Students can visit the media center to research, discover, and correct the error.
1. Oklahoma—History 2. Oklahoma—Description and travel.

976.6
The Twin Territories. (Videocassette). Sigma Educational Media, 1987. (The Story of Oklahoma). 1/2" VHS, (21 min.). $100.00. (Interest level: 5-9).

The Twin Territories emphasizes the Native Americans' quest for sovereignty, land openings, and the establishment of educational and cultural advancements under each of the territorial governors. The narration is dry but contains the most thorough and accurate information about the territories available in nonprint format.
♦ Have students imagine themselves to be a leader of the Five Civilized Tribes in 1905 and write letters to the U.S. Congress trying to persuade the government to create a separate Indian state.
1. Oklahoma—History 2. Indians of North America—Oklahoma.

976.6
Walker, Jerald C. *The State of Sequoyah: An Impressionistic Look at Eastern Oklahoma.* Illus. by Daisy Decazes. Lowell (0-913504-95-5), 1985. 106p. Color illus. (Interest level: 4+).

Concise text documents the history of eastern Oklahoma, the portion of the state that in 1905 proposed admission to the Union as the Indian state of Sequoyah. Sensitive color photographs combine with Walker's narrative to yield a striking image of the eastern half of the Sooner State.
♦ Students may write a brief paper describing an event or locale included in the book. Have students select photographs from a picture file or take a series of original photographs to extend and support that writing.
1. Oklahoma—History, Local 2. Oklahoma—Description and travel.

976.6
Wise, Lu Celia. *Oklahoma's Blending of Many Cultures.* Lu Celia Wise (No ISBN), 1974 (out of print). 176p. Color illus. (Interest level: 3+).

A montage of Oklahoma facts and art presents the land and people from earliest white influences through the early 1970s, giving a sense of the Oklahoma character. This busy overview offers brief glimpses into various aspects of the state's colorful history and will appeal to intermediate readers.
♦ Students may select individual topics they feel would be appropriate if they were to write a similar book on their school or community. Have each student prepare a page with text and original illustrations and compile all contributions into a book.
1. Oklahoma—History 2. Social life and customs—Oklahoma.

976.6 (Reference)
Wright, Muriel H. *A Guide to the Indian Tribes of Oklahoma.* University of Oklahoma (0-8061-0238-1), 1986, 1951. 300p. B/W illus. (Interest level: 8+).

General articles on over 60 Indian tribes are arranged alphabetically, and most contain specific information on the location, population, history, government, and culture of the group. Population figures are dated, but the other data in this encyclopedic work justify its inclusion in the modern reference section. The guide includes a bibliography and an index.
♦ Students can explore their genealogy through personal documents and interviews. Then those students with Native American ancestors can use this volume to research those connections. Students without Indian

roots may choose or be assigned a tribe so that they may participate in the experience.
1. Indians of North America—Oklahoma.

976.605
Wise, Lu Celia. *Oklahoma's First Ladies.* Evans (0-934188-10-6), 1983. 88p. Sepia illus. (Interest level: 4+).

Thumbnail sketches of the wives of Oklahoma governors from Haskell to Nigh are accompanied by photographs of each first lady in her inaugural gown. The author's research gleaned personal glimpses of the first ladies that often indicate the influence each wielded in her husband's administration. A bibliography is included.
♦ Urge students to use media center materials to update information on the more recent first ladies such as Donna Nigh and Molly Boren, or those first ladies not included in the collection, i.e. Rhonda Walters. As an alternative, classes in Oklahoma can arrange a field trip to view the First Ladies' Gown Collection at the Kirkpatrick Center Museum Complex in Oklahoma City.
1. Oklahoma—Governors—Wives 2. Oklahoma—History.

976.66
Shirley, Glenn. *Purple Sage: The Exploits, Adventures, and Writing of Patrick Sylvester McGeeney.* Barbed Wire (0-935269-04-5), 1989. 202p. B/W illus. (Interest level: 8+).

The exploits of McGeeney, railroad man, deputy marshal, and filmmaker, are chronicled by a noted Oklahoma historian. Older readers will be intrigued by both the accounts of outlaws and lawmen in Oklahoma and Indian territories and of early movie production. An index is provided.
♦ Students may wish to script and produce a film based on one of McGeeney's adventures. Students may work with the media specialist and drama teacher to cast, rehearse, and videotape the production.
1. Oklahoma—History 2. McGeeney, Patrick S., 1873-1943.

Biography

92 Mankiller, Wilma P.
Glassman, Bruce. *Wilma Mankiller: Chief of the Cherokee Nation.* Blackbirch (0-8239-1208-6), 1992. 64p. B/W and Color illus. (Interest level: 3-7).

The life and career of the first woman to be elected chief of the Cherokee people is portrayed in simple text and photographs. The concise, large-type text makes this biography accessible to young readers. A bibliography, a glossary, and an index are included.
♦ After reading about Mankiller's dedication and accomplishments, send a group of students to the media center to find the address of the Cherokee tribal center. Let students write and mail letters to Ms. Mankiller, being sure to enclose a self-addressed, stamped envelope so that she may reply.
1. Mankiller, Wilma P., 1945- 2. Cherokee Indians—Biography 3. Cherokee Indians—Kings, queens, rulers, etc. 4. Indians of North America—Biography.

92 Moore, Adam
Moore, Adam. *Broken Arrow Boy.* Illus. by author. Landmark (0-93384-9249), 1990. 29p. Color illus. (Interest level: 2-5).

A young author describes his recovery from a serious brain injury through the efforts of medical personnel and the support of his family. Youthful readers and writers will find encouragement and inspiration in Adam Moore's story, told in the clear, straightforward style of a child.
♦ After reading the book, lead the children in a class discussion about why the title was selected. Read other short tales, asking the students to write appropriate titles for each, and finish by having children write and title original stories.
1. Moore, Adam, 1979- 2. Brain 3. Child authors.

92 Rogers, Will
Keith, Harold. *Will Rogers, a Boy's Life.* Illus. by Karl S. Woerner. Levite of Apache (0-927562-08-1), 1991, 1937. B/W illus. (Interest level: 4-7).

The life of the well-known humorist from boyhood to his early twenties is detailed. Rogers' relatives and friends supplied the author with personal accounts that lend authenticity to the tale.
♦ As a follow-up, have students select scenes containing large amounts of dialogue and prepare a brief play or reader's theater script. Perform the play or script for another class to introduce them to Rogers' early years.
1. Rogers, Will, 1879-1935.

92 Rogers, Will
Rogers, Betty. *Will Rogers.* University of Oklahoma (0-8061-1526-2), 1979, 1941. 318p. B/W illus. (Interest level: 7+).

The life of the beloved humorist is related by the person who perhaps knew him better than anyone, his wife. The author speaks lovingly of the homespun philosopher, giving more insight into his personal life and emotions than many biographers. An index is provided.
♦ After reading, students may wish to view *Ropin' Fool* (Bennett Media, 1988), a video transfer of a 1921 silent film starring Rogers and focusing on his roping skills. Students may wish to experiment with rope tricks and knot tying as demonstrated in the film.
1. Rogers, Will, 1879-1935.

92 Ross, Glen
Ross, Glen. *On Coon Mountain: Scenes from a Childhood in the Oklahoma Hills.* University of Oklahoma (0-8061-2405-9), 1992. 185p. (Interest level: 7+).

Episodic chapters reveal the resourcefulness, humor, and determination of rural Oklahomans in the Great Depression and World War II. Ross vividly portrays the bygone lifestyle in the Cookson Hills in the first half of the twentieth century.
♦ Students may contrast the author's style with that of noted humorist Garrison Keillor. One of the episodes in the book can be adapted into a radio monologue similar to those Keillor delivered on National Public Radio.
1. Ross, Glen, 1929- 2. Teachers 3. Authors, American—20th century—Biography 4. Oklahoma—Social life and customs.

92 Sequoyah
Klausner, Janet. *Sequoyah's Gift: A Portrait of the Cherokee Leader.* HarperCollins (0-06-021236-5), 1993. 111p. B/W illus. (Interest level: 4-7).

Authentic quotes and information are distinguished from probable conversations and thoughts in this fictionalized biography. Cherokee words are written phonetically, and the difference between the Cherokee syllabary and the English alphabet is explained.
♦ Students may recognize the similarity between Sequoyah's syllabary and the syllabary form used in many personalized automobile license plates. Have the children experiment with writing English words in syllabary forms, as explained on pp. 47-48 of the text, or in picture rebuses.
1. Sequoyah, 1770?-1843 2. Cherokee Indians—Biography.

92 Sequoyah
Petersen, David. *Sequoyah: Father of the Cherokee Alphabet.* Childrens Press (0-516-04180-0), 1991. 32p. B/W illus. (Interest level: 2-5).

The life and accomplishments of the Indian silversmith, painter, soldier, and scholar are explored, focusing on his development of the Cherokee syllabary. Although Sequoyah lived most of his life in other states, Oklahomans are justly proud to claim him, and this simple biography makes his story accessible to primary readers. The book includes a chronology and an index.
♦ After reading this, students may wonder how the English alphabet came to be and may wish to research the topic in the media center. Have children write their names in the English alphabet, and above each letter, draw the earliest known form of that letter.
1. Sequoyah, 1770?-1843 2. Cherokee Indians—Biography.

92 Speer, Bonnie, and Speer, Jess
Speer, Jess Willard and Speer, Bonnie. *Hillback to Boggy.* Reliance (0-9619639-5-6 pbk), 1991. 199p. B/W photos. (Interest level: 5+).

This is a first-person account of a family's struggle for survival in depression-era Oklahoma. The author's use of written dialect adds to the authentic flavor of the book but may cause difficulty for many readers.
♦ Students may research John Brown and write a paragraph speculating why Henry Speer used Brown's name as a derogatory adjective. Older readers may wish to compare and contrast the Speer family with the depiction of "Okies" in John Steinbeck's *The Grapes of Wrath* (see p. 59).
1. Frontier and pioneer life—Oklahoma 2. Depressions—1929—Oklahoma.

92 Thorpe, Jim
Bernotas, Bob. *Jim Thorpe: Sac and Fox Athlete.* Chelsea House (0-7910-1722-2), 1992. (North American Indians of Achievement Series). 111p. B/W illus. (Interest level: 4-8).

Text and photographs recount the life and achievements of Jim Thorpe, the man many consider to be the greatest all-around athlete the world has ever known. Intermediate readers will find inspiration in the determination and attitude of Thorpe, who left the legacy of a true

champion. A chronology, a bibliography, and an index are included.
- Students may visit the media center to research Thorpe's athletic career. The children may use the almanac to discover how many other athletes have won both the Olympic pentathlon and the decathlon.

1. Thorpe, Jim, 1887-1955 2. Athletes—United States—Biography 3. Indians of North America—Biography.

Fiction

Bauer, Marion Dane. *Shelter from the Wind.* Houghton Mifflin (0-8164-3160-4), 1979, 1976. 109p. (Interest level: 4-7).

Twelve-year-old Stacy runs away from her Oklahoma panhandle home after an argument with her father and stepmother and is befriended by an elderly woman who lives alone in the harsh land. The author's strong command of language and insight into the thought processes and emotions of adolescents enhance the brief tale.
- Young people may write an additional chapter which details Stacy's return, including the conversations and reactions of her family.

1. Oklahoma—Fiction.

Bess, Clayton. *Tracks.* Houghton Mifflin (0-395-40571-8), 1986. 180p. (Interest level: 7-9).

Two young brothers, Monroe and Blue, meet memorable characters and grave danger as they ride the rails from depression-era Oklahoma. The reader must face some bitter truths about people and prejudice, but this fast-paced adventure will hook young adults as it gives startling insight into the seamier side of a bygone era.
- Students may write a poem or a rap song about the book or its characters using a "clickety clack" ostinato rhythm. Students may also wish to create a hobo dictionary, listing and defining the colorful terms used by hobos.

1. Depressions—1929—Fiction 2. Southwest, New—Fiction 3. Voyages and travels—Fiction 4. Brothers—Fiction.

Far and Away. (Videocassette). MCA/Universal, 1992. 1/2" VHS, (140 min.). $19.98. (Interest level: 7-8).

A young tenant farmer leaves Ireland for the United States, where he participates in the Cherokee Outlet Run in 1893. This is a long film, and only the last half-hour or so applies to Oklahoma and the Land Rush. Beautiful color cinematography and excellent direction set this video apart.
- After viewing excerpts from the video, students may follow-up on the Irish influence in Oklahoma by reading Patrick Blessing's *The British and Irish in Oklahoma* (University of Oklahoma, 1980). Share the information by preparing a chart showing noted Oklahomans of Irish descent and Irish contributions to the state.

1. Oklahoma—History—Land Rush, 1893—Fiction.

Ferber, Edna. *Cimarron.* Lightyear (0-89968-279-0), 1992, 1951. 388p. (Interest level: 7+).

A southern aristocrat joins her husband in the struggle for law and order in Oklahoma Territory. Ferber captures the indomitable spirit of the pioneers, and through the Cravets' experiences readers share the ambience, extremes, and major conflicts of a society in the making.
- Students may write an advertisement that they feel might have been placed in an early newspaper or magazine urging settlers to move to the new territory, choosing words and phrases designed to appeal to a particular audience, i.e. women, itinerant workers, or immigrants. Also, some students may wish to read the excerpt on Elva Shartel Ferguson, the model for Ferber's heroine, in Glenda Carlile's *Buckskin, Calico, and Lace* (see p. 47).

1. Oklahoma—History—Fiction.

Heck, Bessie Holland. *Danger on the Homestead.* Illus. by Peggy Perry Anderson. Levite of Apache (0-927562-00-6), 1991. 142p. B/W illus. (Interest level: 4-7).

Young Todd matures quickly when he helps his father stake and protect their claim during the Oklahoma Land Run of 1889. The viewpoint lends intensity to this tale of the run for the unassigned lands.
- The author foreshadowed Todd's danger by stating that if people knew the future, "we might not be brave enough to face it." Have students write a paragraph in which they discuss the pros and cons of knowing the future.

1. Oklahoma—History—Land Rush, 1889—Fiction.

Heck, Bessie Holland. *The Year at Boggy.* Illus. by Paul Frame. World (ISBN not available), 1966 (out of print). 156p. B/W illus. (Interest level: 4-7).

The difficult life of tenant farmers in post-pioneer Oklahoma is revealed through young Millie Holliway and her family. The author accurately and vividly portrays the setting and the hardships and joys of life in rural Oklahoma.
♦ After reading, urge students to discuss how Millie's life was similar and different from their own. Record student responses on a chart; teachers in Oklahoma might label the chart "Oklahoma Life, Then and Now."
1. Oklahoma—Fiction.

Hinton, S. E. *The Outsiders.* Viking (0-670-53257-6), 1967. 188p. (Interest level: 7+).

Fourteen-year-old Ponyboy struggles to find his place in a world of "haves" and "have nots." This young adult novel by a 17-year-old Oklahoma high school student shook the publishing world by looking beyond school proms and dating to see the anguish in young lives.
♦ After reading the novel, students can discuss the theme of Robert Frost's poem "Nothing Gold Can Stay." Encourage the young people to compare and contrast their ideas to Johnny's interpretation in the final chapter of Hinton's book.
1. Brothers and sisters—Fiction.

Hinton, S. E. *Taming the Star Runner.* Delacorte (0-440-50058-3), 1988. 181p. (Interest level: 7+).

After a violent fight with his stepfather, Travis is sent to live with his uncle on an Oklahoma horse ranch, where he forms a bond with Casey, a teenage horse trainer. As in Hinton's other novels, the writing style is concise and characterization is particularly strong.
♦ Students may wish to research the life of the author and reexamine the text to discover similarities between the protagonist and Hinton herself. As a further extension, have the young people assume the role of casting director, selecting actors to portray the major roles in a film of the novel, justifying their choices based on the text.
1. Authorship—Fiction 2. Horses—Fiction.

Hinton, S. E. *Tex.* Delacorte (0-440-08641-8), 1979. 194p. (Interest level: 7+).

Two teenage brothers discover that "love doesn't solve" everything but "it helps a whole lot." Characterization is the strong point of this first-person realistic novel about teens coping with the harsh realities of modern life.
♦ Students may discuss how the point of view affects the course of the novel by limiting the perception of characters and events. Students may wish to rewrite one or more scenes from the viewpoint of another character in the book or that of an omniscient narrator.
1. Brothers and sisters—Fiction 2. Self-reliance—Fiction.

Keith, Harold. *Komantcia.* Levite of Apache (0-927562-03-0), 1991, 1965. 299p. (Interest level: 4-9).

A young Spaniard must learn to adapt after he is taken captive by a Comanche war party. This new edition of an old favorite authentically depicts Comanche life and features an original cover illustration by Native American artist "Doc" Tate Nevaquaya.
♦ Students and teachers may bring Indian artifacts or artwork from home to prepare a display. As a further extension, invite a classical guitarist to visit the school and perform for the students, playing some of the Spanish-style music at which Pedro excelled.
1. Indians of North America—Fiction.

Keith, Harold. *The Obstinate Land.* Levite of Apache (0-927562-15-4), 1993. 214p. (Interest level: 6-9).

A reprint of the earlier (1977) edition in which a young teen assumes responsibility for his family when his father dies shortly after homesteading in the Cherokee Strip. Authentic dialects and detailed description add to this tale of the frustrations and hazards of life in Oklahoma for the early settlers.
♦ Have students locate the Cherokee Strip (often known as the Cherokee Outlet) on a historical map of Oklahoma. Note towns mentioned in the book, and use other locational clues from the text to find the approximate location of the Romberg homestead.
1. German Americans—Fiction 2. Oklahoma—History—Fiction 3. Frontier and pioneer life—Oklahoma—Fiction.

Keith, Harold. *Rifles for Watie.* HarperCollins (0-690-70181-0), 1957. 332p. (Interest level: 5-8).

Youthful optimism gives way to the grim reality of civil war when a young Kansas recruit takes part in the western campaign in and around Indian and Oklahoma territories. Strong characterization and thorough details highlight this compelling Newbery Award-winning novel.

♦ Students can go to the library media center, research the military contributions of Native Americans like Stand Watie, and share their findings with the class. Introduce the concept of a bibliography and have students compile individual bibliographies on Native Americans, the Civil War, Harold Keith, or other topics.

1. Watie, Stand—Fiction 2. United States—History—Civil War, 1861-1865—Fiction 3. Newbery Medal Books, 1958.

Keith, Harold. *Suzy's Scoundrel.* Illus. by John Schoenherr. Thomas Y. Crowell (0-690-00496-6), 1974 (out of print). 209p. B/W illus. (Interest level: 4-6).

A coyote adopted as a pup by an Amish girl in Oklahoma returns to the wild, where life is both playful and perilous. The author's speculations into the emotions and thoughts of coyotes are balanced by strict adherence to animal nature and behavior with no hints of anthropomorphism.

♦ Students may select and research an animal indigenous to their state. Then they may write a story about the animal that includes the information found in the research.

1. Coyotes—Fiction.

Kirschstein, Carolyn. *Hooray for Oklahoma 1889.* Illus. by David Merrell. B.C. Publishers (0-926521-00-4), 1989. 72p. Sepia illus. (Interest level: K-4).

Young Joey accompanies his father on the Land Run of 1889 to stake the Taylor homestead in Oklahoma Territory. Brief chapters and a concise story line make the story of the run accessible to young readers and listeners.

♦ After sharing the tale, allow children to act on the story, making edible wagons by layering graham crackers for the body and using frosting to attach round candy wheels, pretzel wagon tongues, and canvas tops of thin fruit rolls. As an alternative let the students create a wagon from miscellaneous art materials such as matchboxes, buttons, and paper.

1. Oklahoma—History—Land Rush, 1889—Fiction.

Myers, Anna. *Red-Dirt Jessie.* Walker (0-8027-8172-1), 1992. 112p. (Interest level: 4-7).

Twelve-year-old Jessie watches and tries to ease the suffering of her depression-era family after her sister dies from pneumonia. The characterization and setting are exceptionally strong in this novel, evoking intense responses from readers.

♦ Students may participate in creative dramatics based on a favorite scene from the novel. Children can use paint, crayons, or other media in earth tones reminiscent of the red dirt of Jessie's Oklahoma farm to create a mural to use as a backdrop for dramatics.

1. Oklahoma—Fiction 2. Depressions—1929—Oklahoma—Fiction.

Oklahoma Passage. (Videocassette). Oklahoma Educational Television Authority, 1989. 5 videocassettes, 1/2" VHS, (Parts I-V, 60 min. each). $75.00 each. (Interest level: 4+).

One hundred fifty years in the life of the Benton family, from New Echota to Indian Territory and Oklahoma, is recounted by a grandmother to her children. Excellent production values are evident throughout this work, which brings historical truths to life through the eyes of a fictional family.

♦ After viewing the initial segment of the production, students may conduct a debate on the question of Cherokee removal to Oklahoma. One side should take the stand of the Dream-speakers; the other, the Sun-catchers.

1. Oklahoma—History—Fiction.

Rawls, Wilson. *Summer of the Monkeys.* Doubleday (0-385-11450-8), 1976. 239p. (Interest level: 4-8).

A 14-year-old boy determines to capture a troop of escaped circus monkeys in order to earn a reward with which to purchase his heart's desire. The Cherokee Nation in turn-of-the-century Oklahoma Territory is the setting of this humorous, yet touching novel.

♦ Grandpa and Jay Berry did library research in order to help them trap the monkeys. Students may choose an animal, research it in the media center, and use the information obtained to design a trap to capture that animal without injuring it.

1. Monkeys—Fiction.

Rawls, Wilson. *Where the Red Fern Grows: The Story of Two Dogs and a Boy.* Doubleday (0-385-05619-2), 1961. 212p. (Interest level: 4-8).

Billy works to make his dream of owning prize-winning coon dogs a reality, but his victory is short-lived, ending in calamity. This moving story rings true on all levels, with character and setting being especially strong.

♦ Before reading, introduce the concept of foreshadowing; then ask students to listen or read for and note elements or phrases that

seem to give clues to succeeding events in the story. Stop reading with the chapter that describes the hunting contest, and have children predict what will happen based on those clues.
1. Dogs—Fiction.

Steinbeck, John. *The Grapes of Wrath.* Viking (0-14-018640-9), 1939. 640p. (Interest level: 8+).

The Joad family unsuccessfully fights to save their dust bowl farm and joins the tide of "Okies" migrating to California. Oklahomans have long struggled with the demeaning image Steinbeck portrays and only recently have begun to accept his contention that avarice and stupidity contributed to the dust bowl tragedy.
♦ Students should discuss the term Okie, its origins, and its pejorative use. Have students compare the negative image of Okies with the portrayals of Okie children in Jerry Stanley's *Children of the Dust Bowl: The True Story of the School at Weedpatch Camp* (*see* p. 41).
1. California—Fiction 2. Oklahoma—Fiction 3. Depressions—1929—Fiction.

Thomas, Joyce Carol. *Golden Pasture.* Scholastic (0-590-33681-9), 1986. 144p. (Interest level: 5+).

Three generations of a family are united by their relationship with a beautiful horse. The preface, rich in figurative language, sets a lyrical tone that is maintained throughout this tale of male bonding.
♦ Reread the lines from the preface that begin "I'll be that steadfast in all I begin" and conclude with ". . . for I am young and full of chances." Ask each student to write a brief paper about his or her dreams and the steps that must be taken to fulfill them.
1. Fathers and sons—Fiction 2. Grandfathers—Fiction 3. Horses—Fiction 4. African Americans—Fiction.

Thomas, Joyce Carol. *Marked by Fire.* Avon (0-380-79327-X), 1982. 160p. (Interest level: 8+).

From the moment of her birth during an Oklahoma tornado, storms swirl around Abyssinia Jackson, but her strength of character and the support of other black women allow her to overcome with dignity. Thomas's portrayal of a strong black heroine sings with poetic intensity in this first novel of a trilogy.
♦ As an extension to the book, students can learn to tell a story, such as the story of Lubelle and the snake that Abby told on pp. 102-106. Students may select a folktale from a collection in the media center, prepare, and tell it to the class.
1. Folk medicine—Fiction 2. African Americans—Fiction 3. Oklahoma—Fiction.

Wallace, Bill. *Beauty.* Holiday House (0-8234-0715-2), 1988. 177p. (Interest level: 4-8).

A preteen boy is distraught by his parents' divorce and by being forced to move to his Grandpa's farm but finds solace in his relationship with an old mare named Beauty. First-person narration enhances realism and immediately snares young readers, many of whom identify with the young protagonist's pain.
♦ Read to the students Jill Krementz's *How It Feels When Parents Divorce* (Knopf, 1984). Have the children compare and contrast the accounts from actual youngsters with the reactions of Luke in Wallace's book.
1. Horses—Fiction 2. Farm life—Fiction.

Wallace, Bill. *A Dog Called Kitty.* Holiday House (0-8234-0376-9), 1980. 153p. (Interest level: 3-7).

A dog attack has left Ricky terrified of canines, but he finds himself reluctantly drawn to a starving, abandoned pup. Dialogue and narration filled with phrases and idioms common in Oklahoma conversation heighten the sense of place and reality.
♦ Students can locate the setting of the novel on a state map. Send a group of children to the media center to research the author and discover why many of his books are set in or around Chickasha.
1. Dogs—Fiction.

Wallace, Bill. *Trapped in Death Cave.* Holiday House (0-8234-0516-8), 1984. 170p. (Interest level: 4-7).

Gary embarks on a search for hidden gold and his grandfather's murderer in Oklahoma's Wichita Mountains. Action fills the pages of this rapidly paced adventure that holds sure appeal for young people.
♦ Have students locate the Wichita Mountains and Medicine Park on a map and then mark the probable site of Death Cave. Students also may make a diorama or other visual display to interest other readers.
1. Mystery and detective stories 2. Buried treasure—Fiction.

Periodicals

050
Oklahoma Today. Oklahoma Department of Tourism and Recreation. Bimonthly. B/W and Color illus. (Interest level: K+).

Stunning color photography on high-quality paper extends the text of articles about people, places, and events in the Sooner State. Beautiful landscape photography appeals to even the youngest students, while regular columns on food, art, and literature and an entertainment calendar highlight the magazine for older readers.
- Have students examine current and back issues of the magazine to find articles in which the photographs are especially vital in presenting the information. Let the young people use photography in a similar manner to document a report or extend a creative-writing project.

1. Periodicals—Oklahoma.

050
Outdoor Oklahoma. Oklahoma Department of Wildlife Conservation. Bimonthly. B/W and Color illus. (Interest level: K+).

Articles and regular columns are complemented by outstanding color photography of Oklahoma scenery and wildlife that will attract all ages. Hunting and fishing license revenues finance this publication, so hunting and fishing form a large portion of its content.
- Encourage students to use this periodical to research a subject of their choice. Have students locate at least two articles on the subject spanning a period of several years and compare and contrast the opinions expressed on the issue at different periods of time.

1. Periodicals—Oklahoma.

976.605
Chronicles of Oklahoma. Oklahoma Historical Society. Quarterly. B/W illus. (Interest level: 7+).

This periodical is an outstanding source for articles and essays on the state and its history. The informative articles found in this periodical are invariably historically accurate and often are surprisingly humorous.
- Students may use the cumulative indexes to this periodical to find an article on a subject of their choice. Each student should rewrite the article in simple and brief text, illustrate it, and compile it into a book for elementary readers.

1. Oklahoma—History—Periodicals 2. Periodicals—Oklahoma.

Professional Materials

016.976
Oklahoma Image Materials Guide. Oklahoma Department of Libraries (No ISBN), 1981. 190p. (Interest level: Professional).

This annotated guide to the Sooner State includes books, articles, and a limited amount of audiovisual materials. This guide is somewhat dated and does not suggest interest levels for the material but nevertheless remains an invaluable tool for professionals seeking to develop specific areas of the Oklahoma collection. A bibliography and an index are included.
- Teachers and librarians will want to consult this volume while planning units of study or selecting materials for purchase. The sections listing audiovisual materials will be especially useful because the entries give sources for rental or checkout.

1. Oklahoma—Bibliography 2. Oklahoma—History—Bibliography 3. Oklahoma—Social life and customs—Bibliography.

Texas

by Anita S. Baker

Nonfiction

030 (Reference)
1992-93 Texas Almanac. Illus. by Sue Ellen Brown and Steve Chambers. A. H. Belo Corporation (0-914511-14-9), 1991. B/W illus. and photos. Accompanying teacher's guide. (Interest level: 3-8).

In its 56th edition, this reference book gives up-to-date information and facts on all aspects of Texas, including history, cities and towns, dinosaurs that lived in Texas, crime in the state, even the entire state constitution. Succinct and informative, the *Texas Almanac* is essential for a study of Texas, and the accompanying teacher's guide includes 31 activities using the almanac.
♦ Using the almanac, students may design their own set of questions to challenge each other in a game of Texas Fact and Trivia.
1. Almanacs—Texas 2. Texas—Statistics.

398.2
de Paola, Tomie. *The Legend of the Indian Paintbrush.* Illus. by author. Scholastic (0-590-44706-8), 1988. Unpaginated. Color illus. (Interest level: 2-6).

Little Gopher finds true satisfaction as he captures the colors of the sunset, and the brushes he uses sprout into the spectacular wildflower seen on Texas highways, the Indian Paintbrush. The simply told legend with its large, spectacular illustrations typical of de Paola will prove delightful to any reader.
♦ Using tempera paint, students can capture such natural scenes in their environment, as sunrise, rising moon, cloudy sky, native flowers, etc.
1. Wild flowers—Texas 2. Indians of North America—Legends.

398.24
de Paola, Tomie. *The Legend of the Bluebonnet: An Old Tale of Texas.* Illus. by author. Putnam (0-399-20937-9 pbk), 1983. Unpaginated. Color illus. (Interest level: 2-4).

She-Who-Is-Alone sacrifices her prized possession, a warrior doll, to ensure that the Great Spirit again restores life to the earth and to the people, the Comanche. The fields of bluebonnets promise renewal of life, and de Paola's impressive full-color illustrations capture the reader and enhance the straightforward story.
♦ After listening to or reading the story and discussing the concept of legend, the students can choose a class or school flower and create a legend about its origin.
1. Legends—Texas 2. Comanche Indians—Legends 3. Wild flowers.

597
Grimmer, Glenna. *Things That Swim in Texas Waters Alphabetically Speaking: and in Other Coastal States of the Gulf of Mexico.* Illus. by H. Dickson Hoese. Eakin (0-89015-694-8), 1989. 37p. Color photos. (Interest level: 4-7).

This book presents photographs and descriptions of 26 animals that inhabit the lakes, rivers, and gulf waters of Texas and other Gulf of Mexico coastal states. Excellent photographs, scientific names, common names, length, weight, and habitat are all included with a discussion of the animal and its characteristics. A glossary and bibliography are included.

♦ Creating an A-Z listing of other forms of life in the student's locale could be the first step in a research study. Students can then locate details on descriptions and habitats of the local entries in the media lab.
1. Marine animals—Texas 2. Alphabet.

598.2
Grimmer, Glenna. *Texas Birds from A-Z.* Eakin (0-89015-533-X), 1985. (Stories for Young Americans). 36p. Color photos. (Interest level: K-6).

This alphabet book associates a Texas bird with each letter of the alphabet. This book is an unusual but useful and attractive way to introduce Texas ornithology, and the color photos help students identify birds.
♦ Students may sketch birds or other animals from their state that they have identified using this book and other media center resources. Students may also write a brief description or story about each.
1. Birds—Texas 2. Alphabet.

641.5
The Melting Pot: Ethnic Cuisine in Texas. The University of Texas Institute of Texan Cultures (0-86701-050-9; 0-86701-006-1pbk), 1989. 243p. Sepia photos and illus. (Interest level: 1-8).

This cookbook includes contemporary recipes from 27 ethnic and culture groups that settled in Texas. Each set of recipes is introduced by a two-page discussion of a group and its history in Texas; archival photographs of early Texans of each ethnic/culture group add to the interest. This comprehensive recipe book will extend the study of cultures in Texas.
♦ Small groups of students can select and research a culture, prepare representative costumes, and cook a recipe for a classroom culture fair.
1. Cookery—Texas 2. Texas—History.

641.5
Schlosberg, Hedda, ed. *Company's Coming.* Illus. by Nikki Austin. The University of Texas Institute of Texan Cultures (0-86701-025-8), 1984. 118p. (Interest level: K-8).

Published by the volunteer group associated with the Institute of Texan Cultures, this book includes some recipes indigenous to Texas and the Southwest such as cactus jelly, cowboy bread, and tamales; other recipes are more general in nature. Special Texas recipes in this spiral-bound cookbook could be useful for the classroom. There is an index.
♦ Students can elect appropriate recipes to prepare and to compare with recipes in their own locale. Additionally, if students do not live in Texas, studies of recipes and ingredients could prompt a recipe or ingredients exchange with a class of Texas students of the same age.
1. Cookery—Texas 2. Food—Texas.

719
Finley, Russ. *Big Bend National Park.* (Videocassette). Finley Holiday Film Corp., n.d. (National Park and Monument Series). 1/2" VHS, (30 min.). $24.95. (Interest level: 5-8).

The video takes the viewer on a trip through the three great canyons of Big Bend National Park, the land the Spanish explorers called El Despoblado—the uninhabited land. Color, fast pacing, music, and a strong narration make this a valuable video for the classroom.
♦ Before viewing, the students can generate a list of questions they want answered from the film, predicting the information they will gain from the experience. After viewing, they can evaluate their ability to predict and the information they gained.
1. Big Bend National Park (Tex.) 2. National parks and reserves—Texas.

781.63
Songs Texas Sings: Texas Centennial Songbook. Turner Company, 1986. Unpaginated. Sepia illus.; some photos. (Interest level: 2-7).

This book contains 29 songs, primarily Texas cowboy songs, that Texans and others have enjoyed singing over the years. A brief narrative makes the life of the ranch and cattle trail real to the reader/singer, and the songs will be familiar to many.
♦ Singing these traditional songs will be enjoyable and provide integration of social studies, music, and language arts.
1. Cowhands—Songs and music 2. Songs, Texas 3. Ranch life—Songs and music.

811
Jernigan, Gisela. *Agave Blooms Just Once.* Illus. by E. Wesley Jernigan. Harbinger House (0-943173-46-9; 0-943173-44-2 pbk), 1989. Unpaginated. Color illus. (Interest level: K-6).

Not just a book for preschoolers learning the alphabet, this alphabet book presents vegetation and animals that thrive in the Texas desert, making it a comfortable initial source for older

students studying the arid regions of Texas and the Southwest. This visually stimulating book provides much detail for studying the desert.
♦ Younger students who have mastered a more traditional manuscript handwriting style could create a written alphabet of their own and illustrate it with plants and animals with which they are familiar. Older students could work on placing the subjects mentioned in the book into larger classification groups.
1. Alphabet 2. Deserts—Texas.

910.4
Treasure, People, Ships, and Dreams: A Spanish Shipwreck on the Texas Coast. The University of Texas Institute of Texan Cultures (0-933164-20-3), 1981. 4 sets of 35mm filmstrips with audiocassettes, teacher's guide, free-standing exhibit. $35.00 each; $225.00 for 30-day rental. (Interest level: 5-8).

This set of materials details a voyage of four ships that left Mexico for Spain in 1554, the conditions on shipboard, the shipwreck during a storm, and life of the passengers and crew who managed to survive the disaster. The set of materials includes music and narration which make this historical event come alive for students.
♦ Ask students an open-ended question such as "What would you need to survive in a (jungle, desert, ocean, large city, etc.)?" Students can brainstorm ideas and then, working as survivors in geographically specific locations chosen from a list, collaboratively plan a survival guide.
1. Texas—History 2. Shipwrecks—Texas 3. Buried treasure.

917.3
The Southwest. (Videocassette). National Geographic, 1983. (United States Geography Series). 1/2" VHS, (27 min.). $79.00. (Interest level: 4-8).

The video contrasts the physical, cultural, and economic aspects of the geography of Texas, Oklahoma, Arizona, and New Mexico. Outstanding video photography is complemented by the informative narration in this outstanding documentary.
♦ Using a map of the United States, students can mark key sites and events that occur in the film. They can write the Chamber of Commerce in each major area to receive key information on that area and then create a travel guide listing important places to visit.
1. Southwestern States—Geography.

917.6
Robinson, Charles M. *Frontier Forts of Texas.* Gulf Publishing Company (0-88415-597-8 pbk), 1986. 84p. B/W photos. (Interest level: 4-8).

In this interesting book, Robinson discusses the history and current restoration situation of the forts in Texas which held a key role in the Indian campaigns. Students interested in frontier life, in major and minor battles in Texas, and in the construction of protective forts will find this book extremely interesting. The illustrations include both historic and contemporary views of the forts. An index is provided.
♦ Students may write a daily diary for a week as if they lived in a fort on the frontier.
1. Frontier and pioneer life—Texas 2. Texas—Military history 3. Texas—Description and travel 4. Fortification.

917.6
Texas on My Mind. Falcon Press (0-937959-69-3), 1989. 120p. Color photos. (Interest level: All levels).

This coffee table-size book illustrates the beauty and vast expanses of the state of Texas. Handsome photographs in full color show the range of Texas sights, from city to countryside, cowboys to oil wells, and more.
♦ Have the class take photos or assemble newspaper pictures of their city or neighborhood to create a photographic essay on their community.
1. Texas—Description and travel 2. Texas—Pictorial works.

917.64
Foster, Nancy Haston. *The Alamo & Other Texas Missions to Remember.* Illus. by David Price. Gulf Publishing (0-88415-033-X), 1984. 88p. B/W photos and illus. (Interest level: 4-8).

Architecture, history, events, tours, tips, and maps about Texas missions are included in this guide to Spanish churches, which were often also forts. This book is designed to give a quick reference guide to the missions, many of which are restored and available for visits. A bibliography and an index are provided.
♦ Students can start or add to a card collection of famous churches by collecting postcards of Texas missions. A local newspaper can publish an article about the class's interest, encouraging community people to send cards from their travels.
1. Texas—Description and travel 2. Missions, Spanish—Texas.

917.64
Whisenhunt, Donald W. *The Five States of Texas: An Immodest Proposal.* Eakin Press (0-89015-563-1), 1987. 98p. (Interest level: 6-8).

This book's premise is that Texas is too big and should be divided into five smaller states. The author's reasoning for suggesting dividing up the second largest state in the United States is interesting, and his ideas will elicit provocative questions.
♦ Texas students will be intrigued by the proposal and could determine the location of their city and propose a state government, a state flag, and a song. Out-of-state students can write letters to the author stating their viewpoint and giving reasons for their opinion.
1. Texas—Politics and government 2. Texas—Boundaries 3. Texas—Geography.

929.9
Gilbert, Charles E., Jr. *Flags of Texas.* Illus. by James Rice. Pelican (0-88289-721-7), 1989. 96p. Color illus; B/W photos. (Interest level: 3-6).

This concise history of Texas is told through the stories behind 33 flags that played a vital part in the state's past. Each flag is shown in color with a brief explanation of the background of the flag and its use.
♦ Using the pictures of the flags in the book, students could reproduce either large or to-scale models, adopt the persona of the individual(s) who marched under the flag, and in collaborative groups extend their research to become "experts" on the historical events surrounding the flags.
1. Flags—Texas—History 2. Texas—History.

973
Catalano, Julie. *The Mexican Americans.* Chelsea House (0-87754-857-9), 1988. 95p. B/W and Color photos. (Interest level: 4-7).

The history, culture, and religion of the Mexican people; the factors that encouraged their emigration; and their acceptance as an ethnic group are traced in this volume. The photos in this fact book provide interesting information.
♦ Students can investigate ethnic groups in their community to determine their history, culture, and contributions to the development of the community. If there are Mexican Americans in the community, they may be willing to be interviewees and resource people for the classroom multicultural studies.
1. Mexican Americans 2. Mexico—Immigration and emigration 3. United States—Immigration and emigration.

976.4
Adams, Carolyn. *Stars over Texas.* Illus. by Virginia Scott Gholson. Eakin Press (0-89015-441-2), 1983. 105p. B/W illus. (Interest level: 3-7).

This story-based Texas history textbook details the experiences of early colonists in their struggle to gain independence from Mexico, to establish Texas as a nation, and finally to create a state. Written in chatty vignettes with controlled vocabulary and short, choppy sentences, each historically accurate story is accompanied with three levels of questions—matching, fill in the blank, and discussion.
♦ Students can examine the contributions of different ethnic groups that assisted Texas through the processes to statehood. After studying their own cultural heritages, students could address the question "Does my family have roots in Texas history?".
1. Texas—History 2. Texas—Foreign population 3. Immigration and emigration—Texas.

976.4
The Afro-American Texans. The University of Texas Institute of Texan Cultures (0-86701-036-3), 1975. (The Texians and the Texans). 32p. B/W photos and illus. (Interest level: 3-6).

This book examines the change in the role of African American Texans from the days of slavery to the present. Through historical research and illustrations, the emphasis in this slight but useful volume from the Institute of Texan Cultures is the treatment of the African American and the contributions of individuals from the African American community to Texas and the nation. An index is included.
♦ Investigative reporting on the issue of slavery allows students to gather data, prepare reports, and produce an edition of a newspaper dedicated to the issues. The paper should include editorials, political cartoons, advertisements, news, and human-interest articles.
1. African Americans—Texas—History 2. Texas—History—Biography.

976.4
Anderson, Sylvia and **Riddle, Patricia.** *All about Texas.* Illus. by Diane Fisher. International Publishing (0-88026-0-13-0), 1986. 74p. Color illus. (Interest level: 3-6).

This volume includes information on the history, government, geography, industry, agriculture, transportation, education, wildlife, plants, geology, climate, population, and culture of the Lone Star State. Teachers and students will find that this book adds to a resource data bank on the state.
♦ Students and teachers can use this as a resource book for developing a trivia game, an expanded version of the game developed for *Getting to Know Texas* (*see* following entry). Alternatively, students may study the format of the book and compile a data book about their city or state.
1. Texas—History 2. Texas—Reference books.

976.4
Anderson, Sylvia and **Riddle, Patricia**. *Getting to Know Texas*. Illus. by Diane Fisher. International Publishing (0-88026-021-1), 1986. 80p. Color illus. (Interest level: 4-6).

Interesting facts about Texas history, government, geography, and economics are included in this reference resource, and a glossary and index make it especially useful. As an informational reference book to accompany a study of Texas, this book will be a useful data source.
♦ Students may develop a trivia game using important facts from this source and other media center resources. After developing a marketing strategy and conducting a feasibility study, the class could mass-produce the game for other classrooms. Then issue a challenge to other classes to compete in the Texas trivia game.
1. Texas—History 2. Indians of North America—Texas 3. Explorers—Texas.

976.4
The Anglo-American Texans. The University of Texas Institute of Texan Cultures (ISBN not available), 1975. 27p. B/W photos and illus. (Interest level: 4-8).

The first Anglo-American Texans were persons from the United States who emigrated to Texas before Texas was a state. Today Anglo-American Texans are considered to be persons who immigrated from England, Scotland, Wales, and Ireland. Because the Anglo-American Texans have exerted a dominant influence in law, language, religion, and social customs, this brief account of their immigration is important.
♦ After tracing their heritage, students create a family tree that traces their lineage.
1. Anglo-Americans—Texas.

976.4
Baker, T. Lindsay. *The Polish Texans*. The University of Texas Institute of Texan Cultures (0-933164-98-X; 0-933164-99-8 pbk), 1982. 113p. B/W photos and illus. (Interest level: 4-8).

This book traces the immigration of Polish nationals to Texas and extends the study to Polish people living in Texas in the twentieth century. The scholarly text and historic photographs present a proud culture that has made definite contributions to the settling and progress of Texas, and the documentation is extensive. An index and a bibliography are included.
♦ Students may wish to design and make a bulletin board with information about the contributions of the many ethnic and culture groups that live in their area.
1. Polish Americans—Texas 2. Texas—History—Polish Americans.

976.4
The Belgian Texans. The University of Texas Institute of Texan Cultures (0-933164-97-1), 1975. (The Texians and the Texans). 32p. B/W illus. (Interest level: 3-6).

Studying Belgian influence in Texas, adds to the understanding of cultural diversity, and the focus of this pamphlet is the history and personal contribution of this group. With biographical sketches and historic photographs, this publication from the Institute of Texan Cultures helps children understand the importance of Belgians in Texas.
♦ Have students create a mural depicting contributions of various ethnic and culture groups that settled their area of the state.
1. Belgian Americans—Texas 2. Texas—History—Biography.

976.4
Bustard, Ann. *T is for Texas*. Photos by author. Voyageur Press (0-89658-113-6), 1989. Unpaginated. Color photos. (Interest level: 1-6).

This is a collection of vivid photographs of typical Texas people and places, arranged alphabetically. The up-to-date photos, on a dramatic black background, are examples of excellent camera composition. The book effectively serves both the beginning reader learning the alphabet and the more advanced reader using the visuals to learn about the state.

♦ Students may create their own alphabet book using terms related to their school, city, or state. After learning basic camera techniques, they may take photographs to illustrate the book, or they may instead locate photos in periodicals such as Texas Highways.
1. Alphabet 2. Texas—Photography.

976.4
Callihan, D. Jeanne and **Nesmith, Samuel**. *Our Mexican Ancestors: Vol I*. The University of Texas Institute of Texan Cultures (0-933164-38-6), 1981. 124p. B/W illus. and photos. (Interest level: 3-6).

This book gives the history of the Mexican influence felt in almost every aspect of the state of Texas. Easy-to-read, concise, and accurate, this collection of information helps students understand the role Mexicans played in the development of Texas.
♦ Using this book as a springboard to additional research, students could expand on the stories, collecting data to write and perform a puppet play featuring one or more historical characters.
1. Mexican Americans—Texas—Biography 2. Texas—History—Biography.

976.4
The Chinese Texans. The University of Texas Institute of Texan Cultures (0-933164-91-2), 1978. (The Texians and the Texans). 21p. B/W photos and illus. (Interest level: 3-6).

This small paperback book discusses the many ways Chinese immigrants have contributed to the history and heritage of Texas. The value of this book lies in its concise, accurate data about the Chinese immigrants and the archival illustrations.
♦ Students can use this book to begin a study of Asian influence in art, music, medicine, economics, etc.
1. Chinese Americans—Texas 2. Texas—History—Biography.

976.4
Cox, Mike. *The Texas Rangers: Men of Action and Valor*. Eakin Press (0-89015-818-5), 1991. 126p. B/W photos. (Interest level: 4-6).

Ten action-packed stories of the Texas Rangers, the famous law enforcement agents, provide fascinating reading for intermediate grade students. These factual accounts are well written and valuable for classroom research on the activities of this special law enforcement agency.
♦ Assign 10 collaborative groups one story each to read, and then have each group write a newspaper article, with headlines and a sketch of key events in the story. Combine the articles into a tabloid to be shared with other classes.
1. Texas Rangers 2. Texas—History.

976.4
Crawford, Ann Fears. *New Life, New Land*. Illus. by Betsy Warren. Eakin Press (0-89015-560-7), 1986. 40p. B/W and Color illus. (Interest level: 3-4).

This picture book presents very simple life stories of seven courageous women who helped settle the Texas frontier. Approximately half of each page is devoted to illustration. Short, easy-to-read stories about women who were heroic are especially welcome in a media center or classroom collection that is usually replete with stories of the male heroes of Texas. A bibliography is included.
♦ Students may compare and contrast information provided in various biographical accounts using data retrieval charts. Enter the names of the women horizontally across the top of the chart, and enter sources used vertically down the left side.
1. Women pioneers—Texas 2. Frontier and pioneer life—Texas 3. Texas—Social life and customs.

976.4
Cutrer, Thomas W. *The English Texans*. The University of Texas Institute of Texan Cultures (0-867701-012-6), 1985. 187p. B/W photos and illus. (Interest level: 4-8).

Through this book, readers and listeners may experience the interaction between the rough Texas settlers and the polished English colonists. The book shows the humor that helped the settlers and the colonists as they sought to live together in the new land. Archival photographs aid the study of these Texans.
♦ The English Texans introduced barbed wire, dipping vats, steel windmills, Johnson grass, and the Jersey Lilly saloon. Students can predict the contributions that Americans might make if they helped settle a new frontier. What is there in our country that would be most helpful in a new society?
1. English Americans—Texas 2. Texas—Biography.

976.4
The Czech Texans. The University of Texas Institute of Texan Cultures (0-86701-011-8), 1972. (The Texians and the Texans). 32p. B/W photos and illus. (Interest level: 3-6).

The Czechs first organized colonies around Galveston in 1852, and by 1900 there were 40,000 Texans who claimed Czech as their mother tongue. In this pamphlet, discussions of the history, culture, and contributions of Czech Americans are combined with biographical sketches. An index is provided.
♦ Students may enjoy learning the polka to recordings sung in the Czech language, expecially if the text of the songs is translated for students by a bilingual Czech Texan invited to visit the class.
1. Czech Americans—Texas 2. Texas—History—Biography.

976.4
Davis, John L. *The Danish Texans*. The University of Texas Institute of Texan Cultures (0-933164-56-4),1979. 122p. B/W photos and illus. (Interest level: 4-8).

This book presents the general story of Danish immigration to Texas with an overview of the impact the Danes had on Texas. Easy-to-read text and the many archival and contemporary photos provide information about the people and their culture.
♦ Since the book discusses the major areas of Danish settlement in Texas, students may locate and mark these settlements on an overhead transparency map. Several cultures could be similarly plotted using different colored overlays.
1. Danish Americans—Texas 2. Texas—Biography.

976.4
Fradin, Dennis. *Texas in Words and Pictures*. Illus. by Richard Walls. Childrens Press (0-516-03943-1), 1981. 48p. Color photos. (Interest level: 2-6).

This book provides a brief introduction to the land, history, cities, industries, and famous sites of the Lone Star State. This is an excellent resource for the classroom because it combines solid, concise information with useful illustrations.
♦ Collaborative groups of students may compile a source book on their state or city using a variety of resources and organizing the data in the concise, readable manner shown in this model.
1. Texas—Pictorial works.

976.4
The French Texans. The University of Texas Institute of Texan Cultures (0-86701-046-0), 1973. (The Texians and the Texans). 32p. B/W photos and illus. (Interest level: 3-6).

This monograph allows the reader to see the French influence in many areas of Texas. With historical information, illustrations, and biographical sketches, this book enables students to see the contributions of the French immigrants to Texas.
♦ If there is a French bakery in the area, students may enjoy a field trip and could study the career of chef or baker.
1. French Americans—Texas 2. Texas—History—Biography.

976.4
The Greek Texans. The University of Texas Institute of Texan Cultures (0-86701-007-X), 1974. (The Texians and the Texans). 32p. B/W photos and illus. (Interest level: 3-6).

From two Greeks listed in Texas in the 1860 census to the major immigration after 1890, many Greeks came to Texas to begin a new life. This pamphlet book adds valuable information to the students' understanding of cultural diversity with extensive use of historical photos and its emphasis on early and modern pioneers and their institutions. An index is included.
♦ Because this book presents an overview of the Greek Orthodox religion, students can engage in a survey of religions in America. They can create a data retrieval chart with the different religions written in the horizontal grids at the top, and key beliefs and demographic data written in the vertical grids on the side.
1. Greek Americans—Texas 2. Texas—History—Biography.

976.4
Grider, Sylvia Ann. *The Wendish Texans*. The University of Texas Institute of Texan Cultures (0-86701-000-2), 1982. 119p. B/W photos. (Interest level: 4-8).

Focusing on the customs and traditions of the Wendish Texans, this book helps to answer questions about this unique Texas immigrant group whose European relatives today have German citizenship. The fact that this group is little known will pique the interest of the readers, and the book includes fascinating data such as an abstract of the original ship's registry for the ship *Ben Nevis* on which a group of Wendish colonists came to Texas in 1854,

which includes their birthdate, village or city, and vocation. An index is provided.
♦ Using the ship's registry from the book, students may compute the age of each person on the ship, tally the number of persons in the group with vocational skills needed in the new community, and write a letter as if from one of the families back to their home city or village to tell about the new Texas home.
1. Wendish Americans—Texas 2. Wendish Americans—Social life and customs.

976.4
Guderjan, Thomas H. and **Canty, Carol S**. *The Indian Texans*. The University of Texas Institute of Texan Cultures (0-86701-038-X), 1970. (The Texians and the Texans). 32p. B/W photos and illus. (Interest level: 3-6).

Native Americans were the first Texas immigrants, and their many stories are exciting for students. With its black-and-white photos and illustrations, this pamphlet is arranged by tribes in Texas, with information concerning the location of the tribe, major beliefs, and social life and customs.
♦ "What would it be like to be the first settlers in...?" Students may discuss or write about being one of the first settlers in their community.
1. Indians of North America—Texas—History 2. Texas—History—Biography.

976.4
Gurasich, Marj. *Benito and the White Dove*. Eakin Press (0-89015-693-X), 1989. 104p. (Interest level: 3-6).

The White Dove, Jose Antonio Navarro, tells his story from the walls of the dreaded Ulloa Prison, where he was placed as a traitor to Mexican leader Santa Anna. While the story will capture the reader, the greatest value lies in reading through to the epilogue and author's notes, which provide insight into the background of the story.
♦ Students can study Navarro's influence on Texas as they read about his life, then write about the impact they personally will have on the future, and place their predictions in a time capsule to be buried on school grounds or stored in the school safe.
1. Navarro, Jose Antonio, 1795-1871 2. Statesmen—Texas—Biography 3. Texas—History—Republic 4. Texas—Biography.

976.4
Gurasich, Marj. *Did You Ever . . . Meet a Texas Hero?*. Eakin Press (0-89015-819-3), 1992. 90p. B/W photos and illus. (Interest level: 4-6).

This invaluable, easy-to-read classroom reference provides biographies of important figures in Texas history. This book includes biographies of both women and men who were Texas heroes, word lists with short definitions accompanying the biographical chapters, and a bibliography.
♦ Teachers can use this book, along with other books about heroes from Texas or in general, to discuss the concept of "hero." Students can predict who the heroes of today will be, and then they can do local research and write "Did You Ever Meet a Hero from (their town or city)?".
1. Texas—Geography 2. Heroes and heroines—Texas—Biography.

976.4
Hancock, Sibyl and **Venable, Fay**. *Texas: Yesterday and Today*. Eakin Press (0-89015-304-3), 1982. 50p. B/W photos. (Interest level: 3-5).

Large black-and-white photographs and simple text provide an introduction to Texas history, geography, weather, industry, and 11 major cities. Most of this material is found elsewhere, but the numerous photographs, large print, and straightforward, declarative sentences make this an accessible book.
♦ Students can select a Texas city to study, beginning their research in the media center and writing the chamber of commerce or tourism bureau for additional material.
1. Texas—Geography 2. Texas—Description and travel.

976.4
The Italian Texans. The University of Texas Institute of Texan Cultures (0-86701-033-9), 1973. (The Texians and the Texans). 32p. B/W photos and illus. (Interest level: 3-6).

This pamphlet discusses Italian immigration and influence in Texas, with a focus on individuals, families, and institutions that have been significant to the state and nation. Historic photographs and illustrations personalize the information given in this interesting, well-researched pamphlet.
♦ A discussion of the economic reason for much of the Italian immigration could prompt a study of demographic change in the United States, along with a study of prob-

ability, cause and effect, and prediction of the future. The students' ideas may be recorded and placed in a time capsule to be opened upon their graduation.
1. Italian Americans—Texas 2. Texas—History—Biography.

976.4
Jakes, John. *Susanna of the Alamo: A True Story*. Illus. by Paul Bacon. Harcourt Brace Jovanovich (0-15-200592-7), 1986. Unpaginated. Color illus. (Interest level: 3-6).

This book chronicles the story of Susanna Dickinson and her young daughter Angelina who survived the 1836 Battle at the Alamo and were allowed to leave the Alamo after the battle because Santa Anna wanted the news of the fall of the Alamo to reach Sam Houston. Though this book includes minimal details of the famous battle, the story provides a valuable glimpse into the heart and mind of a survivor.
♦ Students can create a time line of the events found in the story. Students could do additional research on the 1836 Battle at the Alamo to elaborate on the story, and then create a mural based on the tale.
1. Alamo (San Antonio, Tex.)—Biography 2. Dickinson, Susanna 3. Frontier and pioneer life.

976.4
The Jewish Texans. The University of Texas Institute of Texan Cultures (0-86701-024-X), 1992, c1974. (The Texians and the Texans). 32p. B/W illus. and photos. (Interest level: 3-6).

Jewish immigration to Texas was spurred by economic dislocation and political unrest, and most of the new immigrants settled in commercial centers of Galveston, Houston, and San Antonio. This pamphlet book discusses traditional institutions of Jewish life and focuses on the careers of Jewish individuals who have contributed significantly to Texas life. An index is included.
♦ Invite a Jewish Texan to speak to the class about his or her family's immigration to the United States.
1. Jews—Texas 2. Jews—Social life and customs 3. Texas—Jews—Biography.

976.4
The Lebanese Texans and the Syrian Texans. The University of Texas Institute of Texan Cultures (ISBN not available), 1988. (The Texians and the Texans). 29p. B/W photos and illus. (Interest level: 4-8).

This revised edition of a 1974 book entitled *The Syrian and Lebanese Texans* provides an introduction to the substantial numbers of immigrants from Arabic-speaking countries who began arriving in Texas in 1880. Students will find the historic photographs, easily referenced materials, and short biographical sketches on influential persons of Syrian and Lebanese descent useful. A bibliography and an index are also provided.
♦ Students can study their own ethnic heritage, discovering special customs that survived or disappeared in their family celebrations and perhaps learning some key phrases in the native language.
1. Syrian Americans—Texas 2. Lebanese Americans—Texas 3. Texas—History—Biography.

976.4
Lich, Glen E. *The German Texans*. The University of Texas Institute of Texan Cultures (0-933164-84-X), 1981. (The Texians and the Texans). 240p. B/W photos and illus. (Interest level: 4-8).

This extensively documented book introduces many aspects of the German Texan heritage, including biographical sketches of individuals who contributed to the success of Texas. Each chapter in this book is followed by a picture essay related to German Americans. A chronology of Central European colonization in Texas, an index, and a bibliography are additional materials included in this scholarly book.
♦ Students could use scrapbooks kept by families or found at flea markets to study styles of dress, aspects of family life, etc., shown in the photos.
1. German Americans—Texas 2. Texas—History—Biography.

976.4
Marsh, Carole. *Texas Jeopardy: Answers and Questions about Our State's History, Geography, People & More*. Gallopade Publishing Group, 1991. (Interest level: 3-6).

This book presents a variety of questions and answers about Texas history, geography, people, and trivia. The presentation of this fascinating information appeals to students and adults because it is interdisciplinary and random.

♦ After surveying the existing board game market and evaluating best-sellers, students can produce their own board game using information from this book.
1. Texas—Games 2. Texas—History.

976.4
Martinello, Marian L. and **Field, William T., Jr.** *Who Are the Chinese Texans?*. The University of Texas Institute of Texan Cultures (0-933164-47-7), 1979. 80p. B/W photos and illus. (Interest level: 4-6).

Chinese Texans helped create the multiethnic tapestry of Texas, and this book will enhance students' understanding of significant contributions by Chinese immigrants and their families to the state. Through a question-and-answer format simulating interviews with Chinese Americans about their life in Texas, students learn little-known facts about Chinese immigration to the United States and Texas and the rich heritage of Chinese Americans. No index is available.
♦ Students may write question-and-answer simulated interviews, patterned on the ones given in the book, about their own lives.
1. Chinese Americans—Texas 2. Texas—History—Biography.

976.4
The Mexican Texans. The University of Texas Institute of Texan Cultures (0-86701-030-4), 1975. (The Texians and the Texans). 32p. B/W photos and illus. (Interest level: 3-6).

This book profiles significant Mexican Texans who played a role in the Lone Star State, from the first explorers to the 1970s. The pamphlet book has historic photographs of Mexicans in Texas and provides significant information to students about this minority population, which is becoming the majority ethnic group in Texas. An index is included.
♦ Students can examine and prepare interior Mexican food recipes to compare with the TexMex recipes so popular in the United States.
1. Mexican Americans—Texas 2. Texas—History—Biography.

976.4
The Norwegian Texans. The University of Texas Institute of Texan Cultures (0-86701-029-0), 1971. (The Texians and the Texans). 20p. B/W illus. and photos. Unpaginated. (Interest level: 3-6).

This short paperback chronicles the time between 1840 and 1914 when more than one million Norwegians immigrated to America. Short biographical sketches and archival photographs of men and women who left Norway to immigrate to Texas are given in this pamphlet booklet, along with descriptions of their many outstanding accomplishments.
♦ Students can trace the migration routes on a map, study the time period of the major Norwegian migration to Texas, and generate a diary of a child who made the trip from Norway to Texas.
1. Norwegian Americans—Texas 2. Texas—History—Norwegian Americans.

976.4
The Polish Texans. The University of Texas Institute of Texan Cultures (0-933164-34-3), 1972. (The Texians and the Texans). 32p. B/W photos and illus. (Interest level: 4-8).

This paperback monograph details the Polish immigration to Texas in the early nineteenth century and provides a strong historical background. This short, but useful book has the same excellent quality of text and illustrations that is typical of publications of The University of Texas Institute of Texan Cultures. An index and a bibliography are included.
♦ Students could study Poland in the twentieth century, doing research in the media center's periodical collection concerning changes in the country's political and economic situation.
1. Polish Americans—Texas 2. Texas—History—Biography.

976.4
Rice, James. *Texas Alphabet*. Illus. by author. Pelican (0-88289-692-X), 1988. Unpaginated. B/W and Color illus. (Interest level: 3-5).

A feisty Texas jackrabbit called Texas Jack takes the reader through the alphabet, illustrating one or two individuals or events in Texas history for each letter. Texas Jack's sotto voce comments, though not grammatical, elaborate on and lend humor to the entries, making this book enjoyable for many levels of listeners/readers.
♦ Students can adapt Rice's strategies to alphabetize information about any place or event. They can develop their own character to elaborate on each entry, as Rice uses Texas Jack.
1. Texas—History 2. Alphabet 3. Wit and humor—Texas.

976.4
Scott, Larry E. *The Swedish Texans.* The University of Texas Institute of Texan Cultures (0-86701-042-8), 1990. (The Texians and the Texans). 288p. B/W photos and illus. (Interest level: 4-8).

Many Swedish people came to Texas in 1948, and though they are not the largest group to populate the state, they steadfastly set out to make contributions but also to maintain their ethnic identity. Some of this book focuses on the importance of religion in the lives of Swedish Texans, and the biographical emphasis typical of this series from the Institute of Texan Cultures is very interesting. An index and a bibliography are included.
♦ The Swedish people worked to maintain their language, traditions, and folkways. Students can study their own ethnic backgrounds, investigating their family's own traditions and folkways to see which have been kept and which have been replaced.
1. Swedish Americans—Texas 2. Texas—Biography 3. Swedish Americans—Religion.

976.4
Seale, Jan Epton. *Texas History Classroom Plays—Vol. I.* Illus. by Carolyn Commack Seale. The Knowing Press (0-936927-01-1), 1986. 56p. B/W illus. (Interest level: 3-6).

This drama-based biographical book presents plays and dialogue that might have been used by influential Texans like Erastus Smith, Juan Seguin, and Dilue Rose. The play format of this historical data will capture students' attention, and the stories provide insight into Texas history.
♦ Working in four collaborative groups, students can present the plays with costumes and a set, or they may do reader's theater presentations.
1. Texas—History—Drama 2. Texas—Biography.

976.4
Shaw, Charles. *Indian Life in Texas.* Illus. by author. Photos by Reagan Bradshaw. State House Press (0-938349-21-X), 1987. 202p. (Interest level: 4-8).

The quality illustrations, coupled with the extensive information about Native Americans, make this book very useful for research. Organized for easy location of a particular tribe, this book deserves a place in a classroom or library where students study the Native American tribes of Texas.
♦ Students can create visual and written time lines based on a study of Native Americans in Texas, or they can choose a particular time frame and study Native American events in Texas to compare with events in the nation and world during that time. Either approach could culminate in a newspaper publication that included information articles, political cartoons, and editorials reacting to these events.
1. Indians of North America—Texas—History 2. Indians of North America—Texas—Pictorial works 3. Texas—Description and travel.

976.4
The Spanish Texans. The University of Texas Institute of Texan Cultures (0-933164-14-9), 1972. (The Texians and the Texans). 32p. B/W illus. (Interest level: 3-6).

This informative monograph presents a historical overview of the immigration of Spaniards to Texas. Because the Hispanic population of the state of Texas is the majority population, the students should read of the immigration of Spanish people to the state.
♦ Students can study the language, music, art forms, dance, and other contributions of the Spanish people in their own area.
1. Spanish Americans—Texas 2. Texas—History—Biography.

976.4
Stanush, Barbara Evans. *Texans: A Story of Texan Cultures for Young People.* The University of Texas Institute of Texan Cultures (0-86701-040-1), 1988. 122p. Color illus. Teacher's guide available (0-86701-045-2). (Interest level: 4-6).

Fifteen different cultures that distinctively influence Texas are included in this book of historical fact, interesting information, crafts and activities, and dynamic accounts of people in Texas. Attractive illustrations, clear directions, an index, and a whole-language approach to culture make this a complete resource book for the classroom and media center.
♦ Students may make one of the crafts suggested in this book.
1. Texas—Ethnic groups—Study and teaching 2. Texas—History—Biography.

976.4
Stein, R. Conrad. *America the Beautiful: Texas.* Childrens Press (0-516-00489-1), 1989. 138p. Color illus. and photos. (Interest level: 4-8).

Through full-color photographs, the reader is introduced to the vast and diverse state of Texas. The many photos accompanied by minimal text enable students to visit a wide variety of Texas scenes.
♦ Students equipped with cameras can spread out in their community to take photographs for a photographic montage for the classroom or media center.
1. Texas—Pictorial works.

976.4
Stein, R. Conrad. *The Story of the Lone Star Republic.* Childrens Press (0-516-04735-3), 1988. (Cornerstones of Freedom). 31p. B/W and Color illus. (Interest level: 4-8).

This simple narrative provides an overview of Texas history from the first settlements of Americans on Spanish land in 1828 to the annexation as a state in 1845. The straightforward text and illustrations, which include some historic photographs, will capture the interest of the reader, though the illustrations are not effectively labeled.
♦ Students can discuss and write about how Texas history might have been changed if key events had either not happened or resolved themselves differently. Examples of questions include: What if the Mexican forces had lost the battle of the Alamo? What would you include in a declaration of independence or constitution for a new state?.
1. Texas—History—To 1846.

976.4
Stewart, Gail. *Texans.* Illus. by Joe Nordstrom. Rourke (0-86625-408-0), 1990. Unpaginated. Color and Sepia illus. (Interest level: 3-8).

Brief vignettes trace the turbulent history of the Lone Star State, retelling the struggles of the early Texas settlers and their hard-fought battles for independence. The short glimpses give factual information without overloading the reader, and each one could be used as a springboard for additional research, reading, and writing.
♦ After sharing the book, the students can work in collaborative groups to design and activate a "historical silhouette" or a "human time line," complete with period costumes and narrator description of either an event or individual from the book.
1. Texas—History 2. Frontier and pioneer life—Texas.

976.4
Susanna of the Alamo. (Audiocassette). Listening Library (0-8072-0117-0), 1986. (18 min.). (Interest level: 3-6).

The John Jakes book of the same title (*see* p. 69) chronicles the story of Susanna Dickinson and her young daughter Angelina who survived the 1836 Battle at the Alamo. This unabridged tape version of the book, read by Suzanne Toren, will be interesting to students.
♦ Students will want to see the illustrations by Paul Bacon in the John Jakes book *Susanna of the Alamo: A True Story.*
1. Alamo (San Antonio, Tex.)—Biography
2. Dickinson, Susanna 3. Frontier and pioneer life.

976.4
The Swiss Texans. The University of Texas Institute of Texan Cultures (0-933164-92-0), 1977. (The Texians and the Texans). 23p. B/W photos and illus. (Interest level: 3-6).

This pamphlet monograph describes the contributions made by Swiss immigrants as they came to Texas. The discussion of the immigration of the Swiss to America and the biographical profiles on numerous Swiss Americans assist children learning about the diversity of Texas cultures.
♦ After reading the short booklet, students can research travel routes of the Swiss immigrants and hypothesize conditions of their trip and what they found upon arrival in Texas.
1. Swiss Americans—Texas 2. Texas—History—Biography.

976.4
Symbols of Texas. (Kit). The University of Texas Institute of Texan Cultures (0-867010-32-0), 1986-88. 35mm filmstrip with audiocassette and guide—$35.00; slide set with audiocassette—$50.00; teacher's guide—$4.50; videocassette—$35.00. (Interest level: K-4).

Color photos and narrative present information about more than 20 Texas symbols, some of which are official state symbols; others are custom chosen by the developers as representative of Texas. Useful and interesting facts about symbols are presented in a simple manner, and the variety of types of materials provides excellent teaching resources.
♦ Using school or personal video camera recording equipment, students could create a video of their own school symbols with a

narrative to explain the selection of each item.
1. Texas 2. Signs and symbols.

976.4
Texas, the Lone Star State. (Videocassette). KEDT Instructional Services. 13 videocassettes, (8 part series, 60 min. each). $75.00 each, $600.00 for series. Teacher's supplement available. (Interest level: 3-8).

This series of 13 videos is a historical time line that provides a sequenced overview of important events and influences in Texas history. With titles such as *Armadillos and Pigskins, Cattle Culture,* and *The Oil Boom,* this series is interesting and informative, and the teacher's supplement provides appropriate learning experiences for young viewers. Other titles in the series are *Living the Legend, Land Untamed, A New Republic, Statehood, Cowboys,* and *Politics Texas Style.*
♦ Students can interview adults about their reasons for choosing to live in their state, then compile the reasons on a chart.
1. Texas—History.

976.4
Walls, Thomas K. *The Japanese Texans.* The University of Texas Institute of Texan Cultures (0-86701-021-5), 1987. (The Texians and the Texans). 254p. B/W photos and illus. (Interest level: 4-8).

This scholarly book relates the history and heritage of Japanese Texans through their individual stories and thereby breaks down stereotypes and misconceptions related to the Japanese culture. Part of the well-written series from The University of Texas Institute of Texan Cultures, this volume on the Japanese in Texas is well documented and has many fascinating photographs. It also includes an index and a bibliography.
♦ Students may read a children's book from the media center on Japanese internment, such as *Journey to Topaz* by Yoshiko Uchida (Creative Arts Books, 1985).
1 Japanese Americans—Texas 2. Texas—History—Biography.

976.4
Warren, Betsy. *Let's Remember. . . . Texas, the 28th State.* Illus. by author. Hendrick-Long (0-937460-13-3), 1984. (Let's Remember). 36p. B/W illus. (Interest level: 3-6).

This last book in the Let's Remember series reviews cultural and industrial growth in Texas from statehood in 1846 through the technological advances of the 1970s. This cursory study of Texas during the latter half of the nineteenth and twentieth centuries includes useful information, enhanced by black-and-white photographs.
♦ An interesting study might center on what was happening in the United States or other parts of the world when Texas became a state and/or when the student's state was granted statehood.
1. Texas—History.

976.4
Warren, Betsy. *Let's Remember. . . . When Texas Was a Republic.* Illus. by author. Hendrick-Long (0-937460-09-5), 1983. (Let's Remember Series). 32p. B/W illus. (Interest level: 3-6).

This paperback book examines Texas from its beginnings as a republic in 1836 through its statehood in 1846, outlining key events and concepts of the days of the republic in accessible language. The illustrative style of the Let's Remember series is simple line drawings, and the writing style presents limited, but pertinent factual data in an easy-to-read format, along with numerous activities such as a dot-to-dot and a crossword puzzle.
♦ Students can use the information to construct dioramas of events mentioned in the book, and extend the information by doing additional research in the media center.
1. Texas—History.

976.4
Winegarten, Ruth and **Schecter, Cathy.** *Deep in the Heart: The Lives and Legends of Texas Jews.* Illus. by author. Eakin Press (0-89015-759-6), 1990. 253p. B/W photos. (Interest level: 6-8).

This visual history, with 550 photographs of Texas Jews, provides a record of the past and a vision for the future. In addition to a photographic portrayal of Jews in Texas, the book presents issues of prejudice.
♦ Students may prepare a frequency graph which includes the various types of professions and other fields in which the individuals in this book have made contributions: law, medicine, retailing, etc.
1. Jews—History—Texas 2. Jews—Social life and customs—Texas 3. Texas—Ethnic relations.

976.4
Wooley, Bryan. *Where Texas Meets the Sea.* Photos by Skeeter Hagler. Pressworks (0-939722-25-9), 1985. 95p. Color photos. (Interest level: 5-7).

Through attractive photos and interesting narrative, Bryan Wooley and Skeeter Hagler present the Gulf Coast region, a part of Texas not generally considered typical of the Lone Star State. This comprehensive resource to the land, people, and industry of the Gulf Coast area is readable and provides useful information.
♦ Students can brainstorm to list scenes that are generally considered to be representative of their hometown: the town water tower, the city hall, the scenic riverfront, etc. Then they can go in search of the unusual vista to acquaint one another with surprising aspects of their town.
1. Texas—Coast 2. Texas—Description and travel.

Biography

920
Martinello, Marian L. and **Sance, Melvin M.** *A Personal History: The Afro-American Texans: Stories for Young Readers.* The University of Texas Institute of Texan Cultures (0-86701-005-3), 1982. 104p. B/W photos. (Interest level: 5-7).

This exploration of the life and contributions of African Americans who helped Texas and the nation grow and prosper includes individuals from Esteban, who explored the Southwest in 1528, to Barbara Jordan, who served in the U.S. Congress in the twentieth century. Written in interview style, the book presents excellent information in a fascinating manner, and teaches interviewing techniques through the use of a series of structured interview questions.
♦ Using the method suggested in this book, students may collect personal historical data on themselves, and then interview another person and report on their findings.
1. Texas—History—Biography 2. African Americans—Texas.

920
Munson, Sammye. *Our Tejano Heroes: Outstanding Mexican-Americans in Texas.* Eakin Press (0-89015-691-3), 1989. 86p. B/W photos and illus. (Interest level: 5-8).

This text outlines the accomplishments and contributions of 30 Mexican Americans in Texas, including historic figures, such as Jose Antonio Navarro, and contemporary people, such as Congressman Henry B. Gonzalez. Because this interesting collective biography includes famous and little-known heroes, it enables students to see that common, ordinary people can make significant contributions to society. A bibliography is provided.
♦ Students can respond in writing to the question "If a chapter in a book is written about you and your contributions to your city, county, or state, what would you like the chapter to say?" A follow-up discussion could focus on what must be done to insure the accomplishment of that goal.
1. Mexican Americans—Texas—Biography
2. Texas—Biography.

920
Warren, Betsy. *Twenty Texans: Historic Lives for Young Readers.* Illus. by author. Hendrick-Long (0-937460-17-6), 1985. 114p. B/W illus. (Interest level: 3-8).

This is a collection of fascinating short biographies of 20 men and women important in Texas history, from the Mexican rebel Lorenzo de Zavala (1788-1836), to the author Fred Gipson (1908-1973), to the politician Barbara Jordan (1936-). This group of ethnically diverse Texans have contributed much to Texas and the United States, and the book does justice to them and their work. A glossary is included.
♦ After studying this source and others, students can prepare a script to be taped and create living dioramas to enact one key event in the lives of individuals in this book. The dioramas can be displayed with tape players around the room or school library so that other students can see and hear about Texas and its heroes.
1. Texas—Biography.

92 Bowie, Jim
Flynn, Jean. *Jim Bowie: A Texas Legend.* Illus. by Buddy Mullan. Eakin Press (0-89015-241-1), 1980. 51p. B/W illus. (Interest level: 4-6).

Jim Bowie's life is traced from the Louisiana bayous of his youth to his death at the Alamo as a Texas hero. Even though there are few illustrations, this book is so exciting and well written that students will find it a interesting.
♦ As they read the book, students can predict the events of the next chapter and mark a map

as the story progresses to show Bowie's travels.
1. Bowie, Jim (1796?-1836) 2. Texas—Biography 3. Alamo (San Antonio, Tex.)—Biography.

92 Cisneros, Henry G.
Gillies, John. *Señor Alcalde: A Biography of Henry Cisneros*. Dillon Press (0-87518-374-3), 1988. (People in Focus Series). 124p. B/W photos. (Interest level: 4-6).

This biography of San Antonio mayor Henry Cisneros traces his family's history from its beginnings in the early 1700s, and his career in Texas and U.S. politics through his reelection as mayor in 1987. The final chapter of this well-written biography includes 24 personal guidelines that Cisneros wrote himself, which serve as his personal goals. The B/W photos add interest. A bibliography is provided.
♦ Students may research and write additions to *Señor Alcalde*, including Cisneros's more recent contributions, and they may want to suggest a new title for the book.
1. Cisneros, Henry G., 1947- 2. Mayors—Texas—Biography 3. San Antonio, Tex.—Biography.

92 Houston, Sam
Fritz, Jean. *Make Way for Sam Houston*. Illus. by Elise Primavera. Putnam (0-399-21303-1), 1986. 109p. B/W illus. (Interest level: 4-8).

This biography details key events in the life of Sam Houston, the man destined for leadership in the development of Texas. Fritz's inclusion of little-known stories about the colorful life of Sam Houston make this narrative as exciting as the main character was, and the reading is easy.
♦ Reliving Houston's adventures with the Indians or the capture of Mexican leader, Santa Anna, through a drama written, directed, and produced by students would enable them to appreciate Houston's impact on U.S. and Texas history.
1. Houston, Sam, 1793-1863 2. Texas—Governors—Biography 3. United States. Congress. Senate—Biography.

92 Houston, Sam
Sam Houston and Texas: A Giant Man for a Giant Land. (Videocassette). AIMS Media, n.d. (American Lifestyle Series). 1/2" VHS, (24 min.). $70.00. (Interest level: 4+).

This production gives an informed view of an interesting and influential man who ran away at 15 to live with the Indians, was commander of an army, governor of two states, a U.S. senator, and president of a country. This is a well-made, fast-moving presentation of a Texas hero whose life was colorful and exciting, and whose influence on Texas was remarkable.
♦ Students can read *Make Way for Sam Houston* by Jean Fritz (*see* entry this page) to compare this videocassette's image of Houston to that provided by Fritz in her book.
1. Houston, Sam, 1793-1863 2. Texas—Governors—Biography 4. United States. Congress. Senate—Biography.

92 Hughes, John R.
Martin, Jack. *Border Boss: Captain John R. Hughes, Texas Ranger*. Drawings by Frank Anthony Stanush. State House Press (0-938349-50-3 pbk), 1942, 1990. 236p. B/W illus. (Interest level: 4-6).

Captain John R. Hughes was a Texas Ranger who carried law and order to the frontier. Full of details, suspense, and humor, this book will intrigue older elementary students who find action stories interesting. A bibliography and an index are included.
♦ The Texas Rangers have maintained detailed records (Texas Ranger Hall of Fame, Waco, Texas). Students can conduct additional research on an event in Texas history mentioned in the book in order to create independent formal reports or jigsaw collaborations, sharing events which allow a group of students to become experts on a given Ranger and then share data.
1. Hughes, John R., 1855-1947 2. Texas Rangers—Biography 3. Texas—History—Biography.

92 Long, Jane
Crawford, Ann Fears. *Jane Long: Frontier Woman*. Illus. by Rose Baxter. Benson (0-87443-090-9), 1990. B/W illus. (Interest level: 2-5).

Many people call Jane Long the "Mother of Texas" because of the time and energy the pioneer woman invested in the early development of the Republic of Texas. This highly readable selection allows students the opportunity to read about the achievements of a female Texas hero.
♦ Students could plan and present still-life human tableau of important events of the story. Older students could do research on key women who have influenced their commu-

nity and map out a campaign to have them honored in some appropriate way.
1. Long, Jane, 1798-1880 2. Women pioneers—Texas 3. Frontier and pioneer life—Texas.

92 Wallace, W. A. A. "Big Foot"
Sowell, A. J. *Life of "Big Foot" Wallace: The Great Ranger Captain.* Drawings by Charles Shaw. State House Press (0-938349-36-8), 1989. 200p. B/W illus. (Interest level: 5-8).

The life of W. A. A. "Big Foot" Wallace, Texas folk hero and Texas Ranger, is detailed in this book, which was originally published in 1899, the year Wallace died. Students should have an opportunity to read the story of the Indiana Jones of Texas contained in this exciting book, though the print size is small. An index is provided.

♦ As a springboard to additional study, students may correspond with the Texas Ranger Hall of Fame, Waco, Texas, to gather additional information about the exploits of the legendary Texas Rangers.

1. Wallace, W. A. A. (Big Foot), 1817-1899 2. Frontier and pioneer life—Texas 3. Texas Rangers—Biography 4. Texas—History.

92 Williams, Lizzie Johnson
Crawford, Ann Fears. *Lizzie: Queen of the Cattle Trails.* Illus. by Cheryl G. Fain. Benson (0-87443-091-7), 1990. 60p. B/W illus. (Interest level: 2-5).

Lizzie Johnson Williams, a pioneer Texas cattle rancher, made her fortune in the cattle industry of the late 1900s. This interesting story of a strong woman from the latter half of the nineteenth and the early twentieth centuries in Texas could encourage both female and male students in the classroom.

♦ In the story, Lizzie keeps a tally book for counting cattle and recording each cowhand's work time. Students can complete tally sheets and graphs of the kinds of cars on the parking lot, cars that pass the school at a prescribed time, lunchroom behaviors, etc., to reinforce math skills.

1. Williams, Lizzie Johnson, 1843?-1924 2. Women pioneers 3. Ranch life—Texas 4. Texas—Cattle trails.

Fiction

Abernathy, Francis Edward. *How the Critters Created Texas.* Illus. by Ben Sargent. E. C. Temple (0-936650-01-X), 1982. 40p. (Interest level: 4-8).

Based on Indian folklore from the Alabama Coushatta tribe, this little book explains the animals' role in the creation of Texas. Students will enjoy the humor and irony of this selection.

♦ The concept of "folklore" is explored, and students can investigate regional folklore related to animals of their region or state.

1. Alabama Coushatta Indians—Legends 2. Folklore—Texas.

Ata, Te and **Moroney, Lynn.** *Baby Rattlesnake.* Illus. by Veg Reisberg. Children's Book Press (0-89239-049-2), 1989. 32p. Color illus. (Interest level: 1-3).

Willful Baby Rattlesnake throws tantrums to get his rattle before he's ready, but he misuses it and learns a lesson. While first and second graders would enjoy the colorful illustrations, they might not understand the overall intended message; third graders would benefit from both the illustrative method and the message.

♦ After reading the section entitled "About Baby Rattlesnake," students may do further research in the media center to learn more about rattlesnakes.

1. Chickasaw Indians—Folklore 2. Rattlesnakes—Fiction.

Baylor, Byrd. *The Best Town in the World.* Illus. by Ronald Himler. Macmillan (0-689-71086-0), 1982. Unpaginated. Color illus. (Interest level: 3-6).

Written from the point of view of the old-timers, the story's character reminisces about events and people, attitudes and interactions, that made the town the best one in the world. Many small-town students will relate to this story with its watercolor sketches; many large-city students can compare and contrast their city to the one described in the book.

♦ After students brainstorm a list of things that made the town in this story unique, divide the list into sections and send interview teams, each taking a section of the list as their interview focus, into the community to gather stories from older citizens, grandparents, and parents. Stories can be compiled into a "Best Town in the World" book about their city/town.

1. Cities and towns—Fiction.

Beatty, Patricia. *Behave Yourself, Bethany Brant.* Morrow Publishing (0-688-05923-6), 1986. 172p. (Interest level: 4-6).

A preacher's daughter with lots of curiosity and a inclination for getting into trouble has an eventful year and a half, all predicted by a fortune-teller at a Texas county fair. This Texas-based selection is action-packed to hold the reader's attention, and Beatty's portrayal of a minister's family is humorous and enjoyable.
♦ Students can compare and contrast the past with the present by analyzing differences and similarities in the role of the circuit-riding preachers in the story with that of ministers in their community, or by examining the differences in medical treatment then and now.
1. Family life—Texas.

Bragg, Bea. *The Very First Thanksgiving: Pioneers on the Rio Grande.* Illus. by Antonio Castro. Harbinger House (0-943173-22-1), 1989. 57p. B/W illus. (Interest level: 3-6).

A comical, trouble-making goat enables 14-year-old Manuel and his younger brother to survive an extremely difficult trip with an expedition through the Southwest desert to the Rio Grande in 1598, culminating in the real first Thanksgiving in America. The humor in this book makes it worthwhile for classroom use, and the geographical study of the trip is an added bonus. A glossary is included.
♦ After students research the expedition trek described in the text, they can create maps with permanent magic marker on brown mail wrap paper, then wad the paper to create wrinkles, and wash with diluted india ink to create an antique-looking parchment map.
1. Goats—Fiction   2. Explorers—Fiction
3. American exploration—Fiction.

Bruni, Mary Ann Smothers. *Rosita's Christmas Wish.* Illus. by Thom Ricks. TexArt (0-935857-00-1), 1985. Unpaginated. Color illus. (Interest level: 2-7).

Written to record and celebrate Christmas traditions as they are enjoyed in San Antonio, Texas, this book elaborates on the portrayal of *Los Pastores*, a play about the shepherds' journey to Bethlehem to worship the Niño Jesús, the baby Jesus. This attractively illustrated religious story describes a special Hispanic celebration associated with Christmas.
♦ After reading this book, students could begin a comparison of holiday traditions treasured by their families and discuss the origin of those traditions.
1. Christmas—Texas   2. Christmas—Drama.

Cole, Barbara Hancock. *Texas Star.* Franklin Watts (0-531-05820-4), 1990. Color illus. Unpaginated. (Interest level: 1-3).

This picture storybook shows a family getting ready for and hosting a contemporary quilting party. Dramatic, full-color illustrations of the beautiful Texas Star quilt being made add to the pleasant story.
♦ Students may each plan and make a quilt block advertising a favorite children's book; then the assembled quilt may be displayed in the classroom or library. Geometric quilt patterns created by students using cut paper or other media also provide correlated art and geometry activities.
1. Quilting—Fiction.

Evay, Ethel L. *Stowaway to Texas.* Larksdale (0-89896-102-5), 1982. 201p. B/W illus. (Interest level: 4-6).

Weaving fact, based on actual diary and journal entries, with fiction, Evay portrays Allen Dupree's attempts to get help for his family after he stows away on a ship bound for Texas. The adventures of the young character will keep students guessing about what will happen next in this exciting story.
♦ Using map skills, students can plot Allen's trek on current maps of Louisiana and Texas. Where places are cited in the book that no longer exist, students can estimate where Allen was on the basis of travel time.
1. Adventure and adventurers—Fiction
2. Voyages and travels—Texas—Fiction.

Fowler, Zinita. *Ghost Stories of Old Texas.* Illus. by author. Eakin Press (0-89015-407-4), 1983. 61p. B/W illus. (Interest level: 4-6).

The events in these 27 spine-tingling ghost stories purportedly happened in Texas or to Texans. Some stories specify Texas locations, and most have an oral, folkloric quality to them. Each story follows the one before with only a double-spaced break for a new title.
♦ After examining the concept of folklore, students can gather folklore of either this genre or others from their community by visiting with grandparents, other relatives, or friends.
1. Ghosts—Fiction   2. Texas—Ghosts—Fiction.

Garza, Carmen Lomas. *Family Pictures=Cuadros de Familia.* Illus. by author. Children's Book Press (0-89239-050-6), 1990. 32p. Color illus. (Interest level: 2-6).

Using a bilingual text and original paintings, the author describes her experiences growing up in Kingsville, Texas, and visiting her extended family in Mexico. The illustrations portray a South Texas Hispanic family in traditional activities, such as a piñata party and making tamales, and are attractively done in a colorful, simple style. The English/Spanish text describes the activities well.
♦ Students can study Grandma Moses and other illustrators who created art in American primitive style to evaluate process and product. Then students can write and illustrate their own story about their life. Networking with a bilingual class in Texas would allow students to experience recordings of "audio pen pals."
1. Family life—Texas 2. Hispanic Americans—Texas 3. Bilingual books.

Gipson, Fred. *Old Yeller*. Drawings by Carl Burger. HarperCollins (0-06-011545-9), 1956. 158p. B/W illus. (Interest level: 3-6).

Fourteen-year-old Travis accepts almost overwhelming responsibility as the head of his family, and he is both assisted and deterred by his yellow hound dog. Through this eloquently simple modern classic, students can appreciate the trials of early Texas settlers and the literary achievement of a great author.
♦ Students can discuss the differences between Travis's life and theirs. If the video is available, they may compare the novel and the video.
1. Dogs—Fiction 2. Texas—Fiction 3. Frontier and pioneer life—Fiction.

Gipson, Fred. *The Trail-Driving Rooster*. Illus. by Nancy Grobe. Eakin Press (0-89015-620-4), 1955. 94p. B/W illus. (Interest level: 3-6).

Dick, a trail-driving rooster, herds longhorns through Texas to Dodge City during days of the Old West. Taken from true accounts, this book by the author of *Old Yeller* will add fun to a study of the events of a cattle drive. The story has an oral, tall-tale quality.
♦ Students may read more than one Gipson novel and do a comparison. Teachers could rent *Old Yeller* (Walt Disney, 1957) to show.
1. Frontier and pioneer life—Texas—Fiction 2. Longhorn cattle—Texas.

Gire, Ken. *Adventures in the Big Thicket*. Illus. by Elizabeth Miles. Focus on the Family Publishing (0-929608-72-0), 1990. 115p. Color illus. (Interest level: 3-5).

This collection of 14 Aesop-like fables involves personified creatures living in East Texas's Big Thicket. Attractive full-page illustrations introduce each story, and a Bible verse from Solomon concludes each. The literary quality of the tales is high.
♦ After reading a story, but before sharing Gire's moral statement at the end of the story, allow students to generate a statement of the moral of the story. Teachers could also encourage students to write and illustrate their own fables about animals in a local park, zoo, or wildlife preserve.
1. Animals—Fiction 2. Texas—Fiction.

Gurasich, Marj. *Red Wagons and White Canvas: Mollie Bailey, Circus Queen of the Southwest*. Illus. by Francis Hill. Eakin Press (0-89015-646-8), 1988. 83p. B/W illus. (Interest level: 4-6).

Based on events of the Mollie Bailey traveling circus, this story chronicles the adventures of a young boy who leaves home to be a part of the show as it probably was in 1890. While the black-and-white illustrations do not do justice to the colorful circus scene, the historical fiction story is enjoyable for the reader, and the inclusion of a glossary of circus terms and a bibliography is useful.
♦ After reading the book, students may employ their new vocabulary to create a circus advertisement or newspaper article about a circus coming to town.
1. Circus—Fiction 2. Mollie A. Bailey Show—Fiction.

Hancock, Sibyl. *Spindletop*. Illus. by Patty Rucker. Eakin Press (0-89015-265-9), 1984. B/W illus. (Interest level: 1-3).

In a typical setting of the era, a fictitious family experiences the excitement of bringing in an oil gusher at Spindletop, the famous oil field in Texas. The discovery of this pocket of "black gold" altered the social, political, and economic status of the state; therefore, the information is vital to a study of the state.
♦ Bravery is an underlying theme in the book; students may write and illustrate a story of another account of bravery, perhaps their own.
1. Texas—History—Fiction 2. Oil wells—Fiction.

Hicks, Grace Robertson. *The Critters of Gazink*. Illus. by Bruce Hicks and Karen Ashcraft.

Eakin Press (0-89015-816-9), 1991. 61p. Color illus. (Interest level: 4-6).

A rhyming text describes animal inhabitants of the imaginary town of Gazink, Texas. This book's humor and wordplay appeal to older elementary students, and the illustrations hold the attention of younger listeners.

♦ After listing the book's critters and analyzing both their endearing and not-so-delightful attributes, the students can scour the local paper or a book such as *Harriet the Spy* by Louise Fitzhugh (Dell, 1987) for ideas on behaviors of human beings; they then can create fictitious critters of their own and write a poem about the behaviors based on the analyses made.

1. Animals—Fiction 2. Texas—Fiction 3. Stories in rhyme.

Jernigan, Gisela. *One Green Mesquite Tree*. Illus. by Wesley Jernigan. Harbinger House (0-943173-39-6 pbk), 1989. 24p. Color illus. (Interest level: K-6).

This book presents the numerals one through 20 in rhymed text, and it supports a number of concepts through illustrations of various plants and animals found in Texas. With its unusual botanical drawings, this text would be useful in the early grades for number concept development and in the upper elementary grades as students study vegetation in Texas.

♦ Younger students could draw their own picture book of plants in their schoolyard or home to show number awareness. Using a map of Texas, older students can plot the location of the plants, write the Texas Soil and Wildlife Commission for samples of these plants, and investigate the advisability of growing them in their locale.

1. Deserts—Texas 2. Plants—Texas 3. Counting.

Jones, Martha Tannery. *The Great Texas Scare: A Story of the Runaway Scrape*. Illus. by Donna Loughran. Hendrick-Long (0-937460-31-1), 1988. 95p. B/W illus. (Interest level: 3-5).

When fighting begins in Texas in 1836, the approach of the Mexican Army sends Manda and her family fleeing their home to seek refuge in the open countryside. This story creates an understanding of the variety of survival skills that were necessary for pioneer settlers in the early development of Texas.

♦ After discussing the concept of courage as it manifests itself in this story, the students can choose the character they consider to be most courageous and create an acrostic using either the word "courageous" or the character's name and adjectives relating to courage. Students may also create shoebox dioramas of their chosen character's courageous actions.

1. Texas—History—Fiction 2. Frontier and pioneer life—Fiction.

Jones, Marvin E. *Danger in the Big Thicket*. Illus. by Tim Czarnecki. Eakin Press (0-89015-752-9), 1990. 83p. B/W illus. (Interest level: 3-5).

Potential changes in a familiar environment create challenges for the human and animal characters of this story set in the east Texas Big Thicket. This book creates valuable awareness of environmental issues for students, and it will extend discussions of personal involvement in saving national wildlife preserves.

♦ Students can investigate environmental issues indigenous to their locale, write letters to editors of local newspapers stating facts and opinions about environmental issues, and research endangered species of their immediate area.

1. Raccoons—Fantasy 2. Big Thicket National Preserve (Tex.)—Fiction 3. Environment—Wildlife conservation.

Jones, Marvin E. *The Enchanted Valley*. Illus. by Tim Czarnecki. Eakin Press (0-89015-750-2), 1990. 104p. B/W illus. (Interest level: 3-5).

Three human children and their raccoon playmates are main characters in this story, set in the Big Thicket of Texas, involving the capture of the raccoons' mother. Elements of legend, folklore, and fantasy will intrigue young listeners as this story unfolds.

♦ Students can listen for words that paint pictures in their minds and, without seeing the book's black-and-white illustrations, draw their own pictures based on the words in the story. Make the book available for students to view after student drawings have been completed.

1. Raccoons—Fantasy 2. Big Thicket National Preserve (Tex.)—Fiction.

Jones, Marvin E. *Gory Gary Strikes Back*. Illus. by Tim Czarnecki. Eakin Press (0-89015-751-0), 1990. 85p. B/W illus. (Interest level: 3-5).

This second adventure in a trilogy involves an attempt to trap a raccoon family befriended by a human family living in the east Texas area called the Big Thicket. The adventure-legend format of this book will make it interesting for elementary students.

♦ Students can generate a list of additional adventures in which these characters could be involved and then choose one adventure about which to write.
1. Raccoons—Fantasy 2. Big Thicket National Preserve (Tex.)—Fiction.

Kellogg, Steven. *Pecos Bill.* Illus. by author. Scholastic (0-590-41110-1), 1986. Unpaginated. Color illus. (Interest level: 3-8).

This tall tale adds a Texas flavor to the outrageous adventures of Pecos Bill, who manages to conquer rattlesnakes, develop the western rodeo, and ride a beautiful white stallion named Lightning. Steven Kellogg's humorous illustrations and preposterous story provide just the right background for students to understand the tall tale genre.
♦ Students may write their own tall tale featuring an unsuspecting classmate or a fictitious character.
1. Tall tales—Texas 2. Pecos Bill (Legendary character).

Kerr, Rita. *The Alamo Cat.* Illus. by author. Eakin Press (0-89015-639-5), 1988. 49p. B/W illus. (Interest level: 3-5).

Ruby, a calico cat, becomes the undisputed mascot of the patrol rangers who are caretakers at the Alamo, and some folks say her spirit still pads the walkways of the historic church fortress. Cat lovers in the class will be intrigued by this story. The pen-and-ink sketches enhance the story.
♦ Students can create their own short story featuring a favorite animal, perhaps in a historic place.
1. Cats—Texas—Fiction 2. Alamo (San Antonio, Tex.)—Fiction.

Kerr, Rita. *Christopher and Pony Boy.* Illus. by author. Eakin Press (0-89015-843-6), 1991. 90p. B/W illus. (Interest level: 2-6).

Ten-year-old Christopher Schuchart, an orphan from Germany, is adopted by Joseph and Mary Bader of Castroville, Texas, in 1846. Though the black-and-white illustrations are not of excellent quality, the historical fiction story of Christopher's life on the Texas frontier is engaging, and the epilogue tells of the accomplishments of the determined young orphan. A bibliography is provided.
♦ Students can create a compare/contrast chart using book events and personal experiences in caring for a pet or other animal.
1. Texas—History—Fiction 2. Horses—Texas—Fiction.

Kerr, Rita. *The Ghost of Panna Maria.* Illus. by author. Eakin Press (0-89015-791-X), 1990. 86p. B/W illus. (Interest level: 4-7).

Fact, fiction, and folktale blend together in this story about 12-year old Anna Maria and the other Polish immigrants who settled in south Texas. Although there are limited illustrations, this easy-reader book makes a traditional Polish tale accessible to the elementary reader.
♦ Students could find and interview immigrants in their community to record the folktales that pass from one generation to another within the culture.
1. Polish Americans—Fiction 2. Frontier and pioneer life—Fiction 3. Panna Maria (Tex.)—Fiction 4. Ghosts—Fiction.

Kerr, Rita. *Girl of the Alamo.* Eakin Press (0-89015-447-3), 1984. 64p. (Interest level: 4-7).

Susanna Dickinson, the only Anglo-American woman at the Alamo, survives the siege at the Alamo to tell Sam Houston and his army about the defeat. In somewhat flowery prose, this historical fiction story portrays the strength and courage of individuals.
♦ Using this dramatic story, students may write a play for themselves or for puppets to perform for another class.
1. Texas—History—Biography 2. Dickinson, Susanna 3. Alamo (San Antonio, Tex.)—Siege.

Kerr, Rita. *The Immortal 32.* Eakin Press (0-89015-538-0), 1986. 51p. (Interest level: 4-7).

Fully aware of the peril they would face, 32 brave men rushed to San Antonio and the Battle of the Alamo to help their fellow Texans. The riveting account of the battle will hold the attention of upper elementary to middle school readers. A bibliography is included.
♦ Linking this book to others with the theme of bravery, students can compare and contrast motivation for the behavior of the participants.
1. Texas—History—Fiction 2. Alamo (San Antonio, Tex.)—Fiction.

Kerr, Rita. *Juan Seguin: A Hero of Texas.* Eakin Press (0-89015-502-X), 1985. 54p. (Interest level: 4-7).

Juan Seguin, a citizen of the Republic of Mexico, finds himself in disagreement with dictator Santa Anna and chooses to fight on the side of the Americans to free Texas. Written as historical fiction, the story is interesting, though misspellings and other errors mar the text. A bibliography is provided.

♦ Students should be able to discuss the conflict of values and the difficulties involved in making a decision in conflict with the culture group.
1. Seguin, Juan Nepomuceno, 1806-1890 2. Texas—History—Fiction 3. Alamo (San Antonio, Tex.).

Kerr, Rita. *Texas Cavalier.* Eakin Press (0-89015-714-6), 1989. 61p. (Interest level: 4-7).

With 180 men and a sense of adventure beating in his heart, James Bonham joined his friend William Travis to forge the Republic of Texas. Students will enjoy the historical adventure of real heroes set in a fictional genre.
♦ Students can discuss key issues related to making a difference and having a positive influence in a new situation, using Bonham's life as an example. Students can prepare a flowchart to put story events and underlying decisions in graphic form.
1. Bonham, James Butler, 1807-1836 2. Heroes and heroines—Texas 3. Texas—History—Fiction 4. Alamo (San Antonio, Tex.)—Fiction.

Kerr, Rita. *Texas Rebel.* Illus. by author. Eakin Press (0-89015-695-5), 1989. 76p. (Interest level: 4-7).

This account of the author's relatives and the part they played in settling Texas includes Civil War-era decisions the family members had to make. Students, aware that this story is based on actual experiences of Kerr's family, will be impressed with her ability to present events and facts in an interesting, though fictional manner.
♦ After reading this book, students may imagine that they are living in Civil War Texas, and write a letter telling a friend about what they might have experienced.
1. Roberts, Churchill—Fiction 2. United States—History—Civil War, 1861-1865—Fiction 3. Texas—History—Fiction.

Kerr, Rita. *Texas Rose: Dilue Rose Harris.* Eakin Press (0-89015-578-X), 1986. 64p. (Interest level: 3-5).

The experiences of eight-year-old Dilue Harris are woven into this fictional story. Students encountering the exciting, but threatening events in Texas's struggle for independence from Mexico will value the efforts of the heroine of the story.
♦ Students can make journal entries of their activities for a given period of time, then weave the events into fictitious stories of their own lives.
1. Harris, Rose Dilue, 1825-1914—Fiction 2. Texas—History—Fiction 3. Frontier and pioneer life—Fiction.

Kerr, Rita. *A Wee Bit of Texas.* Illus. by author. Eakin Press (0-89015-809-6), 1991. 71p. B/W illus. (Interest level: K-2).

While Grandfather Mouse, the smartest mouse in Texas, reads "A Wee Bit of Texas" to the mice at one of their weekly meetings, the old tomcat creeps closer and closer. The suspense, illustrations, and textual quality of this book will keep younger elementary students' attention.
♦ There are enough characters in this story to create a puppet play using paper-bag puppets that will allow every student to share in the production. A reader's theater presentation of the story would also be appropriate.
1. Mice—Fiction 2. Texas—Fiction.

McDonald, Archie. *When the Corn Grows Tall in Texas: A Story of the Texas Revolution.* Illus. by Joe Peacock. Eakin Press (0-89015-808-8), 1991. 89p. B/W illus. (Interest level: 2-4).

In the winter of 1836, young Albert sees his father ride off to help fight the Mexican soldiers at the Alamo to secure independence for Texas. Younger elementary students will be able to understand this historical fiction book, which portrays the Texas Revolution through the eyes of a young boy who loses his father in the fight for independence.
♦ Putting the story's main events in chronological order enables young students to understand the passage of time, so the class can create a time-line mural.
1. Texas—History—Fiction 2. Alamo (San Antonio, Tex.)—Fiction.

Martinello, Marian L. and **Nesmith, Samuel.** *With Domingo Leal in San Antonio 1734.* The University of Texas Institute of Texan Cultures (0-933164-52-1; 0-933164-40-8 pbk), 1979. 78p. Color illus. (Interest level: 3-6).

Domingo and his family struggle daily to survive in the Spanish colony of San Antonio. A valuable addition to a collection of juvenile literature, the book chronicles a boy's life in eighteenth-century San Antonio, and the preface gives fascinating information about the first 16 families who came as settlers from the Canary Islands, even giving a list of the supplies they brought.

♦ Students may begin their own family history by interviewing relatives, looking at old Bibles and genealogical records, etc.
1. San Antonio, Tex.—Fiction 2. Texas—History—Fiction.

Meador, Nancy and **Harman, Betty**. *Paco and the Lion of the North*. Illus. by Leslie Perna Kell. Eakin Press (0-89015-598-4), 1987. 117p. B/W illus. (Interest level: 5-6).

After being abducted by General Pancho Villa and his band, 14-year-old Paco becomes a scout who aids the general in his fight against the Mexican government. This fast-moving, interesting account of a young man who changed his mind helps students understand how difficult it is to make decisions in the middle of a conflict over loyalties. A bibliography and glossary are included.
♦ Students may discuss concepts of prejudice, stereotyping, and decision making based on best information gathered. Then students can write about events in their lives where they changed their mind about someone after time and experience intervened.
1. Villa, Pancho, 1878-1923—Fiction 2. Mexico—History—Revolution.

Michener, James A. *The Eagle and the Raven*. Drawings by Charles Shaw. State House Press (0-938349-57-0), 1990. 210p. B/W illus. (Interest level: 6+).

This historical narrative recalls one of the most exciting periods of Texas history, when a firebrand renegade named Sam Houston came to help lead the Texas Revolution against Santa Anna. Juvenile readers may read this as an introduction to James Michener's writing, but they should be prepared to deal with his wordiness and some adult situations.
♦ Michener provides an opportunity to compare and contrast the personalities and leadership styles of two very forceful men. Students should also analyze the events in the story, compare this fictionalized version with factual information available on the two characters, and discuss how Michener went about combining the two.
1. Santa Anna, Antonio López de, 1794-1876—Fiction 2. Houston, Sam, 1793-1863—Fiction 3. Texas—History—Fiction.

Milligan, Bryce. *Battle of the Alamo: You Are There*. Illus. by Charles Shaw. Texas Monthly Press (0-87719-156-5 pbk), 1990. 201p. B/W illus. (Interest level: 3-7).

Written as a plot-your-own-story of the fictional events in the life of 14-year-old Thomas Benton, who is determined to fight in the Texas Revolution, this book provides excitement in form and in story. Students will enjoy the interactive aspect of the story, and they get to participate in the decisions the main character makes leading up to the Battle of the Alamo.
♦ Students may add adventures that expand this story, perhaps adding characters.
1. Alamo (San Antonio, Tex.)—Siege—Fiction 2. Texas—History—To 1846—Fiction 3. Plot-your-own stories.

Milligan, Bryce. *Comanche Captive: You Are There*. Illus. by Charles Shaw. Texas Monthly Press (0-87719-157-3 pbk), 1990. 167p. B/W illus. (Interest level: 3-7).

Written as a plot-your-own story of the fictional events in the life of a 12-year-old Texas Hill Country resident captured by the Comanche in 1870, this book provides excitement in form and in story. Students will enjoy the interactive aspect of the story. Native Americans are shown as both fearsome and kindly.
♦ Students may add adventures that expand this story, perhaps adding characters.
1. Comanche Indians—Captivities—Fiction 2. Indians of North America—Captivities—Fiction 3. Plot-your-own stories.

Montgomery, Charlotte Baker. *The Trail North: Stories of Texas' Yesterdays*. Illus. by Mark Mitchell. Eakin Press (0-89015-701-4), 1990. 135p. B/W illus. (Interest level: 3-6).

Each chapter tells a story set in a different period of Texas history from 1000 A.D. to 1990 A.D., and each chapter has a different storyteller, sometimes human, sometimes animal. The oral quality of these stories and the connection with a specified time in Texas' history make this an interesting book.
♦ Student groups may do a chronological study and use their research to write stories, and present the story to classmates with their additional knowledge of the time period in Texas history.
1. Texas—History—Fiction.

Peary, William, ed. *21 Texas Short Stories*. University of Texas Press (0-292-73452-2). 264p. (Interest level: 4-6).

This collection of short stories is filled with colorful characters and interesting events, and they are all stories by Texans. This is a good source for easy-to-read Texas lore.

♦ Students can study the short story genre and create similar short stories about their locale.
1. Short stories—Texas.

Rice, James. *Gaston Drills an Offshore Oil Well.* Illus. by author. Pelican (0-88289-289-4), 1982. Unpaginated. B/W and Color illus. (Interest level: 3-6).

The green-nosed alligator from Louisiana named Gaston embarks on an adventure while drilling for oil in the Gulf of Mexico. Large color illustrations alternate with black-and-white drawings in this picture-book examination of the offshore oil industry in Texas, and special oil well drilling terminology is included in the glossary.

♦ Students can survey key industries in their area and write and illustrate a similar story based on another industry.
1. Oil well drilling, Submarine—Fiction 2. Alligators—Fiction.

Rice, James. *Gaston Goes to Texas.* Illus. by author. Pelican (0-88289-204-5), 1978. Unpaginated. Color illus. (Interest level: 3-6).

Gaston the 'gator is hurled into west Texas by a Louisiana hurricane and becomes the first alligator cowboy. This picture book, written in rhyme, presents an unusual and captivating Texas-based tall tale.

♦ Students can investigate many rhyming procedures, choose one, and rewrite a prose story in rhyme. The class can then have choral readings using the poetry generated by classmates.
1. Alligators—Fiction 2. Stories in rhyme 3. Ranch life—Fiction.

Rice, James. *Gaston Lays an Offshore Pipeline.* Illus. by author. Pelican (0-88289-177-4), 1979. Unpaginated. B/W and Color illus. (Interest level: 3-6).

Gaston, the green-nosed alligator who has been a cowboy and worked at other Texas jobs, heads offshore with a hard hat and steel-toed boots to help workers lay a pipeline. Students who enjoyed other Gaston adventures will find this rhyming tale equally entertaining and informative, but somewhat more difficult to understand.

♦ Use this story to begin researching the environmental issues related to drilling for oil in the offshore waters.
1. Alligators—Fiction 2. Oil well drilling, Submarine—Fiction 3. Stories in rhyme.

Rice, James. *Prairie Night Before Christmas.* Illus. by author. Pelican Press (0-88289-603-X), 1986. Unpaginated. (Interest level: 3-8).

When his reindeer abandon their job in the midst of a Texas storm, Santa enlists the help of two lonely cowboys so that he can finish his Christmas Eve rounds. Rice takes a Texas look at Clement Clarke Moore's familiar poem and tickles the reader's funny bone.

♦ Establishing contact with students in a classroom in another area of the country to exchange audio recordings of this poem or another regional poem may interest students in studying idiosyncrasies in their own pronunciations.
1. Texas—Fiction 2. Santa Claus—Fiction 3. Christmas—Fiction.

Rice, James. *Texas Jack at the Alamo.* Illus. by author. Pelican (0-88289-795-X), 1989. B/W and Color illus. Unpaginated. (Interest level: 3-6).

Texas Jack, the long-eared jackrabbit who is an expert on Texas, tells of the events leading to the Battle of the Alamo. Because the famous story is told from a jackrabbit's perspective in a humorous way, the story is amusing, and the illustrations add to the enjoyment.

♦ Students can research historical events of their community, and then choose a favorite animal and tell their story from that perspective, not omitting the humor!
1. Alamo (San Antonio, Tex.)—Fiction.

Rice, James. *Texas Night Before Christmas.* Illus. by author. Pelican Press (0-88289-603-2), 1986. Unpaginated. (Interest level: 3-8).

With a team of recalcitrant longhorns pulling his sleigh, Santa Claus pays a visit to a family on the Texas prairie, bringing appropriate gifts and Christmas cheer. Students will enjoy this Texas takeoff on Clement Clarke Moore's famous poem, and Rice's hilarious drawings add to the fun.

♦ Students can generate a different set of circumstances for the famous poem: a sleigh pulled by whales, alligators, etc.
1. Texas—Wit and humor 2. Christmas—Wit and humor.

Rosenberg, Marjorie Von. *Max and Martha: The Twins of Fredericksburg.* Illus. by Richard Petri. Eakin Press (0-89015-539-9), 1986. Unpaginated. B/W illus. (Interest level: 1-3).

Twins Max and Martha enjoy their log cabin their Indian friends, the wildlife, and their family as they make their home in Fredericksburg, Texas. Simple, pleasant adventures are fea-

tured in this selection, which has an English/German text.
- With the text presented in both English and German, a resource person could read the text in German while students follow along with the English text on a overhead projector; then students may compare words that are similar in the two languages and learn some basic German vocabulary.

1. German Americans—Texas.

Seale, Jan Epton. *The Ballad of the Men at Mier.* Illus. by Bernice Coleman. The Knowing Press (0-936927-14-3), 1986. B/W illus. Unpaginated. (Interest level: 3-8).

The fateful Black Bean expedition is the subject of this ballad, which tells the story of the group of Texans who invaded Mexico and were forced to choose black or white beans from a pot, with death waiting for the black bean holders and life for the ones with white beans. Two versions of the poetic ballad are included in this book, one with black-and-white line drawings, and the other printed in choral-reading style with suggestions for grouping students for presentation.
- Students can study the music of Texas during this period, compose and record music for the ballad, and then create either slides or a video to accompany the presentation.

1. Texas—History 2. Ballads—Texas.

Shefelman, Janice Jordan. *A Paradise Called Texas.* Illus. by Tom, Karl, and Dan Shefelman. Eakin Press (0-89015-375-2), 1983. B/W illus. (Interest level: 3-7).

This book begins a trilogy of historical fiction books featuring a young girl called Mina, based on Shefelman's ancestors, who left Germany in 1845 to come to Texas. Students will sense Mina's excitement grow with each part of the preparation, journey, and arrival in the new land. The author's note indicating that the main character is a fictionalized composite of two girls' lives will be an asset for students learning about the genre of historical fiction.
- Students may study contributions of the German immigrants who came to the United States, locating places where they settled on a current U.S. map and researching aspects of German culture.

1. Fredericksburg (Tex.)—Fiction 2. German Americans—Fiction 3. Prejudices.

Shefelman, Janice Jordan. *Spirit of Iron.* Illus. by Tom, Karl, and Dan Shefelman. Eakin Press (0-89015-636-0), 1987. 146p. B/W illus. (Interest level: 3-7).

As 15-year-old Mina continues her adventures begun in *A Paradise Called Texas* and *Willow Creek Home* (*see* entries on this page), she demonstrates her strong-willed behaviors that prompt her father to comment that she has a spirit of iron, a trait that enables her to survive pioneer life in early Texas. This readable account of the hardships endured by Mina and her family will interest students in comparing their situation to that in early Texas.
- After reading the story and studying the artistic medium and the three artistic styles used in the limited number of pen-and-ink sketches in the book, have students draw pictures illustrating other key events of the story.

1. Frontier and pioneer life—Fiction 2. Texas—History—Fiction 3. German Americans—Fiction.

Shefelman, Janice Jordan. *Willow Creek Home.* Illus. by Tom, Karl, and Dan Shefelman. Eakin Press (0-89015-535-6), 1985. 98p. B/W illus. (Interest level: 3-7).

In this sequel to *A Paradise Called Texas*, the reader encounters Papa, the children, and his new wife Lisetta enduring a summer drought, illness, and a frightening relocation deep in Comanche territory. Students will find the account exciting as Mina, the main character, faces new challenges.
- Students may investigate the factual basis of a fictionalized history, and then write their own stories in a similar manner, "thinking of other adventures that *could* have happened," as Shefelman reports doing (p. iv).

1. Texas—History—Fiction 2. Comanche Indians—Fiction 3. German Americans—Fiction.

Teague, Wells. *Theo the Indian Fighter.* Illus. by Nancy Grobe. Eakin Press (0-89015-639-5), 1987. B/W illus. (Interest level: 4-6).

This saga of frontier days in Texas describes an ornery mule named Theo, who saves Gus McCormac from the Corn Train Massacre in 1871. This story of fictionalized history provides a positive view of an Indian boy who helps Gus after he is nearly killed. A glossary and bibliography are included.
- Students are encouraged to illustrate the story in greater detail, and then send their illustrations along with the book as it travels to other classrooms. These illustrations could be produced using a variety of media:

watercolor, charcoal, acrylic, computer graphics, etc.
1. Frontier and pioneer life—Fiction 2. Kiowa Indians—Fiction 3. Mules—Fiction.

Tolliver, Ruby C. *Muddy Banks.* Texas Christian University Press (0-87565-062-7), 1987. 151p. (Interest level: 4-7).

As the impending Battle of Sabine Pass threatens to engulf his part of Texas, a 12-year-old runaway slave is torn between his desire to have freedom and his affection for the woman who has protected him. Students who have had to face dilemmas that forced them to make difficult choices will readily identify with this historical fiction story.
♦ Teachers and students can list events that have at least two possible outcomes, and then discuss the decision-making process.
1. Texas—History—Fiction 2. Decision-making—Fiction 3. Frontier and pioneer life—Texas—Fiction.

Townsend, Tom. *The Battle of Galveston.* Eakin Press (0-89015-713-8), 1989. 72p. B/W illus. (Interest level: 4-8).

In 1863, Luke Cochrane and his father go to Galveston to deliver bales of cotton to the Confederate army and find themselves in the middle of a fierce naval battle. The dialect used in the book adds interest to the story of a young boy's view of the Civil War.
♦ Students can study the way in which dialect is used in the book, examine colloquial dialects, and write an adventure using that vocabulary.
1. Galveston (Tex.)—History—Fiction 2. United States—History—Civil War, 1861-1865—Fiction.

Townsend, Tom. *The Dark Ships.* Eakin Press (0-89015-579-8), 1986. 117p. B/W illus. (Interest level: 4-6).

In this exciting adventure story, mysterious Jem interacts with a cadre of unusual characters and a fictionalized Jean Lafitte, who actually played a part in Texas's history. Students will enjoy the fast-paced plot of this book, and they will go looking for *Where the Pirates Are*, for which *The Dark Ships* is a sequel.
♦ After the concept of sequel is discussed, students can look for other books that are sequels and generate a list of books for which they would like sequels to be written. Students could then write to the authors of these books with suggestions on the desired content of the sequels.

1. Adventure and adventurers—Texas—Fiction.

Turner, Martha Ann. *The Yellow Rose of Texas.* Illus. by author. Eakin Press (0-89015-586-0), 1986. (Interest level: 4-7).

An example of historical research, this book recounts the story and song about Emily Morgan, a captured slave girl who was at the Battle of San Jacinto. The enjoyable song and story combination make this a good choice for sharing with upper elementary and middle school students.
♦ After reading the story and singing the song, students may research and write a story and song about a famous local personality.
1. Folk songs—Texas 2. Morgan, Emily 3. Texas—History—Fiction.

Periodicals

591.05
Texas Parks and Wildlife. State of Texas, Parks and Wildlife Department (ISSN 0040-4586). Monthly. (Interest level: 4-8).

This magazine has a different focus each month, but most of the articles discuss hunting and/or wildlife in Texas. Students would find this periodical's color photography interesting, and the articles are informative.
♦ Students may select a Texas animal and do further research in the media center about its range.
1. Texas—Periodicals 2. Parks—Texas 3. Wildlife—Texas.

976.4
Texas Highways. Texas Highways (ISSN 0040-4349). Monthly. $10.00 per year. (Interest level: 4+).

For its bargain subscription cost, this magazine provides excellent photographs and interesting articles featuring recreational, historical, cultural, and ethnic aspects of the state. This source will enhance a study of the Texas of today and yesterday, and the calendar of Texas events is especially useful.
♦ Students can write for more information about a local fair or other event using the address listed in the *Texas Highways* calendar. Then they can plan a vacation to the event, complete with travel route, budget, and sights to see.
1. Texas—Periodicals 2. Texas—Description and travel 3. Outdoor recreation—Texas.

976.4
Texas Historian. Texas State Historical Association (ISSN 0022-6602). 5 issues annually. (Interest level: 4-7).

This magazine is a collection of historical stories and articles, written by students in Texas schools, on a wide range of Texas subjects. Excellent illustrations and articles by young writers make this especially interesting to students.
♦ Students can write historical stories and articles about Texas to submit for possible publication.
1. Texas—Periodicals 2. Child authors.

Professional Materials

016.9764
DeBoe, David C., Immroth, Barbara F., and Manaster, Jane. *Teaching Texas History: An All-Level Resource Guide.* Texas State Historical Association in cooperation with the Center for Studies in Texas History, The University of Texas at Austin (0-87611-091-X), 1989, 1985. 153p. (Interest level: Professional).

This bibliography of curriculum materials for teaching about Texas includes a variety of print and nonprint publications: instructional media, traveling museum exhibits, juvenile books, journals, and professional resources. This useful resource provides a section of ideas for "bringing history home" and a list of distributors, but publication dates are not given.
♦ At the end of this bibliography, a section gives 44 ideas for the classroom in the categories of community studies, personal focus, fieldwork emphasis, an expanded view of history as past culture, and cultural pluralism.
1. Texas—Bibliography 2. Texas—History—Study and teaching.

016.9764
Immroth, Barbara Froling. *Texas in Children's Books: An Annotated Bibliography.* Library Professional Publications (0-208-02116-7; 0-208-02117-5 pbk), 1986. 187p. (Interest level: Professional).

Many of the selections in this comprehensive, annotated bibliography of books on Texas are now out of print. It does provide an excellent list of older titles, many of which are still available in libraries, and the subject and title indexes are helpful.
♦ Teachers may use this list to collect a variety of children's books featuring Texas; then students may examine the books in conjunction with newer books to compare data given about the state.
1. Texas—Bibliography.

917.6
Texas. Texas Department of Transportation (No ISBN pbk), n.d. B/W and Color illus. 264p. (Interest level: Professional).

This free, up-to-date public relations resource gives data on the key cities, forests, flowers, birds, rocks, minerals, climate, and sites of historical and other interest in Texas. The book comes with supplementary brochures and maps, and it is a valuable tool for research.
♦ Students can use the model set by Texas to design a travel guide and brochures for their city or state.
1. Texas—Description and travel.

Directory of Publishers and Vendors

AIMS Media Inc.
9710 De Soto Avenue
Chatsworth, CA 91311

Aladdin Books/Macmillan
100 Front Street
Riverside, NJ 08075

American Museum of Natural History
Central Park West at 79th Street
New York, NY 10024

American School Publishers
155 N. Wacker Drive
Chicago, IL 60606

Ancient City Press
P.O. Box 5401
Santa Fe, NM 87502

Arizona Game and Fish Department
2221 W. Greenway Road
Phoenix, AZ 85023

Arizona Highways
2039 W. Lewis Avenue
Phoenix, AZ 85009

Arizona State Library Association
P.O. Box 26186
Phoenix, AZ 85068

Atheneum Publishers
866 Third Avenue
New York, NY 10022

Avon Books
1350 Avenue of the Americas
New York, NY 10019

Barbed Wire Press
P.O. Box 2107
Stillwater, OK 74076

Barr Films
Box 7878
12801 Schabarum Avenue
Irwindale, CA 91706-7878

B.C. Publishers
P.O. Box 2102
Broken Arrow, OK 74013

A. H. Belo Corporation
P.O. Box 655237
Communication Center
Dallas, TX 75265

Bennett Media
P.O. Box 9905
Kirkwood, MO 63122

Benson, W. S. & Co., Inc.
P.O. Box 1866
Austin, TX 78767

BFA Educational Media
468 Park Avenue South
New York, NY 10016

Blackbird
1812 Keyway
Dubuque, IA 52001

Bradbury Press
Imprint of Macmillan
866 Third Avenue
New York, NY 10022

Brazos River Authority
P.O. Box 7555
Waco, TX 76714-7555

Bullfrog Films, Inc.
P.O. Box 149
Oley, PA 19547-0149

Carolrhoda Books
241 First Avenue North
Minneapolis, MN 55401

Centre Productions
Box 687
708 W. Ninth Street
Lawrence, KS 66044

Chelsea House Publishers
P.O. Box 914
Broomall, PA 19008

Children's Book Press
6400 Hollis Street, Suite 4
Emeryville, CA 94608

Childrens Press
5440 N. Cumberland Avenue
Chicago, IL 60656

Chronicle Books
275 Fifth Street
San Francisco, CA 94103

Clarion Books
215 Park Avenue South
New York, NY 10003

Cobblehill Books
375 Hudson Street
New York, NY 10014

Cobblesmith
Patterson's Wheeltrack
Freeport, ME 04032

Corona
1037 South Alamo
San Antonio, TX 78210

Coronet/MTI Film & Video
108 Wilmot Road
Deerfield, IL 60015

Coward, McCann & Geoghegan
200 Madison Avenue
New York, NY 10016

Crestwood House
Macmillan Publishing Co., Inc.
866 Third Avenue
New York, NY 10022

Crossroads Communications
P.O. Box 7
Carpentersville, IL 60110

Crowell Junior Books
Imprint of HarperCollins Children's Books
10 E. 53rd Street
New York, NY 10022

Crown Publishing Group
Affiliate of Random House, Inc.
201 E. 50th Street
New York, NY 10022

Delacorte Press
666 Fifth Avenue
New York, NY 10103

Dillon Press, Inc.
Macmillan Children's Book Group
866 Third Avenue
New York, NY 80301

Doubleday
1540 Broadway
New York, NY 10036

Dutton Children's Books
375 Hudson Street
New York, NY 10014

Eakin Press
Box 90159
Austin, TX 78709-0159

E-Heart Press
3700 Mockingbird Lane
Dallas, TX 75205

Encyclopaedia Britannica Educational Corporation
310 S. Michigan Avenue
Chicago, IL 60604

Enslow Publishers, Inc.
Box 777
Bloy Street & Ramsey Avenue
Hillside, NJ 07205

Experience America, Inc.
P.O. Box 250
Cedar City, UT 84721-0250

Facts on File, Inc.
460 Park Avenue South
New York, NY 10016

Falcon Press
7025 E. First Avenue, Suite 1
Scottsdale, AZ 85251-4326

Films for the Humanities & Science, Inc.
743 Alexander Road
Princeton, NJ 08540

Films Incorporated
Public Media, Inc.
5547 N. Ravenswood Avenue
Chicago, IL 60604

Finley-Holiday Film Co.
12607 E. Philadelphia Street
Whittier, CA 90601

Focus on the Family
420 N. Cascade
Colorado Springs, CO 80995

Follet Publishing
1000 W. Washington Boulevard
Chicago, IL 60607

Four Winds Press
Imprint of Macmillan Children's Book Group
866 Third Avenue
New York, NY 10022

Gallopade Publishing Group
235 E. Ponce de Leon Avenue, Suite 100
Decatur, GA 30030

Graphic Arts Center Publishing Co.
Box 10306
3019 NW Yeon Avenue
Portland, OR 97210

Great Plains National
University of Nebraska
P.O. Box 80669
Lincoln, Nebraska 68501

Greenwood Publishing Group, Inc.
Box 5007
88 Post Road West
Westport, CT 06881

Gulf Publishing Co.
Book Division
P.O. Box 2608
Houston, TX 77252-2608

Lucy Hammet, Inc.
3708 Crawford Avenue
Austin, TX 78731

Harbinger House
P.O. Box 42948
Tucson, AZ 85733-2948

Harcourt Brace Jovanovich, Inc.
6277 Sea Harbour Drive
Orlando, FL 32887

Harper and Row
10 E. 53rd Street
New York, NY 10022

HarperCollins Publishers, Inc.
10 E. 53rd Street
New York, NY 10022

Heard Museum Shop & Bookstore
22 E. Monte Vista
Phoenix, AZ 85004-1480

Hendrick-Long Publishing Co.
P.O. Box 25123
Dallas, TX 75225-1123

Holiday House, Inc.
425 Madison Avenue
New York, NY 10017

Henry Holt & Co., Inc.
115 W. 18th Street
New York, NY 10011

Holt, Rinehart & Winston, Inc.
6277 Sea Harbor Drive
Orlando, FL 32821

Houghton Mifflin Co./Houghton Mifflin Software
222 Berkeley Street
Boston, MA 02116-3764

Ideals Publishing Corp.
Children's Book Division
1501 County Hospital Road
Nashville, TN 37218

International Film Bureau, Inc.
332 S. Michigan Avenue
Chicago, IL 60604

In-the-Valley-of-the-Wichitas House Publishers
P.O. Box 6741
Lawton, OK 73506

KEDT Instructional Services
4455 S. Padre Island Drive
Corpus Christi, TX 78410

KIDVIDZ
618 Centre Street
Newton, MA 02158

Knowing Press
P.O. Box 5276
McAllen, TX 78502-5276

Landmark Films
3450 Slade Run Drive
Falls Church, VA 22042

Larksdale
P.O. Box 70456
Houston, TX 77270-0456

Leahy Industries
15 Mission Road
Sedona, AZ 86336

Leisure Time Video
Division of GSI, Inc.
P.O. Box 56757
New Orleans, LA 70156

Lerner Publications Company
241 First Avenue North
Minneapolis, MN 55401

Levite of the Apache Publishing
203 Hal Muldrow Drive,
 Suite 3
Norman, OK 73069

Library Professional Publications
Imprint of Shoe String Press, Inc.
P.O. Box 4327
Hamden, CT 06514

Lightyear
P.O. Box 168
Cutchogue, NY 11935

JB Lippincott Co.
227 E. Washington Square
Philadelphia, PA 19106

Little, Brown & Company, Inc.
34 Beacon Street
Boston, MA 02108

Lodestar Books
375 Hudson Street
New York, NY 10014

Lone Star Books
Imprint of Gulf Publishing
P.O. Box 2608
Houston, TX 77252

Lothrop, Lee & Shepard Books
1350 Avenue of the Americas
New York, NY 10019

Lowell Museum
P.O. Box 8515
Lowell, MA 01853

Doyle McCoy
700 SW 102nd
Oklahoma City, OK 73139

David McKay Company, Inc.
Subsidiary of Random House, Inc.
400 Hahn Road
Westminster, MD 21157

Macmillan Educational Distribution Center
Front and Brown Streets
Riverside, NJ 08370

Macmillan Publishing Co.
866 Third Avenue, 7th Floor
New York, NY 10022

Mariposa Publishing
922 Baca Street
Santa Fe, NM 87501

M.B.O.P.
P.O. Box 12
Hugo, OK 74743

MCA Records/Universal Home Video
70 Universal City Plaza
Universal City, CA 91608

Millbrook Press, Inc.
2 Old New Milford Road
Brookfield, CT 06804

Mountain Press
P.O. Box 2399
Missoula, MT 59806

Museum of Northern Arizona
Route 4, Box 720
Flagstaff, AZ 86001

National Geographic Society
1145 17th Street NW
Washington, DC 20036

Natural History Press
American Museum of Natural History
Central Park West at 79th Street
New York, NY 10024

New Forums Press, Inc.
P.O. Box 876
Stillwater, OK 74076

New Mexico Magazine
P.O. Box 46902
Escondido, CA 92046

Northland Publishing Co.
P.O. Box 1389
Flagstaff, AZ 86002

W. W. Norton & Co., Inc.
500 Fifth Avenue
New York, NY 10110

Oklahoma Department of Libraries
200 NE 18th Street
Oklahoma City, OK 73105

Oklahoma Department of Wildlife Conservation
1801 North Lincoln
P.O. Box 53465
Oklahoma City, OK 73105-4498

Oklahoma Educational Television Authority
7403 N. Kelley Avenue
Oklahoma City, OK 73111

Oklahoma Heritage Association
Refer orders to:
Oklahoma Heritage Book Center
1500 North Robinson
Oklahoma City, OK 73152

Oklahoma Historical Society
Wiley Post Building
2100 N. Lincoln Boulevard
Oklahoma City, OK 73105

Oklahoma Publishing Company
P.O. Box 25125
Oklahoma City, OK 73105

Oklahoma State Department of Education
2500 Lincoln Boulevard
Oklahoma City, OK 73105-4599

Oklahoma State University
Audio Visual Center
121 Cordell North
Stillwater, OK 74074

One West Media
P.O. Box 5766, 559 Onate Place
Santa Fe, NM 87501

A. Y. Owen Studio
Refer orders to:
Oklahoma State University, Audio Visual Center
121 Cordell North
Stillwater, OK 74074

Parents Magazine Press
685 Third Avenue
New York, NY 10017

PBS Video
1320 Braddock Place
Alexandria, VA 22314-1698

Pelican Publishing Co., Inc.
Box 189
1101 Monroe Street
Gretna, LA 70053

Penguin Books
375 Hudson Street
New York, NY 10014

Prentice-Hall Press
200 Old Tappan Road
Old Tappan, NJ 07675

Pressworks
P.O. Box 12606
Dallas, TX 75225

Pruett Publishing
2928 Pearl Street
Boulder, CO 80301

Puffin Books
375 Hudson Street
New York, NY 10014

The Putnam Berkley Group, Inc.
200 Madison Avenue
New York, NY 10016

Rabbit Ears
Imprint of Picture Book Studio USA
Box 9139
10 Central Street
Saxonville, MA 01701

Rand McNally Children's Books
Macmillan Publishing Co.
3131 Mount Pleasant Street
Racine, WI 53404

Random House, Inc.
201 E. 50th Street
New York, NY 10022

Reliance Press
1400 Melrose
Norman, OK 73069

Rourke Corp., Inc.
P.O. Box 3328
Vero Beach, FL 32964

St. Martin's Press, Inc.
175 Fifth Avenue
New York, NY 10010

Scholastic, Inc.
730 Broadway
New York, NY 10003

School of America Research Press
P.O. Box 2188
Santa Fe, NM 87504

Scribner Book Companies/Macmillan
866 Third Avenue
New York, NY 10022

Charles Scribner's Sons
Books for Young Readers
Imprint of Macmillan
866 Third Avenue
New York, NY 10022

Sigma Educational Media
101 W. 22nd Street
Ada, OK 74820

Simon & Schuster
The Simon & Schuster Building
1230 Avenue of the Americas
New York, NY 10020

Southern Hills Press
P.O. Box 209
Dayton, OH 45409

Southwest Media Services
3988 N. Central Expressway, Suite 1200
Dallas, TX 74204

Southwest Series, Inc.
738 N. Fifth Avenue #208
Tucson, AZ 85705

State House Press
P.O. Box 15247
Austin, TX 78761

State of New Mexico
Economic Development & Tourism Department
Box 20003
Santa Fe, NM 87501

Steck Vaughn Publishing/Raintree
P.O. Box 26015
Austin, TX 78755

Sterling Publishing Co., Inc.
387 Park Avenue South, 5th Floor
New York, NY 10016-8810

Sunstone Press
P.O. Box 2321
Santa Fe, NM 87504-2321

E. C. Temple
5030 Champion Drive, Suite 100
Lufkin, TX 75901

TexArt
200 Concord Plaza Drive #550
San Antonio, TX 78216-6940

Texas Christian University Press
Box 30783
Fort Worth, TX 76129

Texas Department of Highways and Public Transportation
Travel and Information Division
P.O. Box 5064
Austin, TX 78763-5064

Texas Monthly Report
P.O. Box 1569
Austin, TX 78767-1569

Texas Parks and Wildlife Department
4200 Smith School Road
Austin, TX 78744

Texas State Historical Association
2/306 Sid Richardson Hall, University Station
Austin, TX 78712

Tonkawa Free Press
P.O. Box 12543
Austin, TX 78711

Trails West Publishing
P.O. Box 8619
Santa Fe, NM 87504-8619

Treasure Chest Publications
1802 W. Grant Road, Suite 101
Tucson, AZ 85745

Troll Associates
100 Corporate Drive
Mahwah, NJ 07430

Turner Publishing
P.O. Box 3101
Paucah, KY 42002

Twayne Publishers
866 3rd Avenue
New York, NY 10022

Unicorn Designs
3707 Litchfield Drive
San Antonio, TX 78230

University of Nebraska Press
901 N. 17th Street
Lincoln, NE 68588

University of New Mexico
1720 Lomas Boulevard NE
Albuquerque, NM 87131-1591

University of New Mexico Press
Journalism Building, Suite 220
Albuquerque, NM 87131

University of Oklahoma Press
1005 Asp Avenue
Norman, OK 73019-0445

University of Oklahoma Stovall Museum
Refer orders to:
Museum of Natural History
1335 Asp Avenue
Norman, OK 73019-0606

University of Texas Institute of Texan Cultures at San Antonio
P.O. Box 1226
801 S. Bowie Street
San Antonio, TX 78205

University of Texas Press
P.O. Box 7819
Austin, TX 78713

Vestal Press, Ltd.
P.O. Box 97
Vestal, NY 13851-0097

Viking Penguin, Inc.
375 Hudson Street
New York, NY 10014

Voyageur Press, Inc.
P.O. Box 338
123 N. Second Street
Stillwater, MN 55082

Walker & Company
720 Fifth Avenue
New York, NY 10019

Franklin Watts, Inc.
95 Madison Avenue
New York, NY 10016

Western Heritage
P.O. Box 5108
Berkeley, CA 94705

Windham Hill Productions, Inc.
P.O. Box 9388
Stanford, CA 94309

Windsor
102 E. 38th Street
Savannah, GA 31401

WINGS/Sunburst
P.O. Box 660002
Scotts Valley, CA 95067

World Publishing Co.
2231 W. 110th Street
Cleveland, OH 44102

Author Index

Abernathy, Francis Edward, 76
Adams, Carolyn, 64
Albert, Carl, 40
Amon, Aline, 7
Anaya, Rudolfo A., 29
Anderson, Joan, 33
Anderson, Sylvia, 64, 65
Argo, Burnis, 45
Armer, Laura Adams, 14, 34
Ashabranner, Brent, 29
Ata, Te, 76
Aylesworth, Thomas G., 11, 46
Aylesworth, Virginia L., 11, 46

Bahti, Tom, 24
Baker, Betty, 22
Baker, T. Lindsay, 65
Bash, Barbara, 5, 6
Bauer, Marion Dane, 56
Baylor, Byrd, 1, 5, 8, 9, 14, 15, 16, 17, 27, 35, 76
Beatty, Patricia, 76
Begay, Shonto, 2
Bentley, Judith, 13
Bernotas, Bob, 55
Bess, Clayton, 56
Bicha, Karel D., 47
Bird, E. J., 15
Blackburn, Bob, L. 47
Blood, Charles L., 14, 16, 18, 35
Blume, Judy, 35
Bragg, Bea, 77
Browne, Vee, 2, 22
Bruni, Mary Ann Smothers, 77
Buchanan, Ken, 16
Burchardt, Bill, 45
Burroughs, Jean M., 35
Busch, Phyllis S., 6
Bustard, Ann, 65

Callihan, D. Jeanne, 66
Canty, Carol S., 68
Carey, Valerie Scho, 2, 22
Carlile, Glenda, 47, 56
Carpenter, Allan, 12, 29, 47
Catalano, Julie, 64
Chavez, Thomas E., 38

Chilton, Lance, 26
Clark, Ann Nolan, 7, 25, 28
Cleaveland, Alice Ann, 31, 37
Cobb, Vicki, 12
Cohen, Caron Lee, 2
Cohlene, Terri, 2, 22
Cole, Barbara Hancock, 77
Cole, Judith, 16
Collings, Ellsworth, 47
Courlander, Harold, 3
Cox, Mike, 66
Cravota, Mary Ellen, 2
Crawford, Ann Fears, 66, 75, 76
Cutrer, Thomas W., 66

Daly, Jay, 44
Davis, John L., 67
de Paola, Tomie, 61
Debo, Angie, 45, 46
DeBoe, David C., 86
Deering, Ferdie J., 44
Doherty, Craig A., 29
Doherty, Katherine M., 29
Duncan, Lois, 35

Ellenbrook, Edward Charles, 45
England, Alma M., 47
Erdoes, Richard, 29
Erickson, John R., 48
Etter, Jim M., 41
Evay, Ethel L., 77

Faulk, Odie B., 48
Ferber, Edna, 56
Ferguson, T. J., 26
Field, William T., Jr., 70
Filbin, Dan, 9
Finley, Russ, 62
Flynn, Jean, 74
Folsom, Franklin, 30
Foster, Nancy Haston, 63
Fowler, Carol, 13
Fowler, Zinita, 77
Fradin, Dennis, 12, 30, 48, 67
Franklin, Jimmie L., 48

Franks, Kenny A., 41
Frazier, Kendrick, 30, 38
Fritz, Jean, 75
Fugate, Francis L., 49
Fugate, Roberta B., 49

Garza, Carmen Lomas, 77
Geis, Jacqueline, 8
George, Jean Craighead, 7
Gherman, Beverly, 13
Gilbert, Charles E., Jr., 64
Gilbert, Claudette Marie, 49
Gillies, John, 75
Gipson, Fred, 78
Gire, Ken, 78
Glassman, Bruce, 54
Goble, Danny, 40
Goins, Charles R., 44
Green, Carl R., 21
Green, Timothy, 17, 36
Greene, Carol, 13
Gregory, Robert, 49
Grider, Sylvia Ann, 67
Gridley, Marion E., 43
Griego, Margot, 4
Grimmer, Glenna, 61, 62
Grossman, Virginia, 17
Guderjan, Thomas H., 68
Guiberson, Brenda Z., 5, 6
Gurasich, Marj, 68, 78

Hancock, Sibyl, 68, 78
Harman, Betty, 82
Hart, E. Richard, 26
Hausman, Gerald, 22
Hayes, Joe, 22, 23
Heck, Bessie Holland, 56
Heinrichs, Ann, 9, 12, 49
Henry, Marguerite, 17
Hicks, Grace Robertson, 78
Highwater, Jamake, 3
Hillerman, Tony, 4, 23, 36
Hinton, S. E., 57
Hoig, Stan, 49
Holmes, Anita, 6
Howard, James H., 40
Hoyt-Goldsmith, Diane, 3, 30
Huber, Peter., 14

Immroth, Barbara F., 86

Jackson, Robert B., 50
Jakes, John, 69, 72
James, J. Alison, 36
Jenkins, Myra Ellen, 30
Jernigan, Gisela, 8, 9, 62, 79
John, Naomi, 17

Johnson, Annabel, 18
Jones, Martha Tannery, 79
Jones, Marvin E., 79

Kawano, Kenji, 26
Keegan, Marcia, 10, 27
Keith, Harold, 54, 57, 58
Kellogg, Steven, 80
Kerr, Rita, 80, 81
Kirgo, Julie, 30
Kirk, Ruth, 7
Kirschstein, Carolyn, 58
Klausner, Janet, 55
Krumgold, Joseph, 36

Lacapa, Michael, 3, 23
Lena, Willie, 40
Lich, Glen E., 69
Link, Martin A., 14, 16, 18
Lister, Florence C., 38
Lister, Robert H., 38
Looney, Ralph, 32
Love, Frank, 12
Lowell, Susan, 18

Mabery, D. L., 14
McCoy, Doyle, 42
McDermott, Gerald, 2, 4, 21, 23
McDonald, Archie, 81
McLerran, Alice, 18
McReynolds, Edwin C., 44
Magley, Beverly, 5
Maher, Ramona, 8
Manaster, Jane, 86
Marsh, Carole, 69
Martin, Jack, 75
Martinello, Marian L., 70, 74, 81
Martinez, Estefanita, 24
Mazzio, Joann, 37
Meador, Nancy, 82
Mell, Jan, 7
Michener, James A., 82
Mike, Jan M., 4
Miles, Miska, 14, 18, 34, 37
Miller, Edna, 18
Milligan, Bryce, 82
Montgomery, Charlotte Baker, 82
Moore, Adam, 54
Morgan, Anne Hodges, 50
Moroney, Lynn, 76
Morris, John W., 44, 50
Munson, Sammye, 74
Myers, Anna, 58

Nason, Thelma C., 21
Nelson, Mary Carroll, 33, 34
Nesmith, Samuel, 66, 81

Nunes, Susan, 19

O'Dell, Scott, 19, 37
Osinski, Alice, 11, 28
Otero, George, 38
Oughton, Jerrie, 4, 24

Paul, Paula G., 37
Peary, William, 82
Perrine, Mary, 17, 19, 36, 37
Petersen, David, 33, 55
Pirtle, Caleb, III, 43

Radlauer, Ruth Shaw, 32
Rawls, Wilson, 58
Reeve, Frank D., 31
Rice, James, 70, 83
Riddle, Patricia, 64, 65
Roberts, Calvin A., 31
Roberts, Susan A., 31
Robinson, Charles M., 63
Rodanas, Kristina, 4, 24
Rogers, Betty, 55
Rosenberg, Marjorie Von, 83
Ross, Glen, 55
Rosser, Linda Kennedy, 42
Rucki, Ani, 4
Rummel, Jack, 34
Ruth, Kent, 45

Sance, Melvin M., 74
Sanford, William R., 21
Savage, William W., Jr., 43
Schecter, Cathy, 73
Schlosberg, Hedda, 62
Schroeder, Albert H., 30
Scott, Larry E., 71
Seale, Jan Epton, 71, 84
Sharmat, Marjorie Weinman, 16, 19
Shaw, Charles, 71
Shefelman, Janice Jordan, 84
Shirk, George H., 52
Shirley, Glenn, 54
Sievert, Gregory, 43
Sievert, Lynnette, 43
Simmons, Marc, 32
Skramstad, Jill, 8
Skurzynski, Gloria, 19
Smith, Jack H., 52
Smith, MaryLou M., 25
Sneve, Virginia Driving Hawk, 11, 28

Sotnak, Lewann, 32
Sowell, A. J., 76
Speer, Bonnie, 55
Speer, Jess Willard, 55
Spencer, Guy J., 5
Stanley, Jerry, 41, 59
Stanush, Barbara Evans, 71
Stein, R. Conrad, 32, 71, 72
Steinbeck, John, 55, 59
Stewart, Gail, 72
Strickland, Rennard, 50, 52
Sutton, George Miksch, 43
Szasz, Ferenc Morton, 24

Teague, Wells, 84
Thomas, Joyce Carol, 59
Thompson, Kathleen, 13, 53
Tolliver, Ruby C., 85
Townsend, Tom, 85
Trimble, Stephen, 12, 25, 33
Turner, Martha Ann, 85

Uchida, Yoshiko, 73

Varney, Philip, 26, 32
Venable, Fay, 68

Walker, Jerald C., 53
Wallace, Bill, 59
Walls, Thomas K., 73
Warren, Betsy, 73, 74
Warren, Scott, 10, 33
Whisenhunt, Donald W., 64
Wiewandt, Thomas, 5
Williams, Jerry L., 26
Wilson, Steve, 45
Winegarten, Ruth, 73
Wise, Lu Celia, 42, 53, 54
Wood, Leigh Hope, 27
Wood, Nancy, 25, 28
Wooley, Bryan, 74
Wright, Muriel H., 53

Yue, Charlotte, 11, 33
Yue, David, 11, 33

Zweig, Phillip L., 41

Title Index

Adventures in the Big Thicket, 78
The Afro-American Texans, 64
Agave Blooms Just Once, 9, 62
The Alamo & Other Texas Missions to Remember, 63
The Alamo Cat, 80
Alice Yazzie's Year, 8
All about Texas, 64
Along Sandy Trails, 7
America the Beautiful: Arizona, 12
America the Beautiful: New Mexico, 32
America the Beautiful: Texas, 71
Amigo, 14, 15
Amigo (sound recording), 14
The Anasazi, 33
Ancient Indian Cultures of Northern Arizona, 10
And It Is Still That Way: Legends Told by Arizona Indian Children, 1
And Now Miguel, 36
And Still the Waters Run: The Betrayal of the Five Civilized Tribes, 46
The Anglo-American Texans, 65
Animal Trackers, 6
Annie and the Old One, 18, 37
Annie and the Old One (videocassette, American School Publishers), 14
Annie and the Old One (videocassette, BFA Educational Media), 14, 34
Annie Wauneka, 34
Anpao: An American Indian Odyssey, 3
Antelope Woman: An Apache Folktale, 3
The Apaches and Navajos, 29
Arizona, 9, 12, 13
Arizona Heritage: Bibliography of Materials and Directory of Authors, Illustrators and Storytellers for Teachers, Librarians and Parents, 20
Arizona Highways, 20
Arizona Wildflowers: A Children's Field Guide to the State's Most Common Flowers, 5
Arizona Wildlife Views, 19
Arizona's Story: A Short History, 12
Armadillos and Pigskins, 73
Arrow to the Sun, 4, 23
Arrow to the Sun (videocassette), 1, 21
At Home with an Oklahoma Author, 43
Atlas of Oklahoma, 45

Baby Rattlesnake 76
The Ballad of the Men at Mier, 84
The Battle of Galveston, 85
Battle of the Alamo: You Are There, 82
Beauty, 59
Before You Came This Way, 35
The Beginnings, 46
Behave Yourself, Bethany Brant, 76
The Belgian Texans, 65
Belly Up: The Collapse of the Penn Square Bank, 41
Benito and the White Dove, 68
The Best Town in the World, 76
Between Me and You and the Gatepost: Rural Expressions in Oklahoma, 41
Big Bend National Park, 62
Billy the Kid, 21
Border Boss: Captain John R. Hughes, Texas Ranger, 75
Born to the Land: An American Portrait, 29
The Boy Who Made Dragonfly: A Zuni Myth, 4, 23
A Brief History of New Mexico, 30
Brighty of the Grand Canyon, 17
The British and Irish in Oklahoma, 56
Broken Arrow Boy, 54
Buckskin, Calico, and Lace, 47, 56

Cactus Hotel, 5, 6
Cactus in the Desert, 6
Carlsbad Caverns, 32
Carlsbad Caverns National Park, 32
Cattle Culture, 73
Chaco Canyon: Archaeology and Archaeologists, 38
The Chaco Legacy, 38
Children of Destiny: True Adventures of Three Cultures, 35
Children of the Dust Bowl: The True Story of the School at Weedpatch Camp, 41, 59
The Chinese Texans, 66
Christmas in Oklahoma: Past and Present, 42
Christopher and Pony Boy, 80
Chronicles of Oklahoma, 60
Cimarron, 56
Cities in the Sand: The Ancient Civilizations of the Southwest, 10, 33
Citizen Soldiers: Oklahoma's National Guard, 41
Comanche Captive: You Are There, 82

The Coming of the Indians, 46
Company's Coming, 62
Corn Is Life, 11
Cowboys, 73
Cowboys of the Wild West, 48
Coyote, 7
Coyote Dreams, 19
Coyote E. Native American Folk Tales, 22
The Critters of Gazink, 78
The Czech Texans, 67
The Czechs in Oklahoma, 47

Daisy Hooee Nampeyo, 13
Dance Hall of the Dead, 36
Dance with Me, Gods, 37
Danger in the Big Thicket, 79
Danger on the Homestead, 56
The Danish Texans, 67
The Dark Ships, 85
The Day It Snowed Tortillas: Tales from Spanish New Mexico, 23
The Day the Sun Rose Twice: The Story of the Trinity Site Nuclear Explosion, July 16, 1945, 24
Deep in the Heart: The Lives and Legends of Texas Jews, 73
Desert Giant: The World of the Saguaro Cactus, 5, 6
The Desert Is Theirs, 5
Desert Life, 7
Desert Seasons, 4
Desert Voices, 15
Desert Voices: A Reading by Byrd Baylor, 16
Did You Ever...Meet a Texas Hero?, 68
Directory of Oklahoma, 41
A Dog Called Kitty, 59
Dragonfly's Tale, 4, 24
The Dust Bowl, 48

The Eagle and the Raven, 82
The Enchanted Valley, 79
The English Texans, 66

Family Pictures = Cuadros de Familia, 77
Far and Away, 56
The Farolitos of Christmas: A New Mexico Christmas Story, 29
A Field Guide to Reptiles of Oklahoma, 43
Fifty Common Birds of Oklahoma and the Southern Great Plains, 43
The Five States of Texas: An Immodest Proposal, 64
Flags of Texas, 64
The Flute Player: An Apache Folktale, 3, 23
The French Texans, 67
Frontier Forts of Texas, 63

Gaston Drills an Offshore Oil Well, 83
Gaston Goes to Texas, 83
Gaston Lays an Offshore Pipeline, 83

Geography Skills in a New Mexico Setting, 37
The German Texans, 69
Getting to Know Texas, 65
The Ghost of Panna Maria, 80
Ghost Stories of Old Texas 77
Ghost Towns of Oklahoma, 50
Gila Monsters Meet You at the Airport, 19
Gila Monsters Meet You at the Airport (videocassette), 16
Girl of the Alamo, 80
Girl of the Navajos, 17, 19, 35, 37
The Goat in the Rug, 35
The Goat in the Rug as Told to Charles L. Blood and Martin Link by Geraldine, 14, 16, 18
Golden Pasture, 59
Gory Gary Strikes Back, 79
Grandmother's Adobe Dollhouse, 25
The Grapes of Wrath, 55, 59
The Great Texas Scare: A Story of the Runaway Scrape, 79
The Greek Texans, 67
A Guide to the Indian Tribes of Oklahoma, 53

Hard Times in Oklahoma: The Depression Years, 49
Harriet the Spy, 79
Haunted Highways, 32
Hawk, I'm Your Brother, 15
Hawk, I'm Your Brother (videocassette), 15, 17
Heart Full of Turquoise, 23
Heart Full of Turquoise (sound recording), 23
The Hidden Life of the Desert, 5
Hillback to Boggy, 55
Historic Oklahoma Map Series, 44
Historical Atlas of Oklahoma, 44
A History of New Mexico, 31
A History of the Indians of the United States, 46
Hollering Sun, 28
Hooray for Oklahoma, 1889, 58
The Hopi, 11
How It Feels When Parents Divorce, 59
How the Critters Created Texas, 76
How the Stars Fell into the Sky: A Navajo Legend, 4, 24

I Am Leaper, 18
An Illustrated History of New Mexico, 38
I'm in Charge of Celebrations, 15, 17
I'm in Charge of Celebrations (videocassette), 17
Images of Oklahoma: A Pictorial History, 47
The Immortal, 32, 80
In My Mother's House, 25
Indian Art of the Pueblos, 24
Indian Artists of the Southwest, 25
Indian Boy of the Southwest, 9
Indian Life in Texas, 71
The Indian Texans, 68
The Indians in Oklahoma, 52

Indians, Outlaws and Angie Debo, 50
The Italian Texans, 68

Jane Long: Frontier Woman, 75
The Japanese Texans, 73
The Jewish Texans, 69
Jim Bowie: A Texas Legend, 74
Jim Thorpe: Sac and Fox Athlete, 55
Journey to Topaz, 73
Journey toward Hope, 48
Juan Seguin: A Hero of Texas, 80
Justice Sandra Day O'Connor, 13

Komantcia, 57

Land Untamed, 73
The Land Where We Belong, 43
The Lebanese Texans and the Syrian Texans, 69
The Legend of the Bluebonnet: An Old Tale of Texas, 61
The Legend of the Indian Paintbrush, 61
Let's Remember. . . . Texas, the, 28th State, 73
Let's Remember. . . . When Texas Was a Republic, 73
Life of "Big Foot" Wallace: The Great Ranger Captain, 76
Listening Woman, 36
Little Boy with Three Names: Stories of Taos Pueblo, 28
Little Giant: The Life and Times of Speaker Carl Albert, 40
Little Herder in Autumn, 28
A Living Desert, 5
Living the Legend, 73
Lizzie: Queen of the Cattle Trails, 76
Look at Oklahoma, 44
Los Pastores, 77

Magnificent New Mexico: Land of Enchantment, 31
Ma'ii and Cousin Horned Toad, 2
Make Way for Sam Houston, 75
Many Winters: Prose and Poetry of the Pueblos, 25
Maria Martinez, 33
Maria Tallchief, 43
Marked by Fire, 59
Max and Martha: The Twins of Fredericksburg, 83
Media Cookbook for Kids, 2
The Melting Pot: Ethnic Cuisine in Texas, 62
The Mexican Americans, 64
The Mexican Texans, 70
Michael Naranjo, 34
Mini Myths and Legends of Oklahoma Indians, 42
Monster Slayer: A Navajo Folktale, 2, 22
Moon Song, 15
The Moon, the Sun, and the Coyote, 16
Mousekin Takes a Trip, 18
Mud Pony: A Traditional Skidi Pawnee Tale, 2
Muddy Banks, 85

My Country: A Navajo Boy's Story, 27
Mystery of Navajo Moon, 17, 36

Names We Never Knew, 50
Nannabah's Friend, 17, 19, 36, 37
Native Americans: The Pueblos, 29
Native Peoples of the Southwest, 10
The Naughty Little Rabbit and Old Man Coyote: A Tewa Story from San Juan Pueblo, 24
The Navajo, 11, 28
Navajo Code Talkers, 26
The Navajo Indians, 27
Navajo Moon, 21
The Navajos: A First Americans Book, 11, 28
New Life, New Land, 66
New Mexico, 29, 31
New Mexico!, 32
New Mexico: A New Guide to the Colorful State, 26
New Mexico: Land of Many Cultures, 31
New Mexico: Portrait of the Land and People, 30
New Mexico Blue Book, 38
New Mexico in Maps, 26
New Mexico in Words and Pictures, 30
New Mexico's Best Ghost Towns, 26, 32
A New Republic, 73
1992–93 Texas Almanac, 61
No Golden Cities, 21
The Norwegian Texans, 70

The Obstinate Land, 57
Oil, 51
The Oil Boom, 73
Oil in Oklahoma, 49
Oklahoma, 45, 47, 49, 53
Oklahoma—A Land and Its People: Early Views and History in Picture Postcards, 52
Oklahoma: Land of the Fair God, 48
Oklahoma: New Views of the Forty-sixth State, 51
Oklahoma, Foot-loose and Fancy-free, 45
Oklahoma Historic Tour Guide, 45
Oklahoma Image Materials Guide, 60
Oklahoma in Words and Pictures, 48
Oklahoma Land Runs, 1889!, 51
The Oklahoma Land Rush of 1889, 49
Oklahoma Legislature—But What Do They Do in There?, 40
Oklahoma Memories, 50
Oklahoma Our State, 51
Oklahoma Passage, 58
Oklahoma Place Names, 52
Oklahoma Prehistory, 49
Oklahoma Run, 51
Oklahoma Seminoles: Medicines, Magic, and Religion, 40
Oklahoma Today, 60
Oklahoma Treasures and Treasure Tales, 45
Oklahoma Wildflowers, 42

Oklahoma Wildflowers, 42
Oklahoma's Blending of Many Cultures, 53
Oklahoma's First Ladies, 54
Old Yeller, 78
On Coon Mountain: Scenes from a Childhood in the Oklahoma Hills, 55
One Day in the Desert, 7
One Green Mesquite Tree, 8, 79
The 100-Year-Old Cactus, 6
The 101 Ranch, 47
One Small Blue Bead, 35
The One Who Came Back, 37
The Other Way to Listen, 8, 9
The Other Way to Listen (videocassette), 9
Our Mexican Ancestors: Vol I, 66
Our Tejano Heroes: Outstanding Mexican-Americans in Texas, 74
Outdoor and Trail Guide to the Wichita Mountains of Southwest Oklahoma, 45
Outdoor Oklahoma, 60
Outlaws and Lawmen, 51
The Outsiders, 57

Pablita Velarde, 34
Paco and the Lion of the North, 82
Panhandle Cowboy, 48
A Paradise Called Texas, 84
Pecos Bill, 80
People of Chaco: A Canyon and Its Culture, 30, 38
People of the Short Blue Corn: Tales and Legends of the Hopi Indians, 3
A Personal History: The Afro-American Texans: Stories for Young Readers, 74
The Plains Indians, 52
The Polish Texans, 65, 70
Politics Texas Style, 73
Portrait of America: New Mexico, 31
Prairie Night Before Christmas, 83
Presenting S. E. Hinton, 44
The Pueblo, 11, 33
Pueblo Boy: Growing Up in Two Worlds, 10, 27
Pueblo Storyteller, 3, 30
Purple Sage: The Exploits, Adventures, and Writing of Patrick Sylvester McGeeney, 54

Quail Song: A Pueblo Indian Tale, 2, 22

The Rainmakers, 15
Rat Is Dead and Ant Is Sad, 22
Red Power on the Rio Grande: The Native American Revolution of 1680, 30
Red Wagons and White Canvas: Molly Bailey, Circus Queen of the Southwest, 78
Red-Dirt Jessie, 58
The Remarkable Ride of the Abernathy Boys, 50
Rifles for Watie, 57
Roadrunner, 17

Roadrunners and Other Cuckoos, 7
Roadside History of Oklahoma, 49
Roadside Trees and Shrubs of Oklahoma, 42
Roadside Wild Fruits of Oklahoma, 42
Robert Oppenheimer: Dark Prince, 34
Roots of Oklahoma, 52
Ropin' Fool, 55
Rosita's Christmas Wish, 77
Roxaboxen, 18

Salt Boy, 37
Sam Houston and Texas: A Giant Man for a Giant Land, 75
Sandra Day O'Connor, 14
Sandra Day O'Connor: First Woman on the Supreme Court, 13
Sandra Day O'Connor: Justice for All, 13
The Scorpion 7
Señor Alcalde: A Biography of Henry Cisneros, 75
Sequoyah: Father of the Cherokee Alphabet, 55
Sequoyah's Gift: A Portrait of the Cherokee Leader, 55
Shelter from the Wind, 56
Sing Down the Moon, 19, 37
Sing for a Gentle Rain, 36
Singing Cowboys and All That Jazz: A Short History of Popular Music in Oklahoma, 43
Songs Texas Sings: Texas Centennial Songbook, 62
Sooner Saga, 52
South Central: Arkansas, Kansas, Louisiana, Missouri, Oklahoma, 46
The Southwest, 9, 44, 63
Southwest Indian Arts & Crafts, 24
Spanish Pioneers of the Southwest, 33
The Spanish Texans, 71
Spindletop, 78
Spirit of Iron, 84
Stars over Texas, 64
The State of Sequoyah: An Impressionistic Look at Eastern Oklahoma, 53
Statehood, 73
Steven Spielberg, 14, 20
Stories at Sundown with Joe Hayes: An Evening of Storytelling in Santa Fe with Joe Hayes at the Wheelwright Museum, 24
The Story of the Lone Star Republic, 72
Stowaway to Texas, 77
Summer of Fear, 35
Summer of the Monkeys, 58
Sun Dagger, 32
Sun Journey: Story of Zuni Pueblo, 28
Surviving Columbus, 27
Susanna of the Alamo (audiocassette), 72
Susanna of the Alamo: A True Story, 69, 72
Suzy's Scoundrel, 58
The Swedish Texans, 71
The Swiss Texans 72
Symbols of Texas, 72

The Syrian and Lebanese Texans, 69

T is for Texas, 65
Talking with the Clay: The Art of Pueblo Pottery, 25
Taming the Star Runner, 57
Taos Pueblo, 27
Teaching about New Mexico History and Culture, 38
Teaching Texas History: An All-Level Resource Guide, 86
Ten Little Rabbits, 17
Tex, 57
Texans, 72
Texans: A Story of Texan Cultures for Young People, 71
Texas, 86
Texas: Yesterday and Today, 68
Texas Alphabet, 70
Texas Birds from A-Z, 62
Texas Cavalier, 81
Texas Highways, 85
Texas Historian, 86
Texas History Classroom Plays—Vol. I, 71
Texas in Children's Books: An Annotated Bibliography, 86
Texas in Words and Pictures, 67
Texas Jack at the Alamo, 83
Texas Jeopardy: Answers and Questions about Our State's History, Geography, People & More, 69
Texas Night Before Christmas, 83
Texas on My Mind, 63
Texas Parks and Wildlife, 85
The Texas Rangers: Men of Action and Valor, 66
Texas Rebel, 81
Texas Rose: Dilue Rose Harris, 81
Texas Star, 77
Texas, the Lone Star State, 73
Theo the Indian Fighter, 84
Thief of Time, 36
Things That Swim in Texas Waters Alphabetically Speaking: and in Other Coastal States of the Gulf of Mexico, 61
This House Is Made of Mud, 16
This Place Is Dry, 12
The Three Little Javelinas, 18
Tiger Eyes, 35
Tortillitas Para Mama: And Other Nursery Rhymes/Spanish and English, 4
Tracks, 56
The Trail North: Stories of Texas' Yesterdays, 82

The Trail-Driving Rooster, 78
Trapped in Death Cave, 59
Trapped in Slickrock Canyon, 19
Treasure, People, Ships, and Dreams: A Spanish Shipwreck on the Texas Coast, 63
Turkey's Gift to the People, 4
Turquoise Boy: A Navajo Legend, 2, 22
Turtle Island Alphabet: A Lexicon of Native American Symbols and Culture, 22
Twenty Texans: Historic Lives for Young Readers, 74
21 Texas Short Stories, 82
The Twin Territories, 53

Untold Tales of New Mexico, 26, 32

The Very First Thanksgiving: Pioneers on the Rio Grande, 77
The Village of Blue Stone, 12, 33

Warriors: Navajo Code Talkers, 26
Waterless Mountain, 14, 34
The Way to Start a Day, 1
A Wee Bit of Texas, 81
The Wendish Texans, 67
The West: Arizona, Nevada, Utah, 11
When Clay Sings, 27
When the Corn Grows Tall in Texas: A Story of the Texas Revolution, 81
Where Texas Meets the Sea, 74
Where the Buffalo Roam, 8
Where the Pirates Are, 85
Where the Red Fern Grows: The Story of Two Dogs and a Boy, 58
Who Are the Chinese Texans?, 70
Wildlife Southwest, 8
Will Rogers, 55
Will Rogers, a Boy's Life, 54
Willow Creek Home, 84
Wilma Mankiller: Chief of the Cherokee Nation, 54
With Domingo Leal in San Antonio 1734, 81
Women in Oklahoma: A Century of Change, 40

The Year at Boggy, 56
The Yellow Rose of Texas, 85

A Zuni Atlas, 26

Subject Index

by Janet Perlman

Acoma Indians, 2, 21, 25
Adobe, 16, 25, 27
African Americans, 48–49, 59, 64, 74
Alamo, 63, 69, 74–75, 80–81, 82
Albert, Carl, 40
Alligators, 83
Alphabet books, 9, 22, 61–63, 65–66, 70
American Indian legends
  Acoma, 2, 21
  Anasazi, 2, 22
  Apache, 3, 23
  Arizona, 2–3, 4
  Chickasaw, 76
  Coushatta, 76
  Hopi, 3
  Navajo, 2–3, 4, 22, 24
  New Mexico, 21, 22, 23, 24
  Oklahoma, 40, 42
  Pawnee, 2
  Pueblo, 2, 3, 4, 22, 23
  Tewa, 24
  Texas, 61
  Zuni, 4, 23, 24
American Indians
  Acoma, 25
  Anasazi, 2, 10, 12, 15, 22, 30, 32, 33, 35, 36
  Apache, 9, 10, 29
  Arizona, 9–11, 12, 14–16, 17, 18
  artists, 13, 25, 33–34
  arts and crafts, 3, 13, 16, 24–25, 27, 33–34, 35
  Cherokee, 46, 54, 55,
  Chiefs, 54
  Cochiti, 30
  Comanche, 57, 61, 82, 84
  Coushatta, 76
  Debo, Angie, 45, 46, 50
  history, 10–11, 26–27, 28–30, 43, 46, 50, 52–54
  Hohokam, 10–11 12, 33
  Hopi, 9–10, 11, 25
  jewelry, 24, 25
  kachinas, 24, 25
  languages, 46, 55
  Mankiller, Wilma, 54
  Mogollon, 10–11, 33
  Navajo, 8, 10, 11, 14–15, 16, 17, 18, 19, 21, 25, 27, 28–29, 36, 37
  New Mexico, 25, 26–30, 33–36, 37
  Oklahoma, 40, 52, 53, 57
  Osage, 43, 49
  Papago, 5, 7
  Plains, 52
  pottery, 3, 13, 25, 27, 33
  Pueblo, 10, 11, 24–25, 29–30, 33, 37
  rug weaving, 16, 35
  sculpture, 34
  Seminole, 40
  Sinagua, 10
  Taos, 25, 27, 28
  Tewa, 25, 34
  Texas, 61, 68, 71, 76, 82
  Tohono O'odham, 6, 10
  Zuni, 25, 26, 28
Anasazi Indians, 2, 10–11, 12, 15, 22, 30, 32, 33, 35, 36
Ancient civilizations. *See* Archaeology
Animals
  Arizona desert, 5, 7–8, 12, 15, 16, 17–18
  Carlsbad Caverns National Park (New Mexico), 32
  Oklahoma, 43
  Texas, 61–62
  See also names of individual animals
Antelopes, 3
Apache Indians, 3, 10, 23, 29
Archaeology
  Arizona, 10, 12
  Chaco Canyon (New Mexico), 30, 31, 33, 38–39
  Indian cultures, 10, 12, 15, 33, 35
  New Mexico, 30, 31, 33, 35, 38–39
  Oklahoma, 47, 49
  petroglyphs, 35
  pottery, 27
  Spiro Mounds (Oklahoma), 47
Arizona, ix, 1–20, 63
  ancient civilizations, 10–11, 12, 15–16, 33
  animals, 5, 7–8, 12, 15, 16, 17–18
  artwork, 24

biographies, 13–14
book publishers and vendors, 87–93
cactus, 5, 6
desert, 5, 6, 7–8
endangered species, 8
fiction, 14–19
geography, 9, 12, 44
history, 9, 12–13, 19
Indian legends, 2–3, 4
Indians, 9–11, 12, 14–16, 17, 18
maps, 9, 13
plants, 5–6, 12
Arkansas, 46
Artists, 25
    Martinez, Maria, 33–34
    Nampeyo, Daisy, 13
    Naranjo, Michael, 34
    Velarde, Pablita, 34
Arts and crafts, 24–25
    kachinas, 24, 25
    quilting, 77
    petroglyphs, 35
    pottery, 3, 13, 25, 27, 33
    rug weaving, 16, 35
    See also American Indians
Asian Americans. *See under* Individual nationalities
Athletes, 55–56
Atlases, 44, 45
Atomic bomb, 24, 34

Ballet, 43
Bank failure, 41
Belgian Americans, 65
Big Bend National Park (Texas), 62
Big Thicket National Preserve (Texas), 79
Billy the Kid, 21, 31
Birds
    Arizona, 7–8, 15, 17–18
    Oklahoma, 43
    Texas, 62
Black Bean expedition, 84
Blacks. *See* African Americans
Books
    almanacs, 61
    alphabet books, 9, 22, 61–63, 65–66, 70
    atlases, 44, 45
    bilingual books, 77–78, 83–84
    counting books, 8, 79
    publishers and vendors, 87–93
Botany. *See* Flowers; Plants; Wildflowers
Bowie, Jim, 74–75

Cactus, 5, 6
Camping, 46
Carlsbad Caverns National Park (New Mexico), 32
Cats, 80

Cattle, 76, 78
Caves, 32
Chaco Canyon (New Mexico), 30, 31, 32, 33, 38–39
Cherokee Indians, 46, 54, 55
Cherokee Outlet (Strip), 56, 57
Chicanos. *See* Hispanic Americans
Chickasaw Indians, 76
Chinese Americans, 66, 70
Christmas
    luminarias, 29
    Oklahoma, 42
    Texas, 77, 83
Circus, 78
Cisneros, Henry, 75
Civil War, 57–58, 81, 85
Cliff dwellings, 11, 33
Cochiti Pueblo (New Mexico), 30
Code Talkers, 26
Comanche Indians, 57, 61, 82, 84
Cookbooks, 43, 62
Corn Train Massacre, 84
Cosmology. *See* Creation tales
Counting books, 8, 79
Coushatta Indians, 76
Cowboys, 48, 62
    music, 43
Coyotes, 7
    fiction, 58
    legends, 2, 15, 16, 19, 22, 24
Creation tales
    Hopi, 3
Cuckoos, 7–8
Czechoslovakian Americans, 47, 67

Danish Americans, 67
De Onate, Don Juan, 21, 33
De Zavala, Lorenzo, 74
Death, 14, 18, 34, 35, 37
Debo, Angie, 45, 46, 50
Depression, economic
    farm labor, 41
    Oklahoma, 49, 55, 58, 59
Desert
    animals, 5, 7, 8, 12, 15, 16, 17–18
    cactus, 5, 6
    plants, 5, 6, 12
    seasons, 4–5
Desert tortoise, 7, 8, 15
Dickinson, Susanna, 80
Dogs, 58–59, 78
Dollhouses, 25
Dolls
    kachinas, 24, 25
Dust bowl, 41, 48, 59
Dwellings. *See* Houses

Ecology

desert, 6, 7
Dust bowl, 48
Endangered species, 8
English Americans, 66
Exploration, 27, 30, 77
Farolitos, 29
Flags, 64
Flowers
   Arizona, 5–6
   Oklahoma, 42
   Texas, 61
   wildflowers, 5, 42, 61
Flute player, 3, 23
Folk art. *See* Arts and crafts
Folk songs. *See* Music; Songs
Folklore. *See* Legends
Foods, 43, 62
Forts, 63
French Americans, 67
Frontier life. *See* Pioneer life

Galveston, Battle of, 85
Games, children's, 51
German Americans, 67, 69, 84
Ghost stories, 77
Ghost towns, 26, 32, 50
Gila monsters, 16, 19
Gipson, Fred, 74, 78
Gold mines, 45
Grand Canyon (Arizona), 17
Greek Americans, 67
Gulf Coast, 74

Hawks, 15, 17
Hiking, 46
Hinton, S. E., 43, 44
Hispanic Americans
   folktales, 23
   New Mexico, 33
   nursery rhymes, 4
   Texas, 64, 66, 70, 71, 74, 77–78
Hohokam Indians, 10–11, 12, 33
"Home on the Range," 8
Hopi Indians, 9–10, 11
   kachinas, 24, 25
   legends, 3
   Nampeyo, Daisy Hooee, 13
Horses, 22, 36, 57, 59
Houses, 3, 16, 17
Houston, Sam, 75, 82
Hughes, John, 75

Indians of North America. *See* American Indians
Insects, 7
Italian Americans, 68–69

Japanese Americans, 73
Javelinas, 18
Jewelry, Indian, 24, 25
Jews
   Texas history, 69, 73
Jordan, Barbara, 74

Kachina dolls, 24, 25
Kangaroo rat, 18
Kansas, 46

Languages
   Cherokee, 46, 55
   rural Oklahoma, 41–42
Latinos. *See* Hispanic Americans
Lebanese Americans, 69
Legends
   Acoma Indians, 2, 21
   Anasazi Indians, 2, 22
   Apache Indians, 3, 23
   Arizona, 2–3, 4
   Chickasaw Indians, 76
   Coushatta Indians, 76
   Hopi Indians, 3
   Navajo Indians, 2–3, 4, 22, 24
   New Mexico, 21, 22, 23, 24
   Oklahoma, 40, 42
   Pawnee Indians, 2
   Pueblo Indians, 2, 3, 4, 22, 23
   Tewa Indians, 24
   Texas, 61
   Zuni Indians, 4, 23, 24
Lizards, 8, 9, 15, 16, 19, 22
Long, Jane, 75–76
Long Walk (Navajo), 19, 28, 29, 37
Los Alamos (New Mexico), 24, 34
Louisiana, 46

McGeeney, Patrick, 54
Manhattan Project, 34
Mankiller, Wilma, 54
Maps
   Arizona, 9, 13
   New Mexico, 26, 38
   Oklahoma, 43, 44, 45, 48, 50
   Texas, 83, 86
   Zuni history, 26
Martinez, Maria, 33–34
Mexican-Americans. *See* Hispanic Americans
Migrant labor, 41
Military history
   Alamo, Battle of, 80
   Code Talkers, 26
   forts, 63
   Galveston, Battle of, 85
   Oklahoma National Guard, 41

Missions, 63
Missouri, 46
Mogollon Indians, 10–11, 33
Montezuma's Castle National Monument (Arizona), 10
Music
  "Home on the Range," 8
  Oklahoma cowboys, 43
  Tallchief, Maria, 43
  Texas, 62, 85
Mythology. *See* Creation tales; Legends

Nampeyo, Daisy Hooee, 13
Naranjo, Michael, 34
National monuments, 10
National parks
  Big Bend (Texas), 62
  Carlsbad Caverns (New Mexico), 32
Native Americans. *See* American Indians
Navajo Indians, 8, 10, 11, 14–15, 18
  Code Talkers, 26
  fiction, 17, 19, 34–35, 36, 37
  history, 11, 27, 28–29
  legends, 2–3, 4, 22, 24
  rug weaving, 16, 35
  silverwork, 25
  Wauneka, Annie, 34
Navarro, Jose Antonio, 68, 74
Nevada, 11
New Mexico, ix, 9, 21–39, 63
  ancient civilizations, 33
  biographies, 21, 33–34
  book publishers and vendors, 87–93
  fiction, 34–37
  geography, 32, 37–38, 44
  history, 21, 27, 29, 30–31, 38–39
  Indian legends, 21, 22, 23, 24
  Indians, 25, 26–30, 33–36, 37
  maps, 26, 38
Nisei. *See* Japanese Americans
Norwegian Americans, 70
Nuclear weapons, 24, 34
Nursery rhymes, 4

O'Connor, Sandra Day, 13, 14
Oil industry
  Oklahoma, 49, 51
  Texas, 78, 83
"Okies," 41, 59
Oklahoma, ix–x, 9, 40–60, 63
  African Americans, 48–49, 59
  animals, 43
  biographies, 40, 54–56
  book publishers and vendors, 87–93
  economy, 44, 49, 51
  fiction, 56–59

geography, 44, 46
history, 44, 45, 46–47, 49–52, 56
Indian history, 46
Indian languages, 46, 55
Indian legends, 21, 42
Indians, 40, 52–53, 57
maps, 43, 44, 45, 48, 50
plants, 42–43
Oppenheimer, Robert, 34
Osage Indians, 43, 49
Outlaw life, 21, 51, 54

Papago Indians, 5, 7
Pawnee Indians, 2
Pecos Bill, 80
Pen pals, 28, 29
Penn Square Bank, 41
Petroglyphs, 35
Pigs, 18
Pioneer life
  forts, 63
  Oklahoma, 47, 57, 63
  outlaws, 21, 51, 54
  Texas, 62, 66, 69, 75, 78, 79, 84–85
Plains Indians, 52
Plants, 8, 79
  desert, 5, 6, 12
  Oklahoma, 42
  Texas, 61
Polish Americans, 65, 70, 80
Pottery, 3, 13, 25, 27, 33
Pueblo Indians, 10, 11, 37
  artwork, 24–25
  history, 29–30, 37
  legends, 2, 3, 4, 22, 23
  Martinez, Maria, 33–34
  Naranjo, Michael, 34
  Velarde, Pablita, 34

Quilting, 77

Rabbits, 24
Ranch life
  New Mexico, 29
  Oklahoma, 47–48
  Texas, 62, 76
Reptiles, 15, 16, 19, 43
Rio Grande (Texas), 77
Roadrunner, 7–8, 17–18
Rogers, Will, 54, 55
Roosevelt Dam (Arizona), 12

Saguaro cactus, 5, 6
San Jacinto, Battle of, 85
Santa Anna, Antonio Lopez de, 82
Santa Fe Trail, 31

Scorpions, 7
Seminole Indians, 40
Sequoyah, 46, 55
Sheep, 17, 19, 28, 29, 36, 37
Silverwork, 24, 25
Sinagua Indians, 10
Skidi Pawnee Indians, 2
Songs
  "Home on the Range," 8
  Oklahoma, 43
  Texas, 62, 85
Sonoran Desert (Arizona), 5, 6, 7
Spanish Americans, 71
Spielberg, Steven, 14
Spiro Mounds (Oklahoma), 47
Stalactites, 32
Stalagmites, 32
Storytelling, 3, 12, 23, 24
Survival stories. *See* Wilderness survival
Swedish Americans, 71
Swiss Americans, 72
Syrian Americans, 69

Tallchief, Maria, 43
Taos Pueblo (New Mexico), 25, 27, 28
Tewa Indians, 24, 25, 34
Texas, x, 9, 61–86
  African Americans, 64
  biographies, 74–76
  book publishers and vendors, 87–93
  economy, 44, 65
  exploration, 77
  fiction, 76–85
  geography, 44, 65, 69, 74
  history, 63–64, 71, 72, 73
  immigrant groups, 64, 65, 66, 67–69, 70, 71, 72, 73
  Indians, 61, 68, 71, 76, 82
  maps, 83, 86
  missions, 63

Texas Rangers, 66, 75, 76
"Three Little Pigs," 18
Tohono O'odham Indians, 6, 10
Tortoise, 7, 8, 15
Trail of Tears, 46
Trees, 42–43
Trinity Site (New Mexico), 24, 31
Tuzigoot National Monument (Arizona), 10

Utah, 11

Velarde, Pablita, 34

Wallace, W. A. A. (Big Foot), 76
Walnut Canyon National Monument (Arizona), 10
Wauneka, Annie, 34
Weaving, 14, 16, 18, 24, 25, 34, 35
Wendish Americans, 67–68
White Sands (New Mexico), 31
Wilderness survival, 15, 19
Wildflowers, 5–6, 42, 61
Williams, Lizzie Johnson, 76
Women
  biographies, 13, 14, 33–34
  Oklahoma, 40, 47, 54
  Texas, 66, 75–76
World War II
  atomic bomb, 24, 34
  Code Talkers, 26
  Oklahoma 45th Infantry Division, 41
Wupatki National Monument (Arizona), 10

Zoology. *See* Animals
Zuni Indians, 4, 23, 24, 25, 26, 28, 36

www.ingramcontent.com/pod-product-compliance
Lightning Source LLC
Chambersburg PA
CBHW080542300426
44111CB00017B/2833